D1161539

PROSPECTS FOR CONSERVATIVES

Russell Kirk

PROSPECTS
for
CONSERVATIVES

A Compass for Rediscovering
THE PERMANENT THINGS

Introduction by Bradley J. Birzer

IMAGINATIVE
CONSERVATIVE
BOOKS

Gateway Editions, Inc. © 1956
Imaginative Conservative Books © 2013
Introduction © Bradley J. Birzer 2013

Imaginative Conservative Books is an imprint of
Angelico Press.

All rights reserved.

No part of this book may be reproduced or transmitted,
in any form or by any means, without permission.

For information, address: info@angelicopress.com
See also: www.TheImaginativeConservative.org

ISBN 978-1-62138-050-4 (pbk: alk. paper)
ISBN 978-1-62138-049-8 (cloth: alk. paper)

"This little book is principally an abridgement of my earlier *Program for Conservatives*. I have included in it, however, a portion of my Bildersee-Maroney Lecture at Brooklyn College on 'Freedom and Responsibility,' and a portion of an article on tradition written for *Collier's Encyclopedia*. I am indebted to Mr. Erik von Kuehnelt-Leddihn and Mr. W. T. Couch for whole paragraphs of the latter."
—RUSSELL KIRK, written for 1956 edition

Cover design: Michael Schrauzer

CONTENTS

Editor's Note

IT IS with great pleasure that we launch *The Imaginative Conservative's* book publishing venture, *Imaginative Conservative Books*, as a special imprint of Angelico Press. It gives us even more pleasure that we do so with a new edition of Dr. Russell Kirk's *Prospects for Conservatives*. *The Imaginative Conservative* is an e-journal of conservative thought. Dr. Kirk's writings are at the heart of our publication and it is appropriate that we begin our book publishing efforts with one of his most essential books.

It is also fitting that Dr. Bradley J. Birzer, co-founder of *The Imaginative Conservative*, has written the introduction to this book. Dr. Birzer, who holds the Russell Amos Kirk Chair in American Studies at Hillsdale College, is a scholar with a great depth of knowledge of the writing and thought of Russell Kirk. His forthcoming intellectual biography of Dr. Kirk promises to become the premier work in Kirk scholarship. Our publishing efforts would not be possible without the inspiration and vision that Dr. Birzer gives to *The Imaginative Conservative*.

We publish this book in the same year in which we celebrate the sixtieth anniversary of the publishing of *The Conservative Mind*, which is Dr. Kirk's most well known book. As Dr. Birzer explains in the introduction, *Prospects for Conservatives* was written as a sequel to *The Conservative Mind*. We offer this book to thoughtful readers with the hope that they will be stimulated to renew their acquaintance with the thought of Dr. Kirk in this important year of commemoration.

It is with immense gratitude that we acknowledge Mrs. Annette Kirk and offer thanks for her gracious permission to republish *Prospects for Conservatives*. Mrs. Kirk has been a friend and inspiration to us. She continues to hold high the torch that lights the way to the True, the Good and the Beautiful, which her husband urged us to conserve.

i

Our appreciation is also offered to Ms. Christen Diehr, Ms. Bailey Arlinghaus, and Mrs. Janice D'Agostino, who worked with commitment and tenacity in preparing this book for publication. We trust they now enjoy the fruit of their work with its publication. Additionally, Mr. John Riess and our friends at Angelico Press have been essential to this endeavor, and we are very grateful to have the opportunity to work with partners so patient and wise.

Publishing *The Imaginative Conservative*, and now *Imaginative Conservative Books*, requires resources, which are often difficult to obtain in a world that seems to be enamored with the ephemeral and the temporary more so than the eternal truths and the timeless. Our sincere thanks go to Mr. Robert C. McNair for his generous support of this and the additional programs of our sponsor, The Free Enterprise Institute.

Thank you to my beautiful and intelligent bride, Barbara J. Elliott, for her insights into the works of Dr. Kirk and her stories of visits to the Mecosta home of Russell and Annette Kirk. We have had the joy of spending the best part of lives together working in the fertile field of conservative thought and seeking the best of the western tradition. The work of *The Imaginative Conservative* would not be possible without her sage advice and assistance.

W. Winston Elliott III
Publisher, *The Imaginative Conservative*
Editor, *Imaginative Conservative Books*
October 4, 2013

Introduction

IN 1954, RUSSELL KIRK wrote and the Henry Regnery Company published one of the most interesting books of the twentieth century, *A Program for Conservatives*. Beautifully and lovingly written, Kirk's book might have easily been called "A Christian Humanist Manifesto," as it bridges in a stunning fashion the ideas of the so-called American "New Conservatism" and the writings of European Catholics (Anglo and Roman) such as T.S. Eliot, Gabriel Marcel, and Christopher Dawson. Its importance lies not in the specific issues it addresses, many rooted in 1954, but in its calling down of timeless truths from the realm of the eternal. In its themes, *A Program for Conservatives* is as relevant in 2014 and 2054 as it was in 1954. Indeed, its central theme is the greatest truth ever revealed or told, and it can be told millions of ways, as it pervades all that is good, true, and beautiful in creation. The following, taken from the end of the first chapter, is well worth repeating at length here:

> The enlightened conservative does not believe that the end or aim of life is competition; or success; or enjoyment; or longevity; or power; or possessions. He believes, instead, that the object of life is Love. He knows that the just and ordered society is that in which Love governs us, so far as Love can reign in this world of sorrows; and he knows that the anarchical or the tyrannical society is that in which Love lies corrupt. He has learned that Love is the source of all being, and that Hell itself is ordained by Love. He understands that Death, when we have finished the part was assigned to us, is the reward of Love. He apprehends the truth that the greatest happiness ever granted to a man is the privilege of being happy in the hour of his death. He has no intention of converting this human society of ours into an efficient machine for efficient machine–operators, dominated by master mechanics. Men are put into this world, he realizes, to struggle, to suffer, to contend against the evil that is in their neighbors and in themselves, and to aspire toward triumph of Love. They are put into this world to live

like men, and to die like men. He seeks to preserve a society which allows men to attain manhood, rather than keeping them within bonds of perpetual childhood. With Dante, he looks upward from this place of slime, this world of gorgons and chimeras, toward the light which gives Love to this poor earth and all the stars.[1]

Kirk originally spoke these words at the annual national conference for the Chi Omega sorority in June 1954, as he was writing *A Program for Conservatives*.[2]

Despite its timeless elements, it would be improper to take the book completely out of its context. It's worth remembering that in 1954, much of the world was communist, and nationalism—at home and abroad—had continued to rear its hideous head. Progressive thought, no matter how worn out the ideas, predominated in the federal bureaucracy, somewhat in foreign policy, and heavily in American schools. Additionally, the so-called "New Conservatism" had caught on as a topic of international importance. As it was debated in the pages of important periodicals and on radio and T.V., a new generation of Americans found answers that had previously eluded them. Though the "New Conservatism" first emerged with the works of the late 1940s by Peter Viereck, Richard Weaver, and August Heckscher, it was Kirk's *The Conservative Mind* that propelled the new school of thought into the limelight and gave it a respectable voice in the media and academia. More than any other work of its time, Kirk's *The Conservative Mind* solidified, however briefly, the post-war Right. His *A Program for Conservatives* served, at least in part, as an answer to his critics of his 1953 better-known work.

The Conservative Mind

When the Henry Regnery Company published Russell Kirk's revised doctoral dissertation from the University of St. Andrews as

---

1. Russell Kirk, *A Program for Conservatives* (Chicago, IL: Henry Regnery Company, 1954), 18–19.

2. The original version can be found in Russell Kirk, "Conservatism, Liberalism, and Fraternity," lecture given in June 1954 to Chi Omega, reprinted with same title, *Eleusis of Chi Omega* 58 (February 1956): 124–125.

The Conservative Mind: From Burke to Santayana, on May 11, 1953, it
playfully but deeply shattered the illusion that liberalism—especially in its Lockean form—offered the only viable and legitimate
tradition in America.[3] A hagiography of sorts, *The Conservative
Mind* presented Anglo-American history from the person and
thought of Edmund Burke to the present as a series of biographical
moments, each of the important persons demonstrating or revealing in his actions, thoughts, and words, some manifestation of a
timeless truth. As Kirk would later write, in a rare and revelatory
historiographic moment: "In every age, society has been relieved
only by the endeavors of a few people moved by the grace of God."[4]
Hence, in *The Conservative Mind*, Kirk discovered a lineage of
seemingly disparate figures: Edmund Burke, John Adams, Samuel
Taylor Coleridge, John Randolph of Roanoke, James Fenimore
Cooper, Alexis de Tocqueville, Orestes Brownson, John C. Calhoun,
Abraham Lincoln, and others. Each of these men, in some way—
some ways already known and in some ways recognized first by
Kirk—had relieved their age through some thought or act, a gratu-
itous gift of God through the person.

That such men existed proved God's love and graciousness, offering hope for the past, and even the present and the future. Given
Kirk's views regarding Providence, two problems arise. First, will
God offer such grace to those around us, thus will He send a leaven
to each generation? Or, must humanity await for untold generations before another person is born who will act according to the
True, the Good, and the Beautiful. Almost certainly, from Kirk's
view, this first problem is not a true problem. Though God works in
His own time, He does so in the immensity of Love and will not forget His people, even for an apostate generation. The second, more
difficult question, instead, asks whether an apostate generation will
look for, recognize, and praise the act of grace, so freely given and

3. "Books Published Today," *New York Times*, May 11, 1953, 25. Kirk would later
reject the label "new conservative," but he himself had used it in 1952 to define his
own position.

4. Russell Kirk, *The Roots of American Order* (La Salle, IL: Open Court Press,
1974), 161.

undeserved. Or, will it dismiss the idea, the person, the work of art, as merely a fiction of our ancestors, a residual memory of irrational times and cultures, unenlightened and, therefore, readily dismissed. In other words, the grace of God is always present, though to varying degrees according to situation and person and time. Man's acceptance of just such a gratuitous gift, especially in a secular age, remains problematic and sporadic at best.

Still, the individual person as well as the race as a whole bears incredible and weighty responsibilities when it comes to his and its relationship to the past and future generations as stewards over the earth and over the human condition. In his insightful and penetrating conclusion to the first edition of *The Conservative Mind*, Kirk wrote:

> Our world may be passing from contract back to status. Whether that process is good or evil, conservatives must prepare society for Providential change, guiding the life that is taking form into the ancient shelter of Western and Christian civilization. For this, they will require the vision of Burke, the common sense of Adams, the courage of Randolph, the tolerance of Tocqueville, the resolution of Calhoun, the imagination of Disraeli, the stern justice of Stephen, the catholic learning of More. Democracy in some form will endure. Whether it is to be a democracy of degradation, or a democracy of elevation, lies with the conservatives.[5]

Vitally, then, conservatism represented not only the best tradition of the Anglo-American past, but it also served as the means for a true progress in the Western world, a means by which distinct and eccentric men could recognize the grace, the beauty, and the truth of the Creator and His creation. It offered a means to sanctify and reinvigorate the soul of a sickly body and a confused mind, balancing, consequently, the passions of the stomach and heart with the rigor and logic of the mind. *The Conservative Mind* was not merely a work of politics, then. It was, equally, a book of cultural criticism, art, philosophy, law, economics, and theology. In its own marketing campaign for the book, Regnery defined Kirk's work as "a definitive

---

5. Russell Kirk, *The Conservative Mind: From Burke to Santayana* (Chicago, IL: Regnery, 1953), 428.

statement of the new conservatism."[6] At the time, Kirk believed one
of its most important components "the ethical aspect of the book,"
explaining that he tried "to transcend pure politics."[7] In this, Kirk
echoed the worries and concerns of almost all other Christian
Humanists of his and of the previous generation. With T.S. Eliot,
Kirk and the other Christian Humanists could write as the great
bard of the twentieth century did in his *Murder in the Cathedral*:
"Destiny waits in the hand of God, not in the hands of statesmen/
Who do, some well, some ill, planning and guessing./Having their
aims which turn in their hands in the pattern of time."[8]

Though many disagreed with Kirk's arguments in *The Conservative Mind*, no journal, magazine, or newspaper worth anything in
the American or British press ignored it. Reviews appeared everywhere that really mattered during the two years following the book's
publication. Some major publications even reviewed *The Conservative Mind* more than once. Praise for Kirk as a writer, if not necessarily as a thinker, pervaded the intellectual world. In 1955, for
example, the famous book reviewer, Harvey Breit of the *New York
Times* enthused over Russell Kirk when the young "man of letters"
from Michigan announced the creation of a conservative journal,
soon to be known as *Modern Age*. "We wish him well," Breit wrote
in the *Times*, "not because we are so wildly conservative but because
we think Mr. Kirk is a thoughtful man with scruples.... We plan to
hang around a while and listen."[9] By 1956, *Time* magazine considered Kirk one of the foremost intellects in America.[10] In short, Kirk
became a national celebrity in the decade following the publication
of *The Conservative Mind*.

Though the author of thirty books and numerous articles and
book reviews, Kirk is best remembered for *The Conservative Mind*

6. Advertisement by Regnery, *New York Times*, May 10, 1953, BR35.

7. Russell Kirk to Henry Regnery, May 20, 1953, in the Russell Kirk Center for
Cultural Renewal, Mecosta, Michigan. Hereafter RKCCR.

8. T.S. Eliot, *Murder in the Cathedral* in *The Complete Poems and Plays*, 1909–
1950 (New York: Harcourt Brace, 1980), 176.

9. Harvey Breit, "In and Out of Books," *New York Times*, November 27, 1955,
324.

10. "Parnassus, Coast to Coast," *Time*, June 11, 1956, 65ff.

(1953), *Eliot and His Age* (1971), and the *Roots of American Order* (1974). Sadly, Kirk's 1954 *Program for Conservatives* often gets neglected, lost in his vast literary output.[11] This is extremely unfortunate, as *Program* might possibly be Kirk's best work, in terms both of writing style as well as intellectual thought and creativity.

History of the Text

In an October 7, 1953, letter to Henry Regnery, Kirk discussed two new book projects to his friend and publisher. The first, written because he not only believed in the subject but also because he hoped he could obtain substantial funding for the project, was a book to be entitled *Academic Freedom*. The Volker Fund might, Kirk thought after a long conversation with its director, Herbert Cornuelle, provide him with at least two years' worth of his Michigan State University salary. In a tactful manner, Kirk had quietly resigned his position as assistant professor of humanities, citing a lack of real standards in the teaching of the western and liberal tradition.[12] The matter became brutally public after the student newspaper interviewed Kirk, probing to the quick of his resignation.[13] A professor at MSU, Kirk complained, "has become a menial who lugs in slides, gives standardized lectures, administers tests prepared by someone else, and grades them with a machine."[14] Though several prestigious universities pursued Kirk, he turned every possibility of a permanent academic position down. In May of 1954, he stated bluntly: "I have severed myself from the world of universities; and I am an individualist in this, if in nothing else, that I play a lone hand."[15] Nearly a year later, he again explained his lack of desire to be in academia. "(1) I would have no time to write, think, or travel;

---

11. An important exception is the excellent James E. Person, Jr., *Russell Kirk: A Critical Biography of a Conservative Mind* (Lanham, MD: Madison Books, 1999), 179–190, which gives serious attention to and analysis of *Program*.

12. Russell Kirk to Henry Regnery, September 10, 1953, in RKCCR.

13. Kirk to Regnery, October 26, 1953, in RKCCR.

14. "MSC Officials Rap Kirk's Statement," *Michigan State News*, October 30, 1953.

15. Kirk to Victor Milione, May 24, 1954, in RKCCR.

(2) I would have no time to edit our review; (3) I don't want to live anywhere except Mecosta; (4) teaching anywhere, under present circumstances, is detestable; (5) expenses considered, it would mean that I would have to make a financial sacrifice."[16]

Regnery had initially offered Kirk the second idea. "I am much attracted, O Henry, to your plan for a slim volume on conservatism," Kirk wrote on October 7. "Something like *A Conservative Program*." Kirk viewed the book as an opportunity to express fully his views first offered in the final chapter of *The Conservative Mind*. With such a book, Kirk thought, he could capture conservatism and the right from the libertarians as well as the "reformed Marxists" who now proclaimed "Americanism."[17] Kirk even noted in later letters which parts he wrote to counter certain claims of others who believed themselves the proper inheritors of conservatism. In a letter to his publisher, for example, Kirk directed the final section of Chapter 2, "Who are the Conservatives?," against Frank Chodorov, a then-prominent libertarian, claiming the mantle of one of Kirk's heroes, Albert Jay Nock. In *Program*, Kirk wrote, "Several grand realities exist in addition to the individual. The greatest of them is God. Another is our country, and yet another is our family; and still another is our ancestry."[18] Most of those claiming libertarianism or individualism as the true inheritance of the right, Kirk contended, sought after only second-rate thinkers in history. Instead, he stated, real conservatives should "substitute Moses or St. Paul or Lao-tse, Aristotle or Cicero for Zeno, Dante for Milton, Falkland for Locke, Samuel Johnson for Adam Smith, Burke for Paine, Orestes Brownson for Ralph Waldo Emerson, Hawthorne for Thoreau, Disraeli for Mill, and Ruskin or Newman for Spencer." Should they follow this lineage, Kirk argued, "they might make dry bones speak, and kindle the imagination of the rising generation."[19] Should real conserva-

---

16. Kirk to Regnery, January 28, 1955, in RKCCR. Perhaps most tellingly, Kirk turned down a position with the prestigious Committee on Social Thought at the University of Chicago in 1956. See the offer, John Nef to Russell Kirk, May 7, 1956, in RKCCR.

17. Kirk to Regnery, October 7, 1953, in RKCCR.

18. Russell Kirk, *A Program for Conservatives* (Chicago, IL: Regnery, 1954), 48.

19. Ibid., 49.

tives fail in their task of identifying their proper inheritance, the stakes were very high, for it would negate the power of grace, throwing into the world merely another "philosophy of cosmic selfishness."[20]

As of mid-May, 1954, though, a full eight months after agreeing with Regnery to write *Program*, Kirk had still not started working on it. Instead, he had been attempting to get initial writers and interest for a forthcoming journal of conservative opinion, later named *Modern Age.* He also had been "busy with planting and getting the dry rot out of" his cellar.[21] This is especially impressive given that the book would come out on the shelves only five months later, on October 12, 1954.[22] At the end of May, 1954, Kirk assured Regnery he would have the manuscript to him within a month, noting that he was "progressing at a great rate."[23] He began sending Regnery the chapters, one at a time, as he finished them, chapter one going into the mail on May 28, 1954.[24] By June 10, 1954, Kirk had sent a total of five chapters to Regnery.[25] Four days later, he sent chapter six.[26] The following day, June 15, he sent chapter seven.[27] Two days later, June 17, he sent chapters eight and nine. With only three chapters to go, Kirk assessed the feel of the book, and he found himself somewhat surprised by it. "This book is more sober and somewhat longer than I had originally intended, but I think that is to the good," he assured Regnery. "I had feared that it might turn into a partisan and vulgarized affair."[28] Kirk sent the final pages on June 23, 1954.[29] The speed with which Kirk wrote is nothing short of astonishing, a complete book written over a two-month

20. Ibid., 49.
21. Kirk to Regnery, May 11, 1954, in RKCCR; and Kirk to Regnery, May 25, 1954, in RKCCR.
22. "Books Published Today," *New York Times,* October 12, 1954, 25.
23. Kirk to Regnery, May 27, 1954, in RKCCR; and ibid., May 28, 1954.
24. Ibid., May 28, 1954.
25. Ibid., June 10, 1954.
26. Ibid., June 14, 1954.
27. Ibid., June 15, 1954.
28. Ibid., June 17, 1954.
29. Ibid., June 23, 1954.

period. Regnery, as it turned out, made no substantial changes to *Program*, suggesting only minor cuts in the size of the manuscript.

In part, Kirk wrote so quickly because he was full of ideas, each ready to explode from his mind and his typewriter. One can envision an angrier and energetic young Kirk (age 36), ready to answer all of his critics of *The Conservative Mind*, not with policy (despite the ironic title of *Program*) but with poetry, mythology, and imagination. The real secret to life, he argued, is the Christian and Dante-esque observation that all good proceeds from Love, and not from any policy prescriptions.

Other factors allowed Kirk to produce the book so quickly as well. Several of its parts came from articles previously published—from leading journals and periodicals such as *The Sewanee Review*; *Measure*; *Confluence*; *The Review of Politics*; *Faith and Freedom*; *South Atlantic Quarterly*; and *Northern Review*—as well as singular lectures given at the University of Chicago, the University of Michigan, the University of Illinois, and, most importantly, a series of lectures given at the University of Detroit and sponsored by one of Kirk's closest friends and intellectual allies, Peter Stanlis.[30] While lecturing in Detroit, Kirk also met regularly with a Jesuit priest, receiving instruction to become a Roman Catholic. In part, Kirk had been moving toward a Stoic and Augustinian form of Catholicism for years. Stanlis influenced his decision to receive instruction, as well as Kirk's then Catholic girlfriend, the "papist maiden" Mary Moran. Though Kirk would not enter into full communion with the Catholic Church until the second half of 1964, many perceptive readers have found Kirk's *A Program for Conservatives* not only filled with Catholic insights, but they have also seen it as having anticipated many of the Christian Humanist claims of Vatican II.[31] Intriguingly, a more singularly Kirkian voice emerges from the pages of *Program* than from its much more famous predecessor, *The*

30. Taken from the frontispiece of *A Program for Conservatives*; as well as from Charles Brown, ed., *Russell Kirk: A Bibliography* (Mount Pleasant, MI: Clarke Historical Library, 1981), 14–16.

31. On Kirk meeting with a Catholic priest while teaching at the University of Detroit, see Kirk to Peter Stanlis, January 1954, in RKCCR. Many of my own insights regarding the latent Catholicism found in *Program* come from a day-long

Conservative Mind. A work of intellectual history brimming with wise insights, the first edition of *The Conservative Mind* often reads like a sequel to Irving Babbitt's 1924 book, *Democracy and Leadership*. It is a work deeply indebted to a Babbittian Humanism of the 1910s and 1920s. A work of wise insights brimming with historical knowledge, though, *Program* often reads like myth, parable, and poetry. It is a work much more in line with the emergent Christian Humanism of the 1930s, 1940s, and 1950s, the works of T. S. Eliot, Christopher Dawson, and Gabriel Marcel.

From early childhood, Kirk had thought fondly of the importance of story and myth, especially as a means by which a society could and would understand itself. In 1955, the year before *Prospects* came out, and a year after *Program* had come out, Kirk wrote in the Catholic periodical, *Commonweal*:

> All great systems, ethical or political, attain their ascendancy over the minds of men by virtue of their appeal to the imagination; and when they cease to touch the chords of wonder and mystery and hope, their power is lost, and men look elsewhere for some set of principles by which they may be guided. We live by myth. 'Myth' is not falsehood; on the contrary, the great and ancient myths are profoundly true. The myth of Prometheus will always be a high poetic representation of an ineluctable truth, and so will the myth of Pandora. A myth may grow out of an actual event almost lost in the remote past, but it comes to transcend the particular circumstances of its origin, assuming a significance universal and abiding. Nor is a myth simply a work of fancy: true myth is only represented, never created, by a poet. Prometheus and Pandora were not invented by the solitary imagination of Hesiod. Real myths are the product of the moral experience of a people, groping toward divine love and wisdom—implanted in a people's consciousness, before the dawn of history, by a power and a means we never have been able to describe in terms of mundane knowledge.[32]

seminar sponsored by W. Winston Elliott III, Editor of *The Imaginative Conservative*, August 2010. I am especially thankful to W. Winston Elliott III, John Hittinger, Father Donald Nesti, Barbara Elliott, John Rocha, and Clint Brand for their ideas during discussions. Elliott had hosted a similar program on December 16, 2006.

32. Kirk, "The Dissolution of Liberalism," *Commonweal*, January 7, 1955, 374.

In *Program*, Kirk presented a Christian sanctification of the pagan myth of Perseus and his nemesis, the Gorgon, Medusa. Indeed, this myth holds together the entire book. "A man if he venerates the ashes of his fathers and the temples of his gods, will seek out the terror and strike with all the strength that is in him, as Perseus struck," Kirk wrote, paraphrasing a famous lay by Thomas Babington Macaulay, a nineteenth-century British historian. America, in Kirk's understanding, serves as the modern Perseus, striking against the secularization and ideologizing of the post-war world. As with Perseus, America could turn away from its task—as the leading power of the western world—at any moment. Like Perseus, America would need to contend with the problems of power, of self, and of enemy.

While studiously avoiding any specific policy recommendations, Kirk dealt with a significant number of issues in his book. As with the other Christian Humanists of the time, Kirk argued that man, while capable of great good, was equally capable of great evil. If one must reveal the good, he must first recognize sin as a primary fact of existence.[33] Arguing, then, from Ciceronian first principles, Kirk engaged problems of the intellect, community, justice, order, loyalty, tradition, and power. Every issue Kirk presented tied back, in some way, either to the seven classical and Christian virtues or to the seven deadly sins.

Perhaps most interesting and most revealing of his originality and brilliance is Kirk's discussion of social boredom. Derived from literary sources as well as his vast travels throughout America and Europe, Kirk argued that many of the problems of the western world—including, most recently, various forms of socialism and fascism—originated in the boredom of a society that embraced the ugly and the decadent in its literature, art, and architecture. "The most deadly boredom brings on the appetite for the most forbidden diversions," Kirk claimed.[34] Such boredom in society itself comes from the sin of sloth. With the rhythms of society taking on the aspects of the machine rather than the cycles of the seasons, with the cinema replacing the liturgy, and with the family declining in

33. Kirk, *Program*, 14.
34. Ibid., 103.

size, Kirk feared, men embraced first sloth, becoming bored, and then found themselves either seeking annihilation in the whirligig of the abyss or the false certainties of the new religions, fascism or communism or some derivation of either. The solution to these problems, Kirk thought, was relatively simple. A man must be reminded of his humanity.

Equally interesting, if not quite as original, is Kirk's chapter, "The Problem of Power." The atomic bomb, coupled with what he considered the scandals of the New Deal and the internment of the Japanese Americans, convinced Kirk that the United States and, perhaps, much of the western world, wallowed in decadence and corruption.[35] "We crush an insect with the club of Hercules," Kirk recorded shortly after the devastation at Hiroshima and Nagasaki. From the young man's perspective, progress would always lead to dehumanization.

> This doctrine of progress is a most interesting instance of the blind and foolish confidence of Americans in the God Progress. None of them—not Joseph Smith, not William James, not John Dewey—know what this progress is toward, not even what direction it is to take. Thus far, apparently, it has been progress toward annihilation, an end to be accomplished, perhaps, by the improved atomic bomb? We have dealt more death and destruction in the space of ten years than the men of the Middle Ages, with their Devil, were able to accomplish in a thousand.[36]

With our successful conclusion to the Second World War, we had, Kirk lamented, entered into a new world of total war, becoming no better than the totalitarian societies of the world.[37] Indeed, if anything the New Dealers were the worse tyrants, as they practiced oppression under the guise and name of liberty and equality. In reality, though, "policy is determined in offices in Washington, not by popular opinion," Kirk wrote to Bill McCann. "This is totalitarian government."[38]

35. Kirk, diary entry, October 9, 1945, in Gothic Room, RKCCR.
36. Ibid., November 6, 1945.
37. Ibid., September 25, 1945.
38. Kirk to McCann, February 3, 1945, in Dugway.

Worse still, though, was the creation and use of the atomic bombs. The dropping of the bombs was the "trump of doom; it was sounded, and the gulf yawning; and we got on listening to 'the Hit Parade,' striking, drinking, fornicating, cheating, hating." Americans, Kirk wrote, "are miserable animals in the shambles."[39] In *Program*, Kirk wrote bitterly, "We Americans happened to be first in the race for the acquisition of the tools of mass-slaughter, and we used those tools as the Roman used his sword and his catapult against Carthage."[40] Should our power have been employed virtuously, America would have sought a different path from the one it actually chose. "There are circumstances under which it is not only more honorable to lose than to win," Kirk wrote, "but quite truly less harmful, in the ultimate Providence of God."[41]

Both Regnery and Kirk found much to be optimistic about with the publication of *Program*. As the summer of 1954 continued, with reviews of *The Conservative Mind*, now over a year old, still coming out, Kirk offered encouragement to Regnery. "We have" the left "increasingly scared," Kirk wrote. "As Frederick Wilhelmsen writes to me, they don't yet realize, however, that we're only beginning; they think that they are now engaged in a counter-offensive."[42]

Future Editions

A Program for Conservatives went through several editions. An abridged edition (from which this book you now hold in your hand comes) appeared on November 26, 1956, in the relatively new Gateway paperback series, Regnery's imprint designed to attract readers "on the go" and to compete with publishers such as Signet and Penguin.[43] The first edition of *Prospects* sold for $1.25. Kirk initially wanted to rename the book "Conservative Principles" and include his first autobiography, "Reflections of a Gothic Mind."[44] By the

---

39. Kirk, diary entry, January 12, 1946, in Gothic Room, RKCCR.
40. Kirk, *Program*, 266.
41. Ibid., 268.
42. Kirk to Regnery, August 2, 1954, in RKCCR.
43. "Books Today," *New York Times*, November 26, 1956, 24.
44. Kirk to Regnery, May 3, 1956, in RKCCR.

beginning of June 1956, Kirk had settled on "Prospects for Conservatives" as the new title. "I shall have reduced it in length by thirty or forty pages, and shall have much improved some chapters. Two have been virtually re-written by the substitution of my recent essay—lectures on freedom and on tradition."[45] The majority of Kirk's changes to the 1956 version, *Prospects*, came from his simply having deleted large block quotes, especially in his chapter, "The Problem of Order." He also removed several personal anecdotes. The only major change to a single chapter, though, is the final chapter, "The Problem of Tradition." Kirk rewrote a significant portion of it, making the 1956 version almost an entirely new chapter.

Kirk deleted a few of his more controversial points as well. In "The Problem of Power," for example, Kirk removed his caution that government-provided school lunch programs might be the first real step toward some form of socialism being established in the United States. In the same chapter, he also excised his discussion of the over-reaching powers of the presidency. In "The Problem of Loyalty," Kirk removed his rather tame discussion of Senator Joseph McCarthy and McCarthyism. Some would-be allies, such as the other great conservative theorist of the time, Peter Viereck, would later accuse Kirk of having committed a sin of omission, never having used his celebrity to attack McCarthy and McCarthyism.

> If Kirk and his group had repudiated McCarthy in the early 1950s—McCarthy who was dangerous, McCarthy who could strike back at them more than any Bircher, McCarthy who unlike poor Welch had a mass-base—then their McCarthy-corrupted kind of new conservatism would not be discredited today.[46]

Kirk thought little of Joe McCarthy or his populist rabble rousing; he certainly saw no reason for the government to witch hunt. At the same

45. Ibid., June 2, 1956.
46. Peter Viereck, *Conservatism Revisited/The New Conservatism—What Went Wrong?* (New York: Collier Books, 1962), 145–146.

time, he thought McCarthy and McCarthyism unworthy of serious discussion.[47] Far greater problems loomed over western society.

He also, however, removed several sections dealing with the arguments of specific persons, some allies and some not. These cuts included Kirk's scathing analyses of several prominent libertarians, including Frank Chodorov in "Who are the Conservatives?" and Ludwig von Mises in "The Problem of Community." Kirk mentioned neither man in *Prospects*, and, equally surprising, Kirk removed much of his discussion of Wilhelm Roepke as well as his entire discussion of the Taft-Hartley bill. In "The Problem of Social Justice," Kirk removed every mention of economist Bruce Knight or his discussion of "levelling justice," one of the largest single topics of discussion in *Program*. Kirk cut a significant section dealing with de Tocqueville in "The Problem of Wants." Regnery suggested Kirk should remove the several discussions of David Riesman throughout the 1956 edition, but Kirk disagreed.[48] He removed several paragraphs dealing with Riesman in "The Problem of the Heart," but the other discussions of Riesman remained, unchanged. Even in the 1989 edition of *Prospects*, long after Riesman had been forgotten by the American public, Kirk retained his dissection of the sociologist. As Kirk explained in the "foreword" to the 1989 edition, "I have retained much of my discussion of Dr. Riesman's writings, for the reason that I still find him the most interesting representative of latter-day liberalism in America, intellectually considered—which is no excessive praise."[49]

His autobiography, he decided, would do better in a future book "with which it would harmonize better."[50] As it turned out, that

---

47. Kirk rarely discussed McCarthy in his published writings and almost never in his correspondence. The few thoughts Kirk presented on the Wisconsin junior senator can be found in his article, "Conformity and Legislative Committees," *Confluence* 3 (1953): 342–353.

48. Regnery to Kirk, June 6, 1956, in RKCCR.

49. Russell Kirk, *Prospects for Conservatives* (Washington, D.C.: Regnery, 1989), xii.

50. Kirk to Regnery, June 2, 1956, in RKCCR; and Kirk to Regnery, June 5, 1956, in RKCCR.

essay opened his 1963 *Confessions of a Bohemian Tory*, published by Fleet, not Regnery.[51]

A second and final edition of *Program* came out in 1962, and a second edition of *Prospects*, revised, appeared in 1989.[52] The latter reflects, rather significantly, an aged and very wise Kirk, while the 1956 edition offers a tight, cohesive argument, and it also presents the best glimpse possible of a young, energetic, and, at times, rash Kirk.

The Reception of *A Program for Conservatives*

Though *Program* sold well, it never did as well as either Regnery or Kirk had anticipated. It "continues to sell very steadily, but it hasn't caught on as I had hoped it would," Regnery admitted. "It may have been a mistake to title it as we did; many people, I think, having read the first book may have the impression that the second is just more of the same."[53] To this, Kirk replied, somewhat surprisingly, "I think this is doing very well for so sober a book; I was never quite so optimistic about sales-possibilities for this as you."[54] Less than two weeks later, Regnery informed Kirk that sales of *Program* had slowed down so much that *The Conservative Mind* was again outselling it on a weekly basis.[55]

A few public figures—in particular, Vice President Richard Nixon, Senator John Bricker, and Dorothy Thompson—praised it. Book reviewers, few in number, especially when compared to the vast numbers who reviewed *The Conservative Mind*, gave *Program* mixed reviews. They were so mixed, indeed, that one might gently call them schizophrenic or, if conspiratorial, Manichean. More likely than either of these possibilities, though, is the most likely truth. For if nothing else, the responses indicate that Kirk touched a nerve, and each person reacted approvingly or disapprovingly. For, as Kirk himself admitted, the book sobered one. Some greatly appreciated the reminders; others detested them.

Least surprisingly, reviewers for Catholic periodicals saw much

51. Kirk, "Reflections of a Gothic Mind," in *Confessions of a Bohemian Tory* (New York: Fleet Publishing, 1963), 3–30.

52. "Books Today," *New York Times*, October 29, 1962, 26.

53. Regnery to Kirk, December 23, 1954, in RKCCR.

54. Kirk to Regnery, December 28, 1954, in RKCCR.

55. Regnery to Kirk, January 6, 1955, in RKCCR.

to admire in the book. Father Joseph McSoreley, a Paulist, compared *Program* to the best of the writings of Edmund Burke, but set in the modern world. He argued that Kirk's "wide vision" offered a "calm, philosophical diagnosis of the forces that threaten the very existence" of our cultural order.[56] A Benedictine, Bernard Theall, admitted that Kirk's new book, equal in importance to *The Conservative Mind*, would meet with serious opposition, perhaps even galvanizing the anti-Conservatives. Best of all, though, Theall argued, Kirk presented an utterly Catholic view of the world without being officially associated with the Catholic Church, thus appealing "to a group of readers who might be frightened off from the writing of a priest." Theall recommended the duteous reader read Father Thomas Gilby's *Between Community and Society* alongside *Program*. "There is no doubt that Mr. Kirk is on the side of the angels," Theall concluded, and "deserves to be very widely read and thought upon."[57] Monsignor Edwin Sullivan labeled *Program* "a brilliant successor" to *The Conservative Mind*. As with Theall, Sullivan considered *Program* a deeply Catholic work, but he feared that Catholics would want Kirk's Catholicism to be more explicit, while the secularist would readily dismiss Kirk as too Catholic.[58] Jesuit Francis E. McMahon, who reviewed many of Kirk's books in the 1950s, argued that if one did not embrace Thomism, his second best option would be the tradition of Russell Kirk. If Kirk understood the full Thomist tradition, McMahon not so subtly implied, he would reach real truth. As Thomists understand history and philosophy,

---

56. Joseph McSorley, C.S.P., Review of *A Program for Conservatives*, *The Catholic World* 180, December 1954, 234.

57. Bernard Theall, O.S.B., "A Conservative Examines the Problems That Face Us," *Books on Trial*, December 1954, 115–116.

58. Monsignor Edwin V. Sullivan, review of *A Program for Conservatives*, *The American Catholic Sociological Review* 16 (March 1955): 52–53. Aaron I. Abell's review of Kirk's book in Notre Dame's *Review of Politics* somewhat confirmed Sullivan's worries. "Whether he is a believer or, like the late Irving Babbitt, merely a humanist he does not state," a skeptical Abell worried. See Aaron I. Abell, "What's New in the 'New Conservatism?'" *Review of Politics* 17 (January 1955): 153.

[T]here are grave lacunae and equally grave misconceptions in the volume of Mr. Kirk. That precious legacy of Western culture, the Thomistic lexicon, provides certain precisions on such pivotal concepts as social justice, private property, the common good, the person and society, which are missing in his account. His social ethics suffers from the lack of a metaphysics. This appears to be the greatest weakness of the tradition he espouses.[59]

Roman Catholic historian John Lukacs, then a little-known Hungarian immigrant to the United States, praised Kirk's writing abilities. "An excellent essayist," Kirk "is strong in principles and rich in moral content." Lukacs cautioned, however, that Kirk had failed to grasp intellectually much of the modern world, beating upon those things already dead or doomed to fail.[60]

Though ostensibly an ally of Kirk's, Lukacs would certainly not be the last to suggest that Kirk argued nostalgically and fallaciously for a past that never did nor could exist. Kirk would face this criticism for the next forty years of his life. The one Catholic periodical to challenge *Program*, *Commonweal*, called Kirk's book "a lament" and his argumentation so "unreal" as to distort some of the most important questions of the day, creating only more confusion in the modern world. "*A Program for Conservatives* is rich in quotations from these earlier great conservatives, but we cannot redeem a mid-twentieth century world in violent flux by chewing over the gnarled crusts of Burke and Coleridge," William Shannon claimed. "The dough of conservative thought is nourishing but it must be baked again, so to speak, in contemporary ovens," Shannon continued. Real conservatives must step forward, the critic continued, and bring the arguments back to reality and real solutions. Kirk has presented "a hopeless yearning and a barren nostalgia for the irretrievable past of small shops and craft guilds."[61]

59. Francis E. McMahon, *America*, November 13, 1954, 190.

60. J.A. Lukacs, review of *A Program for Conservatives*, *Social Order* 5 (May 1955): 231.

61. William V. Shannon, "The New Conservatism," *The Commonweal*, December 31, 1954, 360–362.

While *The Conservative Mind* presented a valuable argument, Princeton University's H.H. Wilson reluctantly conceded, "the value of the new book is vitiated by his detestation of mass society, especially its cities and industrialization, and his acceptance of the nostalgic myth of rural virtue."[62] H.G.G. Herklots complained that Kirk distorted the definition of "conservatism," confusing its meaning with "tradition." Herklots also uncharitably suggested that Kirk just needed to enjoy "a good time."[63] An anonymous reviewer for the *United States Quarterly Book Review* claimed that Kirk presented nothing but a "sentimental wistfulness, criticizing his own times for failure to hold firm to ideals imagined as having governed a holy squirearchy of preindustrial England." The young author—obviously angry—stood up, merely to cry "woe." Rather than returning us to an idyllic late-eighteenth century English countryside, Kirk's *Program* would most likely lead society back to the industrial savagery of the late nineteenth century, "the great barbecue."[64] Paul Pickrel of Harper's savaged *Program*, calling Kirk's analysis dated, his solutions "pallid," though he clearly saw the author as man of deep moral convictions, superior education, and much talent. Explaining a "mood" rather than a program, though, Kirk could not claim the label "conservative." *Program*, Pickrel insisted, is "the utopianism of the nostalgic right." Once the reader realizes this, the suggestions and the order of the book will become apparent. Sadly, Pickrel concluded, "a utopian spends his life writing the same book over and over."[65] The famous historian, Arthur Schlesinger, Jr., dismissed Kirk's arguments as the most extreme of the so-called "New Conservatives." In reality, Kirk's program was nothing more than impossible meshing of "aristocratic British conservatism" with the predominant "business society of the United States."[66]

---

62. H.H. Wilson, "The New Conservatism," *The Nation*, January 22, 1955, 76–77.

63. H.G.G. Herklots, "American Conservatism," *Church Quarterly* (Jan.–March 1958): 155.

64. Review of *A Program for Conservatives*, *United States Quarterly Book Review* 11 (March 1955): 102–103.

65. Paul Pickrel, "Backward, Turn Backward," *Harper's*, January 1955, 91–93.

66. Arthur Schlesinger, Jr., "The New Conservatism, The Politics of Nostalgia," *New York Reporter* 10, June 16, 1955, 11.

Other criticisms appeared alongside these. J. E. Hodgetts of Queen's University implied that Kirk, a "prophet of gloom," had read too much dystopian literature, especially that of Aldous Huxley and George Orwell, with *Program*, consequently, taking "on the ring of desperation."[67] UPenn's Jeannette P. Nichols argued that Kirk was not only a poor historian, he was also an ineffective writer. His tactic, she believed, was simply to apply "shock treatment" to a problem-riddled western society through "a show of arrogance" and "venomous vocabulary," all the while poring "vials of wrath." When all is said and done, though, Kirk only wants to revive order through the elites, temporal and spiritual.[68] Walter Berns, a political scientist, complained that Kirk's "definition was anything but clear," especially in his identification of Aristotle as a conservative. "Aristotle was not a conservative; he was a political philosopher," Berns prognosticated in a somewhat Gnostic fashion. "To confuse the two is to be guilty of a fundamental error, the confusion of theory and practice." Kirk, the professor from Louisiana State University proclaimed, substitutes "History" (or, would, "if he were more sophisticated") with political philosophy, following in the footsteps of "Hegel, Marx, and Nietzsche." In the end, Kirk was not only foolish, Berns opined, but he was also "yearning for a verdant and innocent and, he would have to insist, 'integral' past," in his hatred of all that is a part of the present world.[69]

Though in smaller numbers, several reviewers praised *A Program for Conservatives* as well. Francis Wilson understood Kirk's work to be a "brilliant" book, first and foremost concerned with the renewal of the individual person's soul. Only with this accomplished, Wil-

67. J. E. Hodgetts, "The New Conservatism," *Queen's Quarterly* 62 (Spring 1955): 115–116.

68. Jeannette P. Nichols, a review of *A Program for Conservatives*, *Pacific Historical Review* 24 (May 1955): 176–177.

69. Walter Berns, review of *A Program for Conservatives*, *Journal of Politics* 17 (November 1955): 684–686. In a much shorter review, Whitaker Deininger, offered just the opposite suggestion. While somewhat critical of Kirk, the reviewer appreciated him and his "more or less Aristotelian conception of Conservatism." See "Whitaker T. Deininger, a review of *A Program for Conservatives*," *Western Political Quarterly* 8 (June 1955): 305–306.

son recognized in a very Platonic fashion, could society begin to reform itself.[70] Whereas *The Conservative Mind* represented a "flanking maneuver of historical analysis," *Program* offered "direct statement," James Burnham contended. Though "cocky" and "cranky," Kirk was "rescuing" the conservative tradition, "both from sterile reactionaries who have degraded it, and from verbalists who by paying out a few modish conservative phrases are at present trying to hitch a ride on the shifting Zeitgeist."[71] The famous professor of rhetoric at the University of Chicago, Richard Weaver, recognized *Program* as a call to arms against the modern "heresies of the time." Kirk's book, Weaver prophesized, would serve as the rallying cry of all strands of conservatism, "who are legion" to awake, organize, and do battle against the forces of modernity.[72] In the same vein, political scientist Raymond English labeled *Program* the "second blast on the conservative trumpet." Correctly arguing the book as more cultural and personal than political, English wrote "Kirk is a gloomy and learned diagnostician rather than a physician for our ills, but his diagnosis is one we cannot afford to neglect." Importantly, contrary to many of Kirk's critics, English claimed that Kirk employed Burke's language and ideas effectively, making them palatable for and relevant to the modern world.[73] In *The New Leader*, James Rorty proclaimed *Program* even better than *The Conservative Mind*, at least in terms of style and language.[74]

The strongest review came from William S. Schlamm in the libertarian journal, *The Freeman*. Schlamm praised Kirk as a person, noting that with such wit, education, and wisdom, Kirk proved,

---

70. Francis G. Wilson, "Past in Present," *Saturday Review*, November 6, 1954, 21. William H. Chamberlin offered a similar analysis. See William H. Chamberlin, "A Powerful New State of the Conservative Case," *Wall Street Journal*, November 3, 1954.

71. James Burnham, review of *A Program for Conservatives*, *The Annals of the American Academy* 298 (March 1955): 216.

72. Richard Weaver, "Battle for the Mind," *Chicago Tribune*, October 24, 1954.

73. Raymond English, "The First Job is Criticism," *New York Times*, November 21, 1954, BR30.

74. James Rorty, "What Conservatives Want," *The New Leader* 37, October 25, 1954, 24–25.

once and for all, that East Coast Ivy League elites held no monopoly on class. Indeed, Schlamm wrote with obvious relish, the Michiganian scholar made all of the "Eastern Seaboard look like intellectual slums." What better test of success could there be, Schlamm asked. But, perhaps more importantly, did Kirk live what he preached? "There is perhaps no more reliable test of a conservative's authenticity than his sense of form," and Kirk's book serves as "an aesthetic delight." Recognizing the title as "sheer irony," Schlamm called *Program* "a forceful, penetrating and witty discussion of the pathetic, and often terrifying, results of liberal programs." Far from being rooted in the past, Schlamm stated, Kirk's book offered American conservatism a protected and protracted future, a true form of moral and ethical progress.[75]

A Final Word

You hold in your hands one of the great books of the twentieth century. Enjoy.

My most profound go thanks to W. Winston Elliott III, with whom I have had many, many conversations about this book—it being a favorite for each of us; Catherine Sims, who did some of the research for this version; Annette Kirk, who continues to be a force of nature and a close friend; Jim Garmhausen, who graciously gifted me with his collection of signed Russell Kirk books; my wife, Dedra, and kids, who gave me space to write this; and to Greg Spawton, David Longdon, Neal Morse, and Matt Stevens for providing the soundtrack to my work.

BRADLEY J. BIRZER
Hillsdale, Michigan
Feast of St. Andrew, 2012

75. William S. Schlamm, "Civilized Conversation," *The Freeman*, December 1954, 233.

The Gorgon's Head

"IN POLITICS, the professor always plays the comic role," says Nietzsche. Once upon a time I was a professor myself, and I must admit the general truth of this impeachment. We are fortunate, indeed, when the professor is content to be the clown, refraining from the presumption of giving commands to armies and decrees to nations. There is no arrogance equal unto the closet philosopher's, when he is afflicted with *hubris* and a wiser and better man than Nietzsche, Edmund Burke, observed that he knew of nothing more wicked than the heart of a pure-bred metaphysician, devoid of reverence and humility, and therefore sheer defecated evil. Hilaire Belloc reminds us that the very eccentricities of professors, their peculiarities of gait, their squint, their oddities of gesture and speech, are a curse put upon them as punishment for their terrible sin of Pride. Yet though I know these dreadful truths, and though I am a doctor of letters, and an historian of sorts, in this little book I venture into the dark and bloody ground of political policy, naked unto mine enemies; and I do this not out of foolhardiness, but because the men of affairs who ought to be applying the tenets of philosophy to the affairs of nations are doing nothing of the sort—or, at least, when they make such an essay at all, they commonly behave as abstractly and imprudently as if they were so many professors.

Not long ago I wrote a fat book, a history of conservative thought in America and Britain. I did not hesitate to make judgments, and to employ terms of value, for I believe that the historian who is afraid of terms of value presently will find himself in a world where no values are recognized. Nevertheless, I endeavored to let the conservative thinkers whose work I discussed speak for themselves, as much as possible, and I had no intention of preaching a neat metaphysics of conservatism, nor of setting up for a prophet. The historian's task is to chronicle, and, if he can, to criticize intelligently; he ought not to be expected to set the world in order. So, at least, I had always thought; and therefore I was somewhat taken aback when certain hostile critics of my book (I was gratified that they were few in number) reproached me for not having produced from my folios a cure for all the ills to which flesh is heir. It was highly flattering, I confess, to find that my opponents actually thought me (or the breed of historians) capable of guiding the destinies of nations, even though they declared that I had failed to fulfill this high duty. No one ever had written or spoken of me so kindly before; and therefore, touched by this simple trust, I made up my mind to retrieve my critics' gauntlets from the dust and give them what they asked for.

This present book is the consequence. Painfully aware that I was not the man to write it, I have waited for some years for that better author, that man practiced in statecraft and glowing with a generous learning, to come forward. But he has not made his appearance; possibly the old-fashioned literary statesman, the philosopher-leader, like Burke or Fox, like Adams or Jefferson, like Disraeli or Gladstone, is banished forever from our world, much as the Athenians shut out Aristides. For all the imperfections of this book, then, I ask the forgiveness of my critics, hoping they will recall Dr. Johnson's remarks on a woman preacher: such a creature, he said, is like a dog walking on its hind legs; we do not expect the thing to be done well, but are surprised that it is done at all. So it is with a professor, or even a *ci-devant* professor, who presumes to meddle with the great complexities of the workaday world.

Now though the professor is a fumbling and meddlesome being when he turns his hand to contemporary politics, still he is infinitely preferable to two other species of human creature: and they are the intellectual, and the ideologue. Out of the infinite mercy of God, I never have been an intellectual; and, if Providence continues kind, I never shall be an ideologue. The scholar and the man of principle deserve to be cherished mightily by us all, for no society ever has enough of them. But the intellectual and the ideologue deserve to be cast into the outer darkness by gods, men, and booksellers. An "intellectual" in our century (though the noun had a less indecent signification in the seventeenth century) is a member of that vain and sorry and shabby class which the Marxists call the "intelligentsia," a man who has but tasted the Pierian spring and is correspondingly puffed up with a ridiculous contempt for everything in heaven and earth but his own notion—who, like Kipling's orangutan, has "too much ego in his cosmos." When a man is both a professor and an intellectual, he is loathsome; when he is professor and intellectual and ideologue rolled into one, he is unbearable.

Napoleon, who detested the doctrinaire reformer, gave us the words "ideology" and "ideologue" as terms of abuse; old John Adams was driven nearly to distraction by "ideology," writing of it, "Our English words, Idiocy or Idiotism, express not the meaning or force of it. It is presumed its proper definition is the science of Idiocy. And a very profound, abstruse, and mysterious science it is. You must descend deeper than the divers in the Dunciad to make any discoveries, and after all you will find no bottom. It is the bathos, the theory, the art, the skill of diving and sinking in government." The ideologue is convinced that in his rigid closet-philosophy all the answers to all the problems of humanity are plain to be discerned. We have but to be governed by his rules, and the earthly paradise is ours. He may be an *a priori* reasoner, or an *a posteriori* reasoner, but in his system no room is left for Providence, or chance, or free will, or prudence. He is the devotee, often, of what Burke called "an armed doctrine." His ancestor was Procrustes, and he is resolved to stretch or hack all the world until it fits his bed. (Conservatism, as Mr. H. Stuart Hughes remarked not long ago, is the negation of ideology—though not, I trust, the negation of principle.)

> "You may break, you may shatter the vase, if you will; But the scent of the roses will cling to it still."

If, then some faint odor of the professor lingers about this little book, redolent of old calf and cheap tobacco and cheaper whiskey, still I think it is quite free of the reek of intellectual and ideologue. I do not profess to be invested with omniscience of that closed corporation called the intelligentsia, nor do I hope to bring to the reader a perfected set of secular dogmas which will make this sad old world into a brummagem utopia. The conservative believes that the individual is foolish, although the species is wise; therefore, unlike the confident intellectual, he declines to undertake the reconstruction of society and human nature upon the scanty capital of his private stock of reason. The conservative believes that the world is not perfectible, and that we poor fallen human creatures, here below, are not made for happiness, and will not find happiness—at least, not if we deliberately pursue it; therefore, unlike the ideologue, he is not under the impression that any single fixed system of political concepts can bring justice and peace and liberty to all men at all times, if uniformly applied. I am of the number of those who would have asked God to conserve chaos, and who would have stormed Olympus with the Titans for the sake of old Cronos' memory; I confess, in short, to being a true-blue conservative; and if any taint of liberalism has crept into these pages, I am infinitely sorry for it. Such is my apology for undertaking this task of which I am unworthy, and such are the limitations the reader must expect to find in these chapters.

Once I was in a bookshop when a perplexed and rather belligerent gentleman of middle years demanded a book: "I want a book that tells how to solve all these social problems in a practical way. I don't want one that has anything to do with religion." If that gentleman has happened to purchase my book, he is bound to be disappointed by what follows. The true conservative knows that the economic problem blends into the political problem, and the political problem into the ethical problem, and the ethical problem into the religious problem. There exists a hierarchy of difficulties, as well as a hierarchy of values. Although I cannot say half so much as I should like, in these pages, about questions of morals and faith, these subjects must be touched upon, for they underlie the conservative view of society.

The conservative understands that the circumstances of men are almost infinitely variable, and that any particular political or economic policy must be decided in the light of the particular circumstances of time and place—an enlightened expediency, or prudence. I am attempting to outline here, rather, the general principles upon which conservatives ought to endeavor to form their opinions of particular issues and make their decisions in particular circumstances. I am not endeavoring to dictate a platform for the Republican party, or for the Democratic party; I am trying, instead, to sketch those general assumptions by which men of conservative inclination in any party try to guide their steps. I have no desire to establish a pattern of politics for the whole world; my aim is to deal with the conservative movement in the United States, for the most part, although my remarks may be applicable in some degree to all states which participate in the Anglo-American tradition of justice and liberty.

Conservatism, I repeat, is not an ideology. It does not breed fanatics. It does not try to excite the enthusiasm of a secular religion. If you want men who will sacrifice their past and present and future to a set of abstract ideas, you must go to Communism, or Fascism, or Benthamism. But if you want men who seek, reasonably and prudently, to reconcile the best in the wisdom of our ancestors with the change which is essential to a vigorous civil social existence, then you will do well to turn to conservative principles. The high-minded conservative believes in Principle, or enduring values ascertained through appreciation of the wisdom of dead generations, the study of history, and the reconciliation of authority with the altered circumstances of our present life. He is a highly reasonable person, although he looks with deep suspicion on the cult of Reason—the worship of an abstract rationality which asserts that mundane planning is able to solve all our difficulties of spirit and community. But the high-minded conservative detests Abstraction, or the passion for forcing men and societies into a preconceived pattern divorced from the special circumstances of different times and countries.

My program, then, is not a series of slogans calculated to enforce conformity to some impersonal pattern of existence; nor is it a congeries of recommendations for legislative enactment. I do not propose, for instance, to tell everyone how to deal with the problem of business cycles, once and for all; but I may suggest the spirit in which the conservative ought to approach such economic matters as the business cycle. I do not propose to instruct the national administration how to deal, to everyone's satisfaction, with the Union of Soviet Socialist Republics; but I may suggest the way in which the conservative thinker endeavors to form a foreign policy. Particular remedies and plans of action are subjects which ought to be generally debated, and often reviewed, not settled by some abstract doctrines; and besides, I simply do not have neat answers to all our modern complexities, and neither does anyone else, however much certain radicals and even liberals try to persuade us that they have. Conservatives always differ a good deal, among themselves, as to the better solution of any particular problem. What they have in common is a similar view of human nature, of the ends of society, and of the most nearly satisfactory *methods* for seeking the common good.

Particular policies ought to be left to the politician; and I do not use the word "politician" in any denigrative sense. I do not happen to be calculated for a politician. But the bookman and the critic and the clergyman, the people whom Coleridge called "the clerisy," have the right and the duty of examining and restating those general principles which are the foundation of any decent social order. Ideas, good or bad, still rule the world; and if the clerisy disdain or neglect their function of advising the politician and the mass of mankind, we will indeed find ourselves, before long, under the Rule of Unreason. The divorce of the life of the spirit and the mind from the life of politics already has been thoroughly accomplished in much of the world, and America slips further and further toward that catastrophe. Not long ago, a professor of history in a state college lectured on the revival of an imaginative conservatism in these United States. He was not himself a conservative, but he remarked with interest and some degree of approval this phenomenon. A student lounging in the back row roused himself from his lethargy, presently, and inquired, with heavy resentment, "Who are these conservatives? Are they the guys we call eggheads?" He did not resent them because of their conservatism; the word itself was new to him; what he resented was any commendation of the works of the mind. Well, Burke says that prejudice is the wisdom of unlettered men; and most of our students in colleges nowadays being conspicuously unlettered men, perhaps this instance of prejudice was a form of conservatism, after all. But it was the kind of conservatism which led Brooks Adams to write that "with conservative

6

populations, slaughter is nature's remedy." It was not the conservatism of reflection which I am describing in the following chapters. A conservatism of reflection is the proper antidote to the conservatism of apathy; and this conservatism of reflection cannot be conjured up by the politician and the publicist unaided. The mind and heart of America, in this tremendous hour, require an inspiration which cannot come out of the party caucus and the editorial room of the daily newspaper.

Mr. T.V. Smith once did me the honor of observing that I espouse conservatism with the vehemence of a radical. Nor can I deny this. The thinking conservative, in truth, must take on some of the outward characteristic of the radical, today: he must poke about the roots of society, in the hope of restoring vigor to an old tree half strangled in the rank undergrowth of modern passions. The conservative does not much enjoy this unaccustomed function, for, with Randolph of Roanoke, he has found the philosopher's stone, which is this formula: never disturb, except under the greatest necessity, a thing that is at rest. That dread necessity, however, is upon us; the conservatism of enjoyment must be exchanged for the conservatism of labor; and it is for us to prove that the conservative can water and prune, if he must, the great tree of society, as well as pick the fruit. In this century the conservative cannot be a lotus-eater. He must perform a higher working if we are all to be saved from that lowest form of work, the servile labor of a proletariat directed by an omnicompetent state.

Now the first task for the imaginative conservative, I think, is the hard duty of frank criticism. The liberal and the radical used to consider this function their peculiar prerogative, though now and then men like Disraeli or Henry Adams would dispute their monopoly. Since no society can prosper without the smart and goad of unabashed criticism, the liberals and the radicals did everyone, especially the conservatives of lethargy, an invaluable service so long as they went at this task with a will. Often their criticism may have been injudicious or malicious; but no matter; they made men think, and they kept a sharp eye out for rogues, and thus they played their part under Providence. For some years, however, the liberals and the radicals have been derelict in the performance of the critical function. The typical liberal or radical of our times is smugness incarnate. He has become, indeed, precisely what he used to denounce, for we become the thing we hate, if we hate without discernment.

The Advanced Social Thinker, during the nineteen-twenties and nineteen-thirties, came unwittingly to take on the characteristics of the being he had so long derided, the complacent conservative of lethargy, the man convinced that this is the best of all possible worlds, and that every day, in every way, matters are getting better and better. If God no longer was in his Heaven, at least the Planner was in the terrestrial paradise, and all was right with the world. The application of scientific methodology to the problems of society, it was assumed, would presently resolve the difficulties of nations and the problems of private life; a beneficent state would supply the wants of everyone; modern psychological theory would supplant the superstitions of religion, teaching men indulgence, rather than constraint; state education would be the great leveller, inducing everyone to conform to an approved pattern, and peacefully accomplishing "social adjustment"; the bitter memories of the Past might safely be forgotten, for Pragmatism would show us how we might move ever onward and upward by devoting ourselves to the practical questions of the present hour.

But why break a butterfly on the wheel? These illusions now are consigned to the dear, dead days beyond recall; the terrible events of our time have buried John Dewey and his generation deeper than any Pharaoh. The most old-fashioned and archaic persons in our nation today are those who still try to believe in the inevitability of Progress and the competence of Reason to make men into gods. There are gods among us, true enough: but they are the gods of the copybook headings, returned with fire and sword to remind us how wise were the old Greeks with their talk of hubris and nemesis and catastrophe. The shock of the First World War disturbed the complacency of the liberal; the rise of the totalitarian states and the Second World War shook this fatuous liberalism to its foundations; and the spectacle of Soviet Russia, together with unmistakable indications of moral and political decay in the rest of the world, put an end to the popular ascendancy of liberalism. The Liberal party of Britain was annihilated at the polls; in America, the words "liberal" and "liberalism," formerly so commendatory, have become terms of derogation or suspicion. As for the radicals, they found themselves in the dismaying situation either of becoming the willing agents of Russian imperialism, or of being cut quite loose from their moorings, to be left at the mercy of every wind of doctrine. Such of them as still are afloat are masterless men, all the heart gone out of them; most of them sank long ago. For the Iliad of their woes, it is sufficient to remark the vicissitudes of such journals as the *Partisan Review*. They have nothing to tell us nowadays, and most of them know it, in their heart of hearts.

To criticize, a man must have some standard to which he can repair, some system of values superior to the fashion of the hour. Our liberals and radicals no longer rally round any such standard; their gods have failed them; and therefore they no longer criticize convincingly. They still can carp, and carping may impart some faint failing ray of warmth to their desolate hearts, but criticism of that low order will not suffice to restrain society from excesses or to light the way for the vast groping masses of humanity.

A pathetic willingness to listen to the criticism of conservatives, however—and an equally pathetic inability to understand that criticism—is apparent just now in certain leaders of liberal opinion, if so inchoate a group can be said to retain leaders. Certain reviewers of my *Conservative Mind* professed an anxiety to find some new solution to the afflictions of modern society in conservatism; but I had disappointed them, they lamented. One could not understand what I was after, if I would embrace neither capitalism nor communism; he seemed to imply that I must be engaged in some dismal Fascist conspiracy. Another, remarking my reluctance to endorse either of these sets of dogmas, asked just what the conservatives do want: "Are they Keynesians?" Now we scarcely can wonder at the bankruptcy of liberalism, when its most articulate spokesmen think of the problems of modern society as no more than an exercise in economic theory, and are unaware that Karl Marx was the popularizer of both the terms "capitalism" and "communism," and seem to be quite ignorant of the existence of Christian social principles, or of private property which is not "capitalistic" in the Marxist sense, or of traditions and political institutions far older than Keynes, or

Marx, or even the modern industrial system. (The late Lord Keynes, the least dogmatic of all economists, doubtless would be greatly perplexed at being asked to define a "Keynesian.") The decay of the historical imagination, and indeed of the simplest historical foundation of fact, among the *illuminati* of the Left, has reduced them to this puerility.

One cannot re-educate a generation through a single book, or a thousand books, and therefore I do not really expect to be able to make my opponents into converts, as Burke converted Mackintosh; for the modern liberal does not have the intellectual discipline of Mackintosh which made it possible to persuade him of his errors. Far more than the thinking conservative, the modern liberal is the slave of his own early prejudices. But, in my small way, I endeavor to do here what Burke did in his grand way: I attest the rising generation. And the rising generation is not sentimentally liberal; no one knows this better than the liberal professor.

With an eye more to the young and unprejudiced reader, then, and to the older reader of conservative tendencies, rather than to the liberals who have dominated our educational system and our publishing industry this past generation, I propose to describe here, very briefly, the awful gravity of the problems which confront conservatives. I do not say that the conservatives are going to solve these problems. The enlightened conservative knows that certain problems of humanity are not susceptible of solution, and that others can be solved only by a great elapse of time, the healer of social wounds. The conservative, moreover, puts only a limited trust in the power of human reason, and knows that our future depends in considerable part upon Providence, or chance, or that infinite combination of tiny causes which we call chance. Nor is it by any means certain that the conservative, despite the decay of liberalism, retains today the courage and hardihood to meet these problems boldly; for in some degree the conservative's mind and will have been corroded by the same acids that have eaten away the vigor of modern liberalism.

Yet, when all is said, the conservative believes that men and nations possess free will, and that if a nation or a civilization tumbles to its ruin, that catastrophe is the consequence, for the most part, of the failure of heart and mind of the people who made up that nation or that civilization. The conservative, unlike certain of our *cognoscenti* of the twentieth century, still clings to his old-fangled opinion that there is such a thing as mind, and that there is such a thing as heart, or will, in the Schoolmen's sense. The conservative may fail to redeem modern society from its perilous state. But if he fails, we have no hope in this world. The liberal and the radical have failed already, and the enormity of their failure is stamped upon the face of Europe and the face of Asia.

To commence the description of a conservative program, we need first to analyze the wasting diseases that menace the survival of order and justice and freedom among us. My liberal critics have asked me for a program; yet I doubt whether they will relish that program as it takes shape. For it has very little of the rosy glow of the characteristic liberal dream of futurity. The truth, in our time, is hard; and if truth still has beauty, it is a beauty so stern and austere that it terrifies the luxurious taste of the liberal. When Perseus, having slain the Gorgon, brought the gristly veiled head to the palace of Polydectes, the king and his company demanded a sight of the trophy, and would take no denial; so that, when they grew menacing, Perseus showed them the awful dead face of Medusa with the snaky locks, and king and courtiers turned to stone before that dread countenance. We throw a decent veil over the origins of society, said Burke, if we are wise; but the modern liberal, although he delights in poking into social origins, commonly has blindfolded himself to the real problems in modern existence. If he insists upon looking at them now, he risks the fate of Polydectes.

Some liberals, indeed, half-aware of this peril, repeat to themselves, like an incantation, certain mumbled cliches to the effect that people are growing kinder, and life is more secure than it used to be, and that our present discontents are no more than so many transitory phenomena. Thus they fancy themselves in the garden of Proserpine. I should be sorry to wake them, were it not that the flowers of Proserpine bloom only in the realm of Hades. A professor of chemistry, to whom I had been describing some very real and immediate symptoms of social decay—the increase in the rate of crime, the debauchery of children's minds, the collapse of law and of order in a great part of the world—inquired, complacently, "But isn't all this just anxiety?" Such beings almost disprove Aristotle's contention that man is a rational creature. The man who was thrust into a gas-oven at Belsen was not suffering simply from a psychological condition of anxiety; the man who is knocked on the head in some dark street of Chicago will not be helped much by his psychiatrist. Nothing but direct and painful personal experience can convince liberals of this stamp that Sin is a literal statement of fact. The conservatives are doing what they can to spare the liberals that rude awakening. But the best way to avert danger is to meet it intrepidly.

If it will not do to gratify our curiosity by looking the Gorgon morbidly in the face, still it is no salvation to pretend that the great claws are an optical illusion, and that the snaky locks are only weeds waving in the wind; nor will we save ourselves by cowering in terror. Persons like Mr. Alfred Kinsey are ever so eager to throw off the veil which hides the worst in our fallen nature; but this prurient inquisitiveness turns the hearts of a generation to stone. Persons like Mr. David Riesman please themselves by whistling in the dark, with only an occasional wince at some shadow there in the corner; but if the shadow takes substance, it will refuse to be whistled down the wind. I think that both of them are wrong. A man, if he venerates the ashes of his fathers and the temples of his gods, will seek out the terror and strike with all the strength that is in him, as Perseus struck.

In the earlier Greek representations, Medusa is raw head and bloody bones, such a face as drifts through dreams, the princess of terrors. But as Greek society softened and sentimentalized, and as Greek freedom trickled down toward servility, Medusa took on a very different aspect. The frightful grin, the flattened nose, the lolling tongue, the eyes with their fixed stare, give way at the end of the fifth century to a frigid beauty, the mask of a woman beyond good and evil; and later, about the beginning of the third century, this fatal beauty loses its impassive quality, a faint sensual smile creeping upon the lips, a hint of terror or of pain haunting the eyes. The Anatolian monster that hunted the early Greeks through their dreams has become the incarnation, in art, of concupiscence struck down in the moment of its evil perfection.

Our time, sick nigh unto death of utilitarianism, and literalness, cries out for myth and parable. Great myths are not merely susceptible of rational interpretation: they *are* truth, transcendent truth. I do not desire to degrade the legend of Perseus into a tract for our times; but the face of Medusa has as much meaning for us as it had for Hesiod, and perhaps more. A nation, in its youth, confronts the menace of nature red in tooth and claw—physical nature and human nature. Its bogies, however fearsome, may be overcome by primitive courage and rude strength. Thus, in a sense, we Americans drew the sword to end the difficulties of our War of Independence and our Civil War; and, Perseus-like, we triumphed through the heroism of youth. But the power of Evil, infinitely subtle, masks itself in fresh guises as a nation grows older; and the sword snaps in the hand, when the nightmare-creature is metamorphosed into the lure of sensuality. By the side of the problems of 1776, or of 1861, our modern distresses loom gigantic. We still need Perseus; but our Perseus, if he is to crush Medusa now, must be endowed with powers of mind and conscience undreamed of in the simple days of our national boyhood.

To descend from fable to sorry immediacy, I am saying that modern American conservatives are confronted by dangers and discontent which exceed, in number and intensity, even the perils which plagued the age of Edmund Burke and John Adams, I hope that conservatives will encounter these troubles in the light of the wisdom of their ancestors; yet precedent alone will not suffice to rescue American society from its present distresses. The modern conservative must improvise and create, as well as obey prejudice and prescription. It seems to me that the most urgent questions which demand some answer from our conservatives are ten in number, and they are these:

(1) The problem of the mind, or how we are to redeem our intellects from the sterility and uniformity of the mass-age.

(2) The problem of the heart, or how we are to resuscitate the aspirations of the spirit and the dictates of the conscience in a time that has supped too long on horrors.

(3) The problem of boredom, or how our industrialized and standardized society may take on refreshed meaning for truly human persons.

(4) The problem of community, or how collectivism may be averted by a restoration of true commonwealth.

(5) The problem of social justice, or how we are to keep avarice and envy from setting every man against his brother.

(6) The problem of wants, or how to satisfy just desires and abjure unjust desires.

(7) The problem of order, or how variety and complexity may be preserved among us.

(8) The problem of power, or how they might which has been given into our hands may be governed by right reason.

(9) The problem of loyalty, or how to teach men to love their country, their ancestors, and their posterity.

(10) The problem of tradition, or how, in this day when Whirl seems to be king, a continuity may link generation with generation.

I have prefaced the discussion of these ten riddles by a chapter on the nature of American conservatism, and the sources of its strength. Whoever happens to read this book to the end will find that I have asked more questions than I have given answers. It is said that a visitor to President Harding's office once found that unfortunate politician tumbling over papers confusedly on his desk, and sighing, mostly to himself, "Somewhere—*somewhere* there's a man who can tell me what to do about all these things. But who is he?" Of course President Harding's omniscient counsellor did not exist; nor can he exist, the problems of modern states being so infinitely varied as they must. I make no pretense to being able to guide our steps aright.

I have tried, rather, to describe the task for conservatives as it is given to me to apprehend it, and to suggest here and there, ends and means. If I thought I stood alone, I should not bother to write this book: one might as well shriek against the hurricane. But I believe there are those who may read these feeble sentences of mine, and perhaps give these thoughts a greater degree of coherence, and in time realize certain of these ideas in action. We all are part of a great continuity and essence, and ought to rest content if we have done our own petty labor in obedience to what seems, according to our imperfect lights, the decree of Providence.

Some readers will be surprised that I have devoted very little of this book to present controversies, and that I do not say much about men of the hour. But it happens to be my opinion that the profound causes of our present discontents lie elsewhere than in the fury of popular passions. If I do not write about the president, or this senator, or that governor, it is because I try not to think in slogans or to argue in personalities. The ephemeral moment, so beloved by the popular journalist and the radio commentator, is too much with us. Without men who take long views, we are in a pathless wilderness. In short, I do not think that the policies of the Federal Reserve Board, or the negotiations between General Motors and the United Automobile Workers, or the struggle between factions of the Republican party, are the causes of our perplexity; they are merely symptoms. These symptoms require intelligent discussion, but that is someone else's work. I am concerned here with first principles— not because I love abstract concepts, but because very few other men have anything to say about first principles just now.

And I shall tell you one secret, before taking arms against a sea of troubles: at the back of every discussion of the good society lies this question, What is the object of human life? The enlightened conservative does not believe that the end or aim of life is competition; or success; or enjoyment; or longevity; or power; or possessions. He believes, instead, that the object of life is Love. He vows that the just and ordered society is that in which Love governs us, so far as Love ever can reign in this world of sorrows; and he knows that the anarchical or the tyrannical society is that in which Love lies corrupt. He has learnt that Love is the source of all being, and that Hell itself is ordained by Love. He understands that Death, when we have finished the part that was assigned to us, is the reward of Love. And he apprehends the truth that the greatest happiness ever granted to a man is the privilege of being happy in the hour of his death.

He has no intention of converting this human society of ours into an efficient machine for efficient machine-operators, dominated by master mechanics. Men are put into the world, he realizes, to struggle, to suffer, to contend against the evil that is in their neighbors and in themselves, and to aspire toward the triumph of Love. They are put into this world to live like men, and to die like men. He seeks to preserve a society which allows men to attain manhood, rather than keeping them within bonds of perpetual childhood. With Dante, he looks upward from this place of slime, this world of gorgons and chimeras, toward the light which gives Love to this poor earth and all the stars. And, with Burke, he knows that "they will never love where they ought to love, who do not hate where they ought to hate."

Who are the Conservatives?

JUST OFF Central Park, in New York, a friend of mine lives in a brownstone house that has fallen upon evil days and is cut up into little apartments. The Puerto Ricans are moving down this way from Harlem, nowadays, and a dozen families of them have occupied the house next to my friend's. Their radios blare all night; their beer-bottles crash down the dumb-waiter all day; through my friend's windows comes an incessant medley of screams, curses, snatches of song, and shrill laughter. But my friend, who cannot afford to pay a higher rent elsewhere without giving up books and certain other touches of civilization, stays on. His apartment is an island of order in this Babel, for he and his family have resources not subject to time and place. They have educated themselves humanely, and do something to preserve the decent draperies of traditional life in a topsy-turvy world. The American thinker whom my friend admires most is Irving Babbitt, perhaps the strongest conservative author in the whole range of modern American letters. For my friend is an enlightened conservative; and he is also a truck-driver.

Another friend of mine is an old-fashioned manufacturer. A religious man, he has a strong will and a strong mind, and a strong respect for the pagan and the Christian virtues. By long experience of the world, he has learnt the true meaning of justice, which is this: "Give to each man the things which nature fits him for." He is not a sentimentalist nor an equalitarian, but he is a generous and honest man. Familiarity with contracts has taught him the necessity for the reign of law. He knows that thrift, diligence, and intelligence deserve their proper rewards, and that any society which denies this presently will cease to be a just society, or to exist at all. Wiser than most educationists, he knows that society is not a machine, to be tinkered with at a whim; society, instead, is a delicate growth, kept in tolerable health only because some conscientious men, ordinarily few in number, devote their lives to conserving the complicated general ideas and political institutions and economic methods which we have inherited from our ancestors. His practicality informs him that slogans like "human rights" and "absolute liberty" and "social justice" and "fair shares for all" do not have any meaning unless they are attached to particular proposals: he distrusts the abstractions of liberalism. My friend, in short, is a working conservative.

A third friend of mine—I am going to describe only three—is a farmer with a face like leather, who owns either eighty or a hundred acres of stony ground, on which, by much exertion, he raises potatoes and beans and cucumbers, and keeps a few cows. Intensely independent in character, he resents any endeavor to convert him into another sort of man than the being he is by nature and circumstance. He wants to live as his father lived before him, and to bring up his children in his own steps. He is well enough satisfied with the cabin that always has been his home. He knows that it is highly imprudent to disturb a thing that is at rest; he has a suspicion of most change, although he understands that society, like the soil, can grow sterile from lack of cultivation. But he is convinced that certain moral axioms never can be cast aside with impunity, and that a mysterious continuity guides the destinies of men, as surely as the seasons follow their cycle. A hater of centralization, a lover of old habits and old stories, in his little community he stands out with some success against the ascendancy of the mass-mind and against the threatened conversion of society into a mere state-supervised economic operation, rather than a way of living. He understands the idea of the Republic, a government of laws and not of men, and would confine the operation of government within prescriptive bounds. Although my farmer-friend is not much read in political theory, and probably could not express his social principles in any very coherent summary, still he is a reflective and genuine conservative.

Now most truck-drivers and manufacturers and farmers do not possess the will and intelligence of these three friends of mine. If they did, preserving justice and freedom in our society would not be so alarming a problem. But the point I am endeavoring to make is just this: the people whom we call "conservative" are not restricted to any social class or any economic occupation or any level of formal education. Some are physicians, and some engine-drivers, and some professors, and some clerks, and some bankers, and some clergymen, and some diemakers, and some soldiers. In a popular magazine, recently, I noticed a passing reference to "the rich conservatives, the well-off liberals, and the poor laboring men." This notion is nonsense. Some millionaires are fanatically radical, and some working men are fiercely conservative, and the well-to-do may be anything under the sun. Conservatism and liberalism and radicalism are states of mind, not of the pocketbook. The United States, throughout most of our history, have been a nation substantially conservative, though rich men have exerted less direct influence upon government here than almost anywhere else in the world. Conservatism is something more than mere solicitude for tidy incomes.

Conservatism, indeed, is a word with an old and honorable meaning—but a meaning almost forgotten by Americans for some years. Even today, although there are many men of conservative prejudices active in national and state politics, few are eager to describe themselves as "conservatives." The people of the United States became the chief conservative nation of the world at the very time when they had ceased to call themselves conservatives at home. For a generation, the word "liberal" had been in fashion, particularly in universities and among journalists. The liberal, in American parlance, has been a man in love with constant change; often he has been influenced directly by the group of ideas called pragmatism and the writings of John Dewey; commonly the liberal has tended to despise the lessons of the past and to look forward confidently to a vista of endless material progress, in which the state will play a larger and larger role, and a general equality of condition will be enforced.

This liberal now is a distraught and frightened man, incapable either of serious leadership or serious criticism. It is time for people who know they are not liberals or radicals to ask themselves just what they do believe, and what they must call themselves. The traditional system of ideas opposed to liberalism and radicalism is the conservative belief. Already the words "conservative" and "conservatism" are being employed as terms of praise in the popular press and by serious critics of society, and books by conservative writers are receiving an attention that they have been denied most of this century. In politics, as in physics, it is scarcely possible to make progress until you have defined your terms. What is conservatism? Who are the conservatives?

Aristotle was a conservative, and so was Cicero, and there have been intelligent conservatives in every age. John Stuart Mill, a century ago, called conservatives "the stupid party." But the conservatives have outlasted their enemies, or most of their enemies. Modern conservatism, as a regular body of ideas, took form about the beginning of the French Revolution. In England, the founder of true conservatism was Burke, whose *Reflections on the Revolution in France* turned the tide of opinion against the levelling and destructive impulse of the French revolutionaries. In America, the founders of the Republic had no desire to turn society upside down; and in their writings, particularly in the works of John Adams and in the *Federalist Papers,* we find a sober conservatism built upon an understanding of history and of human nature. I think a very brief review of the chief sources of modern conservative principles will be of service here.

Historically considered, modern conservatism is a protest against the delusions and excesses of the modern revolutionary impulse, which Mr. D.M. Brogan has described so somberly in *The Price of Revolution.* It is an error to look upon the American War of Independence as the first of the terrible revolutions of the modern era; for our "Revolution" was a movement intended to preserve the traditions of American society against the innovation of George III and his friends, not to create a new order in the thirteen colonies. The French Revolution, instead, with its contempt for social continuity and its exaltation of abstract doctrines, ushered in the disorder which has brought Western society—and now nearly all the world—so close to destruction. "Conservatism" was not a political term until the early years of the nineteenth century, when first Continental thinkers and presently English writers began to employ it to describe those principles of social and moral order which had been so powerfully expounded by Burke in his *Reflections*.

In Parliament, Burke's high and solemn denunciation of the French Revolution at first had little effect. His own friend and fellow-leader of the Whigs, Fox, looked upon the upheaval in France as a splendid triumph of progress and liberty; while the younger Pitt, then in power, thought the eclipse of the French monarchy more an opportunity for English advantage than a menace to established society in England. Perceiving that he must appeal from St. Stephen's Hall to the sound sense of the English public, Burke set to work writing a tremendous answer to a letter from his young French acquaintance Dupont, which soon became that book which is the foundation of conservative principles, *Reflections on the Revolution in France*. Dupont never saw this tremendous epistle until it was published, and then was astounded by it. The immediate effect of the *Reflections* was titanic. The Tories, the Portland Whigs, and some other persons began at once to perceive the terrible danger of revolution, and proceeded to that course of action which in the long run, would crush Napoleon. Fox's Whigs, on the contrary, cried down Burke as an apostate, and the Duke of Bedford was rash enough to accuse Burke of mere self-seeking, so that he provoked Burke's crushing reply called *A Letter to a Noble Lord*. A flood of pamphlets in answer to Burke's great work appeared through Britain and the Continent; in the English language, the two most influential retorts were those of James Mackintosh and Thomas Paine. Mackintosh, as the Revolution progressed, admitted that Burke had been wholly right, and became one of Burke's own disciples; and though Paine never disavowed his own radicalism, his narrow escape from the guillotine in Paris was sufficient refutation of his early high hopes for French liberty and justice.

In the minds of liberals as well as the minds of conservatives, from Woodrow Wilson to Harold Laski, from Samuel Taylor Coleridge to Paul Elmer More, Burke vanquished Paine in this great debate; and certainly he won the immense majority of his countrymen, so that Britain turned all her energies to the defeat of revolutionary violence. That leadership which is inspired by honor, that love of things established which grows out of a high veneration of the wisdom of our ancestors, that profound sagacity which reconciles necessary change with the best in the old order—these things Burke knew to be infinitely superior to all the pretended Rights of Man that Paine extolled; and British and American society, at least, have been incalculably influenced by Burke ever since the *Reflections* was published in 1790.

On first examination, the *Reflections* may seem to be a chaotic book; but really it is nothing of the sort. Burke "winds into his subject like a serpent," blending history with principle, splendid imagery with profound practical aphorisms. All his life, he detested "abstractions"—that is, speculative notions with no secure foundation in history or in knowledge of true human character. What Burke is doing in this book, then, is setting forth a system of "principles"—by which he means general truths deduced from the wisdom of our ancestors, practical experience, and a knowledge of the human heart. He never indulges in "pure" philosophy because he will not admit that the statesman has any right to look at man in the abstract, rather than at particular men in particular circumstances. To understand the greatness of Burke's book, one must read it through, and that with the closest of attention. Written at white heat, the *Reflections* burns with all the wrath and anguish of a prophet who saw the traditions of Christendom and the fabric of the civil social order dissolving before his eyes. Yet his words are suffused with a keenness of observation and a high wisdom which are the marks of an accomplished statesman. This book is polemic at its most overwhelming strength, an undying work of political philosophy, and one of the most influential tracts in the history of civilization.

Today its pertinence is greater, whether for conservative or liberal (Burke himself was both), than it was forty years ago. The revolution of our times has dissipated the shallow optimism of the early years of the twentieth century, and we now perceive in the Russian Revolution the counterpart, still more terrible, of the French Revolution; and we behold in the grinding tyranny of the Soviets the full realization of Burke's prophecies. Having broken with all the old sanctions to integrity, Burke knew, revolutionaries must come down to force and terror, the only influences which suffice to govern a society that repudiates the conservative principles of veneration and prudence. The spirit of religion and the spirit of a gentleman, Burke tells us, gave to modern Europe everything generous and lovely in our culture. A speculative system which detests both piety and just order speedily will repudiate even the pretended affection for equality which gives that system its initial appeal to the masses. "To them, the will, the wish, the want, the liberty, the toil, the blood of individuals is nothing," Burke said of the French zealots. What these pretended humanitarians really sought was power; the human person was as nothing, in their fierce imagination, by the side of an abstract nationalism. In the name of liberty, every ancient freedom would be overthrown; in the name of fraternity, every atrocity excused. And the true moral equality of men would be rejected together with the religious sanction which gave it meaning. We know all too well, in the middle of the twentieth century, the dreadful accuracy of this description, which nineteenth-century optimists took for mere distempered fancy. We, to our sorrow, live that "antagonist world" of madness and despair which Burke contrasted with the traditional order of social existence. Oliver Goldsmith once feared that Burke was giving to his party the noble talents he ought to give to mankind. In the end, it was very different for Burke broke with party and friends and the very climate of opinion, out of "the exigencies of this tremendous reason." Only today are we coming to understand fully the nobility and the wisdom of his act. Burke knew that the Revolution in France was no simple political contest, no culmination of enlightenment, but the inception of a tremendous moral convulsion from which society would not recover until the disease, the disorder of revolt against Providence, had run its course.

Burke's American influence has been incalculably pervasive, North and South. The Federalists—not only Hamilton and Ames and Dwight, but John Adams and his son, these latter somewhat against their will—learned a great deal from him. The Southern conservatism of John Randolph and Calhoun, and so in some measure Southern political opinion to the present day, is rooted in Burke. Tocqueville, Burke's best Continental pupil, reinforced the American appreciation of Burke. "Criticism of literature as criticism of life begins, as a serious matter," Harold Laski wrote, "with James Russell Lowell"; and Lowell, like Arnold, believed Burke be the great master of English prose and the great source of political wisdom. Ever since, social and literary criticism in the United States has borne the mark (sometimes unacknowledged) of Burke.

Yet it will not do to neglect the native American sources of our conservative ideas. The conservative tradition in America is receiving just now a respectful attention long denied it, from the age of the Mathers to the age of Elihu Root and Henry Cabot Lodge. Much still needs to be done. Mr. Daniel Boorstin, in his *Genius of American Politics,* reminds us how American conservation has usually found its expression in a respect for juristic precedent and constitution, beginning with the *Federalist Papers,* rather than in an affirmation of abstract political doctrines. Such substantially, was the conservatism of Chancellor Kent, of Calhoun, of Webster, of Alexander Stephens, of Joseph Choate, to choose some eminent names almost at random. This cast of mind has dominated the class in America which Tocqueville called our best expression of natural aristocracy—our lawyers, who from the beginning have constituted a stabilizing influence upon the American temper.

Both of our early parties, the Federalists and the Republicans, were led by men whose training and mode of expression were those of Anglo-American jurisprudence, rather than of metaphysical speculation. Jefferson, despite the show of French ideas which he made from time to time, founded his idea of liberty and justice upon the writings of Coke and Kames and the other English juridical writers, and upon the tradition of English freedom from the Anglo-Saxons down to the eighteenth century. James Madison, fundamentally conservative both at the time of the framing of the Federal Constitution and in his later years, expressed this prudent and reasoned view of human rights and duties with a high prescience. And the most vigorous and candid of American conservatives, old John Adams, anticipated Burke in a good many things, and did a great deal to establish ineradicably in Americans' minds that attachment to the division and balancing of power which has been our principal achievement in the art of just government. A thorough critical biography of that great man, incidentally, is one of the most conspicuous gaps in American literature. His demolition of the delusion that men are naturally benevolent, his historical examination of constitutional government, and his attack upon centralized power, democratic despotism, and sentimental abstraction are the best expression of the American genius for a practical politics illuminated by historical knowledge.

The founders of the American Republic, knowing that theirs was a conservative task, endeavored to attain to the level of Burke's model of a statesman, who should combine a disposition to preserve with an ability to reform. "They meant to set up a standard maxim for free society," Abraham Lincoln said once, "which should be familiar to all, and revered by all; constantly looked to, constantly labored for, and even though never perfectly attained, constantly approximated, and thereby constantly spreading and deepening its influence and augmenting the happiness and value of life to all people of all colors everywhere." This prudent idea, so remote from the Jacobin dream of absolute rights imposed immediately without respect for established interests and traditions, has remained ever since strong in the minds of our leading statesmen. Lincoln himself, though the object of much misplaced "liberal" adulation was substantially a conservative, as Mr. Stanley Pargellis argues. "What is conservatism?" Lincoln asked, before he was president. "Is it not adherence to the old and tried, against the new and untried?" Lincoln's original allegiance was to the Whigs, then the conservative party of the United States; and, as Mr. Richard Weaver observes in *The Ethics of Rhetoric,* "It is no accident that Lincoln became the founder of the greatest American conservative party, even if that party was debauched soon after his career ended. He did so because his method was that of the conservative."

The best men in our political life usually have desired to be esteemed as conservatives; Lincoln was one, Calhoun another. Our native radical movements, like Populism, commonly have been inspired, however curiously, by certain conservative instincts. Doctrinaire socialism never has been able to win many converts among us. Our occasional professions of egalitarianism have been given the lie by our actual conduct of affairs.

We have submitted ourselves with good will to the most successful conservative device in the history of government, the Federal Constitution, so that it is quite natural for us to be, nowadays, the chief conservative power among the nations. None of our great parties ever has been dominated by true radicals, and all of them always have contained real and influential conservatives. Our native conservatism extends to every class and interest in our society. We Americans were from the first a people endowed with strong conservative prejudices, immeasurably influenced by the spirit of religious veneration, firm in a traditional morality, hostile to arbitrary power whether possessed by a monarch or a mob, zealous to guard against centralization, attached to prescriptive rights, convinced of the necessity and beneficence of the institution of property. We have reason, I think, to be proud of the healthy and continuous existence of conservative principles here, for three centuries; and it is to be hoped that we will act today in the light of this long conservative development, not lusting after abstract new doctrines, whether those doctrines are called "conservative" or "liberal" or "radical." What we most require is an illumination and renewed recognition of the lofty conservative concepts and institutions which have sustained our nation.

Now Mr. Arthur Schlesinger, Jr., writing in the quarterly journal *Confluence*, remarks that "The aim of the New Conservatives is to transform conservatism from a negative philosophy of niggling and self-seeking into an affirmative movement of healing and revival, based on a living sense of human relatedness and on a dedication to public as against class interests, all to be comprehended in a serious and permanent philosophy of social and national responsibility." This is well put. It is important, however, to make sure that we do not draw certain erroneous deductions from Mr. Schlesinger's essay. First of all, true conservatism has not ordinarily been "a negative philosophy of niggling and self-seeking." Many of the people who think this are suffering from a delusion semantic and historical in its sources. Such notions continue to prevail even among professors of history and politics, so that to them the word "conservatism" means a doctrinaire attachment to the accumulation of private wealth, an inclination toward political centralization, and a glorying in ruthless competition. But these beliefs, whether or not they

26

are consonant with one another, are none of them articles of conservative conviction.

Nor do true conservatives seek to harden the conservative impulse into a set of dogmas. They do not despise philosophy; and probably Mr. Schlesinger does not mean by "a serious and permanent philosophy" such a system of abstract doctrines as the Benthamites professed. Prudence and humility are the virtues of the successful conservative statesman, who does not mistake abstractions for principles.

With these qualifications, Mr. Schlesinger's summary of the aims of thinking conservatives is valuable. But Mr. Schlesinger believes that modern American conservatives suffer from impracticality and an historical confusion. One cannot trace a regular line of consistent conservative leaders in American history, he says; besides, "the New Conservatives, for all their ardent conviction that philosophy must be precipitated out of the actual circumstances of society and the concrete life of the people, remain astonishingly indifferent to the actual circumstances of *American* society and to the concrete life of the *American* people." Then, too, America never had a feudal system, and so lacks the aristocratic traditions which gave force to European conservatism. Mr. Schlesinger insists that "as feudalism was the central fact in European conservatism, so the business community must be the central fact in American conservatism." The modern conservatives either must align themselves with the industrialists, therefore, he continues, or else with what he calls "the party of the people" (at present, it appears, the minority party). "The true obligation of the New Conservatives is to illuminate the limits and potentialities of business rule in America, and not to reproduce the agreeable but irrelevant sentiments of European conservatism."

So, after all, Mr. Schlesinger slips into the errors of the Jacobins—especially the Jacobin passion for simplicity. The dominant aspirations of the French revolutionaries were for simplicity of structure and concept; it was no mere coincidence that they detested Gothic architecture. And Mr. Schlesinger, in his desire to reduce the complexity of American politics to black-and-white abstractions, lops away from his concept of the antagonist forces in our country every branch or twig that does not suit his *a priori* system, so that when he has finished, we are left with the Hard, Practical Industrialist confronting the Civil-Liberties, Democratic Liberal. This tableau is impossibly fanciful. First of all, Mr. Schlesinger has confused the Conservatives (who did not exist before 1790, and did not take the name for more than two decades after that) with the Tories; then he has supposed the conservative interest to have been identical with the interest of the landed proprietors in England and Europe, which it never was; then he has quite ignored the conservative interest in America which came from roots very different from mere love of material aggrandizement; then he has eliminated from consideration the conservatives in the Democratic party; then he has implied that the thinking conservatives—unlike Harvard professors—know nothing of real life in these United States; and at last, after such a series of ingenuous bounds, he leaves us with the interesting alternatives of serving Mammon or serving The People.

Now, in sober reality, conservatives are not merely a sect of political economists, but rather a number of persons, of all classes and occupations, whose view of life is reverential, and who tend to be guided by the wisdom of their ancestors, instead of abstract speculation. To attempt to identify the true conservative with the hard-headed man of business is to substitute what sociologists love to call a "stereotype" for careful analysis of American society—in short, it is an error precisely of the sort which Mr. Schlesinger attributes to the conservative writers. The American businessman is a being caricatured insensately by both his enemies and his friends. Far from the existence of a "business rule" in the American Republic, the fact is that the vast majority of American industrialists and entrepreneurs, preoccupied with the intricacies of production, decline to take any substantial interest in politics, and constitute no coherent body of opinion; they are not "conservative" or "liberal" or "radical," but simply busy. And if all men of business should turn political philosophers, or even political managers, next week, we should all be ruined.

Someone has to do the world's work; the man of business, by definition, is not a man of leisure; and although I hope we may count upon his intelligent support, increasingly, of a reflective conservatism, we should be silly to expect him to lead us in politics. Besides, he is not trying to lead; he is desperately eager to follow, if he can follow with confidence; and if sometimes he follows the demagogue and the charlatan, it is because he errs in judgment, more than in heart. And important though the support of manufacturers and bankers and retailers is to the conservative cause, the businessman does not stand alone as a buttress of the conservative interest. The American farmer generally is conservative; and the skilled craftsman; and the lawyer; and the man who goes to church; and the man who owns a house; and a great complex of other groups and interests and occupations, joined in a common conservative belief out of their understanding that they are all safe together within American political traditions and American moral prejudices.

Conservatism, then, is not simply the concern of the people who have a great deal of property and influence: it is a social concept important to everyone who desires equal justice and personal freedom and all the lovable old ways of humanity. Conservatism is not simply a defense of "capitalism," the abstraction of Marx. The true conservative does defend private enterprise stoutly; and one of the reasons why he cherishes it is that private enterprise is the only really practicable system, in the modern world, for satisfying our economic wants; but more even than this, he defends private enterprise as a means to an end. That end is a society just and free, in which every man has a right to what is his own, and to what he inherits from his father, and to the rewards of his own ability and industry; a society which cherishes variety and individuality, and rises superior to the dreary plain of socialism. A conservative society enables men to be truly human persons, not mere specks in a collective tapioca-pudding society; it respects their dignity as persons—or, as Chesterton put it, the right of every man to be "his own potty little self."

Strong though the conservative tradition is in America, it will not suffice for us simply to express a vague opposition to collectivism if, at the same time, conservatives allow the enemies of traditional society to obtain control over the instruments of political and economic survival. Centralization, extension of the economic functions of government, the increase of taxation and national debts, the decay of family-life and local association, and the employment of state education to enforce uniformity of character and opinion—

these influences, and others, are at work among us with dreadful power. We are just beginning to make our way back to the first principles of politics and ethics. The conservative instinct of America, just not reawakening, must draw its vigor from everyone who believes in the enduring truth, in liberty under law, and in the political and economic institutions essential to the preservation of a just and free and tranquil society. Americans have more to conserve, probably, than have any other modern people; and conservative impulses are more general among us than anywhere else.

We all are partners in this gigantic incorporation of American society, whether our material share in the national partnership is large or small; the man with the smallest portion has as much right to that share as the man with the greatest possessions has to what is his own. Correspondingly, we all have the duty of standing by our common heritage of the Republic.

The majority of conservatives, in every country, always have been men of slender means and obscure station. These conservatives are not devoted primarily to "free competition" or "the American standard of living," valuable though those possessions may be. What gives the true conservative his strength in our time of troubles is his belief in a moral order which joins all classes in a common purpose, and through which men may live in justice and liberty. It is high time that the leaders of political conservatism began to speak in terms of ethics, of right and wrong. If they do so, they will find that they enjoy a free field, for their liberal and radical adversaries are morally bankrupt in this fateful year.

The American conservative, priding himself upon his old antipathy toward abstraction, ought to endeavor to define his own terms. Precisely what is the essence of our American conservatism? I think that the old conservative character of the American nation is marked by these qualities:

> (1) A belief in an order that is more human, which has implanted in man a character of mingled good and evil, susceptible of improvement only by an inner working, not by mundane schemes for perfectibility. This conviction lies at the heart of American respect for the past, as the record of Providential purpose. The conservative mind is suffused with veneration. Men and nations,

the conservative believes, are governed by moral laws; and political problems, at bottom, are moral and religious problems. An eternal chain of duty links the generations that are dead, and the generation that is living now, and the generations yet to be born. We have no right, in this brief existence of ours, to alter irrevocably the shape of things, in contempt of our ancestors and of the rights of posterity. Politics is the art of apprehending and applying the Justice which stands above statutory law.

(2) An affection for variety and complexity and individuality, even for singularity, which has exerted a powerful check upon the political tendency toward what Tocqueville calls "democratic despotism." Variety and complexity, in the opinion of conservatives, are the high gifts of truly civilized society. The uniformity and standardization of liberal and radical planners would be the death of vitality and freedom, a life-in-death, every man precisely like his neighbor—and, like the damned of the *Inferno,* forever deprived of hope.

(3) A conviction that justice, properly defined, means "to each the things that go with his own nature," not a levelling equality; and joined with this is a correspondent respect for private property of every sort. Civilized society requires distinctions of order, wealth, and responsibility; it cannot exist without true leadership. A free society will endeavor, indeed, to afford to men of natural abilities every opportunity to rise by their own efforts; but it will resist strenuously the radical delusion that exact equality of station and wealth can benefit everyone. Society longs for just leadership; and if people destroy natural distinctions among men, presently some Bonaparte will fill the vacuum—or worse than Bonaparte.

(4) A suspicion of concentrated power, and a consequent attachment to our federal principle and to division and balancing of authority at every level of government.

(5) A reliance upon private endeavor and sagacity in nearly every walk of life, together with a contempt for the abstract designs of the collectivistic reformer. But to this self-reliance, in the mind of the American conservative, is joined the conviction that in matters beyond the scope of material endeavor and the present moment, the individual tends to be foolish, but the species is wise; therefore we rely in great matters upon the wisdom of our ances-

tors. History is an immense storehouse of knowledge. We pay a decent respect to the moral traditions and immemorial customs of mankind; for men who ignore the past are condemned to repeat it. The conservative distrusts the radical visionary and the planner who would chop society into pieces and mould it nearer to his heart's desire. The conservative appeals beyond the fickle opinion of the hour to what Chesterton called "the democracy of the dead"—that is, the considered judgment of the wise men who died before our time. To presume that men can plan rationally the whole of existence is to expose mankind to a terrible danger from the collapse of existing institutions; for conservatives know that most men are governed, on many occasions, more by emotion than by pure reason.

(6) A prejudice against sudden change, a feeling that it is unwise to break radically with political prescription, an inclination to tolerate what abuses may exist in present institutions out of a practical acquaintance with the violent and unpredictable nature of doctrinaire reform.

American character being complex, along with these conservative threads are woven certain innovating and even radical threads. It is true, too, that national character is formed, in part, by the circumstances of history and environment, so that such a character may alter, or even grow archaic. Certain powerful influences presently at work among us are affecting this traditional character, for good or ill. It is time, nevertheless, that we acknowledged the predominantly conservative cast of the American mind, since the inception of the Republic, and time that we paid our respects to the strength and honesty of that character. We are not merely the pawns of impersonal historical influences; we have it in our power to preserve the best in our old institutions and in our old opinions, even in this era of vertiginous change; and we will do well, I think, if we endeavor to govern ourselves, in the age that is dawning, by the prescriptive values in American character which have become almost our second nature.

Mr. Daniel Boorstin, in his recent study of American political institutions, suggests that the chief merit of them has been that they rose out of the peculiar circumstances of American life, rather than from abstract ideologies; and he is right. He goes on to advise us not to attempt to impose American institutions upon all the world, because one cannot transplant history; and again he is right. It does not follow, however, that we ought to leave our national institutions and character out of consideration in our foreign policy. The conspicuous defect of our course of action abroad since the end of the war against Germany and Japan seems to have been that we have endeavored to espouse and sustain a dim ideology which is neither an expression of the American experience nor a system founded upon the traditional institutions of the nations whose concerns we have busied ourselves with. We have talked windily of "democracy" and "the four freedoms" and "the permanent revolution" and similar abstractions. But we have meant, ordinarily, something very different from anything that exists in America. Too often we have commended, in Europe or Asia, the totalitarian democracy of Rousseau, or a catalogue of non-descript "freedoms" impossible to attain anywhere upon earth, or the destruction of the established ways of life and thought of whole peoples, so long as that revolution was not professedly or initially "Marxist." We cannot afford to be so naive much longer.

It is ridiculous, for instance, to talk of "fighting for democracy" in Indo-China when the people we support there are not democrats at all, and cannot be, in the light of history and the present condition of Indo-China. We owe ourselves and the world candor. We are not struggling to establish universal "democracy" or "capitalism" or "human rights." Our mission in the affairs of nations is not to undertake an eccentric crusade on behalf of these abstractions, but rather the practical task of repelling the menace of Soviet imperialism, and of conserving the freedom and justice and strength of the United States. Most of us are not really so arrogant as to think we have a right to remould the whole world in our image. The best we can do, toward redeeming the states of Europe and Asia from the menace of revolution and the distresses of our time, is to realize our own conservative character, suspicious of doctrinaire alteration, respectful toward history, preferring variety over uniformity, acknowledging a moral order composed of human persons, not of mere political and economic atoms subservient to the state. We have not been appointed the correctors of mankind; but, under God, we may be an example to mankind.

I have heaped a great deal of praise upon conservatism, enlightened conservatism, the conservatism of honor and reflection. There exist varieties of conservatism, however—or, rather, impulses vulgarly called conservative—for which I have no sympathy. One of these is the conservatism of mediocrity, and the other the conservatism of desolation.

By the conservatism of mediocrity, I mean the concept of the *juste milieu,* the middle course, the excluded middle, the way of the trimmer and temporizer, pluming himself on having attained the Golden Mean when in truth he has only split the difference. Unless the conservative adheres to some enduring principles, the middle course will be wherever one extreme or the other decides to put it. If, for instance, a communist faction demands the confiscation of all property, and a "reactionary" group maintain that they do not want any of their property confiscated, it is scarcely conservative to endeavor to compromise by confiscating only *half* the property in question. Such an issue must be settled by an appeal to enduring justice, not by splitting the difference. The real conservative is not a devotee of "expediency," in the modern meaning of that word. Burke, it is true, often commended policies of "expedience"; but what he meant was *prudence,* the avoidance of applying abstract *a priori* doctrines regardless of particular circumstances. Nor is the real conservative a pragmatist. Mr. C. Hartley Grattan, some few years ago, commended a certain Republican senator as a "pragmatic conservative." But there is no such animal.

Pragmatism, in the meaning it has acquired from its adoption by Pierce, William James, and John Dewey, is the policy of judging all things purely from the standpoint of how they "work"—that is, simply in the light of present experience, in contempt of tradition and the past, and in the confidence that somehow vague experiment with everything established will lead to future sure improvement. No conservative can hold with this notion, for the conservative judges all things in the light of authority and the wisdom of our ancestors, tempered by a willingness to accept evidence of altered circumstances. A pragmatist has no faith that abiding principles exist; while the conservative believes that a man without principles is an unprincipled man. A conservative can be an empiricist, however, and many conservatives are—that is, they judge of present things by the light of experience, or history, a very different method from the pragmatic endeavor to act upon sheer experiment and the flickering light of the evanescent present Lincoln, despite the attempts of certain commentators to prove otherwise, was not a pragmatist, and not ordinarily a trimmer; he declared that the endeavor to march smugly between pretended extremes was "a sophistical contrivance." And I am convinced that "conservatives" who think that their whole duty is to play Artful Dodger will end in the vestibule of Hell, where Dante saw them blown about by every wind of doctrine.

By the conservatism of desolation, I mean the forlorn endeavor of certain persons of conservative instincts to convince themselves that they are "individualists"—that is, devotees of spiritual and social isolation. The dreary secular dogma of individualism is the creation of Godwin, Hodgskin, and Herbert Spencer, and it progresses from anarchy back to anarchy again. Any thinking conservative knows it for a snare and a delusion. The real conservative is all in favor of sound individuality; he is all against doctrinaire "individualism," the belief that we exist solely in ourselves, and for ourselves, so many loveless specks in infinite time and space, like the unfortunate youth in Mark Twain's *Mysterious Stranger* to whom Satan reveals that nothing exists except the boy and empty space, and that his very informant is no more than a random thought of the desolate Self. *La vida es sueño, y los sueños sueños son.* Whatever we may say to Calderon, it is well to remember that the emancipated critic of Twain's novel is the Devil, or at least the Devil's nephew. Individualism was born in the hell of spiritual solitude. The conservative knows that he is part of a great continuity and essence, created to do unto others as he would have others do unto him. Godwin's and Spencer's individualism, literally applied, would destroy the whole fabric of civilization. It is nonsense in any age; but in our complex age, with all its apparatus of industry and urban life, it would bring a very speedy and very unpleasant death to almost all men.

We ought not to indulge such childish heroics. We do not really live for our selves, nor unto our selves. Burke and Adams knew that individuality, the dignity of personality and private rights, was a great good, and the product of elaborate conventions, developed by the painful experience of the human race over many thousands of years. They also knew that the doctrine of individualism preached by their enemy Godwin was nicely calculated to wipe out the whole civil social order, should it get a hold upon the popular imagination. Burke was the most courageous opponent of tyranny and the improper extension of the powers of the state; but he knew that just government is the creation of Providence, intended to enable men to live a life, through willing cooperation, which they could not possibly enjoy in a state of anarchy.

The conservative, if he understands himself and his world, is no sentimental humanitarian; but neither is he a swaggering nihilist, jeering at the state, the duties of men in society, and the necessities of modern life. As a reaction against the grim and insensate collectivism that menaces us today, this flight to individualism is understandable; but it is consummate folly, for all that, and even more disastrous to the conservative cause than the policy of unprincipled trimming. There is an order which holds all things in their places, Burke says; it is made for us, and we are made for it. The reflective conservative, far from denying the existence of this eternal order, endeavors to ascertain its nature, and to find his place in it. The shape of that order in the twentieth century, and the way in which conservatives may reconcile their birthright from their forefathers with that change essential to any healthy society, are the subjects of the ten short chapters which follow.

The Problem of the Mind

At the end of the famous tribute to Marie Antionette, Burke exclaims, "But the age of chivalry is gone. That of sophisters, economists, and calculators has succeeded; and the glory of Europe is extinguished forever. Never, never more shall we behold that generous loyalty to rank and sex, that proud submission, that dignified obedience, that subordination of the heart, which kept alive, even in servitude itself, the spirit of an exalted freedom. The unbought grace of life, the cheap defense of nations, the nurse of manly sentiment and heroic enterprise, is gone! It is gone, that sensibility of principle, that chastity of honor, which felt a stain like a wound, which inspired courage whilst it mitigated ferocity, which ennobled whatever it touched, and under which vice itself lost half its evil, by losing all its grossness."

All this enraged Paine. Burke, he said, pitied the plumage but forgot the dying bird; besides Paine could not understand what Burke meant by "the unbought grace of life." Burke employs this idea of the unbought grace of life to describe the great civilizing and ordering influence of a liberal mind, in the old and true sense of the word "liberal"—that is, the disciplined reason and imagination of free men, which were the product of the education of a gentleman. A gentleman, like Cicero's honorable Roman, is essentially the possessor of such a mind, with the habits it encourages—whether or not any particular gentleman is born to great expectations. Without that discipline and those circumstances which have made possible the unbought grace of life in Western civilization, Burke writes in his *Appeal from the New Whigs to the Old*, a natural aristocracy cannot exist among men; and without that aristocracy, soon there is no nation. These, Burke says, are the elements which form that unbought grace, and confer upon society a peace and harmony and justice, drawn from an elevated moral leadership, which the sophister and the calculator cannot restore, once they have destroyed the institutions that have sheltered this grace of life:

> To be bred in a place of estimation; to see nothing low and sordid from one's infancy; to be taught to respect one's self; to be habituated to the censorial inspection of the public eye; to look early to public opinion; to stand upon such elevated ground as to be enabled to take a large view of the widespread and infinitely diversified combinations of men and affairs in a large society; to have leisure to read, to reflect, to converse; to be enabled to draw the court and attention of the wise and learned wherever they are to be found; to be habituated in the pursuit of honor and duty; to be formed to the greatest degree of vigilance, foresight, and circumspection, in a state of things in which no fault is committed with impunity, and the slightest mistakes draw on the most ruinous consequences; to be led to a guarded and regulated conduct, from a sense that you are considered as an instructor of your fellow-citizens in their highest concerns, and that you act as a reconciler between God and man. . . .

A mind and a temper shaped upon this pattern were the ends of old-fashioned liberal education; and as that system of education has decayed among us, our minds and tempers seem to have deteriorated proportionately. Was it indeed the plumage that Burke pitied? Or did Burke discern, Paine notwithstanding, that what was dying in 1790 was not the French people, but all that grace of life which, with religion, raises man above the brutes? This grace is not mere plumage; it is the lifeblood of individuality and of our civilization, Burke knew. When it is lacking, the very sense of justice and the sense of gratitude are effaced, so that Paine himself presently was flung into prison by his "dying bird," the French people, and came very close to sharing the doom of the queen whose cause he had derided. The time has now come, I think, six generations after Burke and Paine, when the remnant of this unbought grace of life which came down to us from our ancestors is nearly exhausted; and if we are to hope at all for a high-minded and talented leadership in the age that is dawning, if we apprehend in any degree the problems of justice and leisure and liberal thought that perplex our time, I think we must turn our minds to the examination of this unbought grace of life: what it is, and whence it comes, and how it may be preserved or restored.

"We are but too apt to consider things in the state in which we find them," Burke writes in the *Reflections*, "without sufficiently adverting to the causes by which they have been produced, and possibly may be upheld. Nothing is more certain, than that our manners, our civilization, and all the good things which are connected with manners and civilization, have, in this European world of ours, depended for ages upon two principles; and were indeed the result of both combined; I mean the spirit of a gentleman, and the spirit of religion. The nobility and the clergy, the one by profession, the other by patronage, kept learning in existence, even in the midst of arms and confusions, and whilst governments were rather in their causes, than formed. Learning paid back what it received to nobility and to priesthood; and paid it back with usury, by enlarging their ideas, and by furnishing their minds." Yet the arrogant man of ideas, Burke continues, in modern times too often has been debauched by ambition, and has turned against both the spirit of religion and the spirit of a gentleman; he has become a neoterist, enamored of purposeless change; he has joined the revolution of enterprising and unscrupulous talents. But the scholar cannot survive the extinction of the priest and the gentleman. "Along with its natural protectors and guardians, learning will be cast into the mire, and trodden down under the hoofs of a swinish multitude."

John Adams flew into a fury at these latter words, calling Burke an impious reviler of the human species. Yet Burke was only paraphrasing the seventh chapter of Matthew, sixth verse: "Give not that which is holy unto the dogs, neither cast ye your pearls before swine, lest they trample them under their feet, and turn again and rend you." When the unbought grace of life is stifled, then indeed will the multitude be swinish, Burke thought; the whole noble essence of an elevated civil social existence evaporates, once the circumstances which made possible the spirit of religion and the spirit of a gentleman are altered fatally by some iron new order. The problem confronts us with a terrible urgency; and the late Professor C. E.

M. Joad, in the concluding chapters of his penetrating book *Decadence,* suggests that the struggle already is concluded in favor of the sensual masses; that whatever survives of the grace of life exists merely upon sufferance, or because unnoticed; and that whenever the attention of the modern multitude is attracted to the cost of things that are not flesh, or whenever the interests of the total state, Tocqueville's "democratic despotism," conflict with the claims of this forlorn grace, the poor remnant of our cultural and social inheritance is crushed mercilessly beneath the hoofs. If Professor Joad is correct, it seems probable, then, that Paine was wrong, and Burke was right.

The practice of the unbought grace of life will not survive the vanishing of its principle, and its principle must be nourished in every generation by the men and women who have wealth, power, and eminence. So long as the complex edifice of sentiment and tradition which we call "the unbought grace of life" still has some attraction for the masters of society—why, as Burke told the Duke of Bedford, "we are all safe together." But if these ideas of duty and honor and right and beauty are treated as so many "ridiculous, absurd, and antiquated" fashions by the men who make our laws and form our tastes, then the cement of society begins to crumble, upon every level of existence; as Burke himself concludes, "nature is disobeyed, and the rebellious are outlawed, cast forth and exiled, from this world of reason, and order, and peace, and virtue, and fruitful penitence, into the antagonist world of madness, discord, vice, confusion, and unavailing sorrow."

Among the causes of the disorder which has fallen upon the modern world, I think that a general contempt for the whole idea of the unbought grace of life has been one of the most efficient. The modern mind has sneered at all these distinctions between man and man which the word "order" signifies, and so has deprived itself of the leadership inspired by sensibility of principle, and inflicted upon itself the ascendancy of cunning or of force. The modern mind has forgotten that there exists an unbought grace more valuable than any degree of material aggrandizement, and so has denied the claims of true leisure, and condemned itself to boredom, until that boredom threatens to extirpate the speculative imagination which inspires any high civilization. The modern mind has done its best to sweep aside those classes and that education which apprehended the meaning of justice, and so is menaced by a power of fraud and violence which no police force can arrest unaided. The modern mind has made utility the basis of its politics, and so has left itself defenseless against the self-interest of the fierce egoist and the hard knot of special interests. The modern mind has failed to understand Burke's admonition that for us to love our country, our country ought to be lovely, and so has subjected us to the most hideous wave of architectural deformity and artistic debasement that any civilization has endured. The modern mind has thought of men as the flies of a summer, and so has deprived itself of the wisdom of our ancestors, and laid waste the portion of our posterity.

I think that all these crimes and follies are closely bound up with the decay of consciousness of what a reality the unbought grace of life has been among men, and what a power for their betterment, though it cannot be weighed or tabulated. I do not mean to forget the part that industrialism, economic levelling, the degradation of the democratic dogma, and secularism have had in this desolation of our heritage. Yet when all allowance has been made for the material and political causes of our modern discontents, in Western society, I think that a confusion about first principles still must be accounted a direct and terrible cause of our perplexities; and I think that an ignorance of the very nature of the unbought grace of life, expressed by Tom Paine when the form of eighteenth-century life had begun to give way, is just such a confusion about first principles. Paine expected to resolve by political adjustment all the ills to which humanity is heir. But politics is indeed the preoccupation of the quarter-educated; and, infatuated with political techniques and sentimental humanitarianism, we have endangered the very springs of human achievement, this past century and a half, by neglecting "the wardrobe of a moral imagination, which the heart owns and the imagination ratifies." While we stand irresolute, this devastation of the higher culture continues with dismaying speed; but if we can attain to some candid understanding of our malady, then possibly we may begin to carry the war into Africa.

The consequences of the neglect or decay of this unbought grace of life being indescribably intricate, any man who begins to examine the problem is oppressed by the dread that his effort will come to no more than a series of bewildered sallies into the boundless desolation of modern apathy, without meaning or achievement. Yet anyone who quotes Burke ought to be suspicious of abstraction, out of deference to his model—as suspicious of abstraction as he is respectful of principle. To be more specific, then, there are two principal aspects to the degradation of the modern mind. One of these is the effect upon the person: the starving of nearly every man's and woman's higher imagination, so that Reason, the faculty which distinguishes the human person in this world from the brutes, is reduced in acuity and in depth; this is the worst thing which can be done to a person, worse than political tyranny or physical injury. And the other aspect is the effect upon the republic, or society: the neglect of those intellectual and moral disciplines which enable us to live together harmoniously, and which are the foundation of free government; this assault upon intelligence, if it is not repelled, must end by subjecting the great majority of men to the mastery of a few managers and manipulators, or else in anarchy.

The people who accept or applaud the educational schemes and the social alterations which accelerate this decay of Reason among us may be ignorant of the grand tendency of their undertaking; commonly, indeed, they think that they are imparting "adjustment" or "democracy" or "enriched appreciation" or some other abstract benefit to the rising generation. But in plain fact, they are doing all they can to deprive modern society of both true leadership and intelligent self-reliance, and all they can to make the inner life of the person one vast utilitarian tedium, peopled only by smug generalizations.

What the church is to the spirit of religion, liberal learning is to the unbought grace of life—the only means for realizing the end. Where there is no liberal learning, in the long run there is no civilization—at least no civilization in our Christian and Western tradition. For some years or even generations after liberal education has been extinguished, in this country or that, the outward signs of civilization may remain, sustained by the dwindling intellectual capital of the generation that is passing, or by borrowing the thought and the moral standards of nations where something of the old grace of life survives. Yet in the end, the mind of man stifles without the liberating influence of humane learning. And in an age which talks windily of "equality of opportunity," we ought to remind ourselves that a liberal education is not designed simply to satisfy the tastes of ready-made gentlemen; instead, liberal disciplines offer to everyone able to undertake them the possibility of becoming a gentleman. Far from being an instrument of "class supremacy," a liberal education has long been a far more effective leveller than any program of positive legislation in America; and, unlike most devices for producing equality through juridical and economic devices, a liberal education levels upward, not downward.

By the spirit of a gentleman, Burke and Newman did not mean simply the deportment of superior rank. They meant, rather, that elevation of mind and temper, that generosity and courage of mind, which are the property of every person whose intelligence and character have been humanely disciplined. They meant that liberal education, and that habit of acting upon principles which rise superior to immediate advantage and private interest, which distinguish the free man from the servile man. There cannot be too many gentlemen among us. Burke and Newman meant by "the spirit of a gentleman" what the later Roman writers called *humanitas*, that ethical discipline acquired through knowledge of great literature and great lives which teaches men the meaning of duty and of continuity. Lacking this, Burke says, all the schooling in the world is of no avail; the principle of continuity ceases to be apprehended; and with the triumph of the vulgar solicitations of the hour over humane disciplines, "No part of life would retain its acquisitions. Barbarism with regard to science and literature, unskillfulness with regard to arts and manufactures, would infallibly succeed to the want of a steady education and settled principle; and thus the commonwealth itself would, in a few generations, be disconnected into the dust and powder of individuality, and at length dispersed to all the winds of heaven."

Paul Elmer More, in his *Aristocracy and Justice*, after praising Sir Thomas Elyot's *Boke Named the Governour*, gives us the best brief description of the ends of humane education that I know: "The scheme of the humanist might be described in a word as a disciplin-ing of the higher faculty of the imagination to the end that the student may behold, as it were in one sublime vision, the whole scale of being in its range from the lowest to the highest under the divine decree of order and subordination, without losing sight of the immutable veracity at the heart of all development, which 'is only the praise and surname of virtue.'" Very few of the people who are in charge of our schools nowadays—indeed, not many of the people who manage our colleges and universities—have the slightest idea of what More is describing.

For humanistic studies, like the influence of the church, have been declining for more than a century; and humane learning, whatever may be said of religious belief in our time, shows few symptoms of resurgence. We all know the power of the forces against which humane studies have contended in our time. The ascendancy of Benthamite ideas, the triumph of mechanical and industrial uniformity, the decay of those classes which formerly had leisure and means to pursue liberal studies without much impedi-ment, the demands of total war, and the hostility of the mass-mind—all these have hacked and battered those intellectual disci-plines which are calculated to encourage contemplation, a sense of duty, and obedience to inherited moral precepts. Yet as no class ever falls from power without some considerable degree of fault within its own ranks, so no discipline of the mind ever succumbs to the encroachments of rival systems without a degree of internal decay. This has been true of liberal learning in our time. Irving Babbitt, some fifty years gone, prophesied the retreat of humane studies before the demands of the technologist and the social engineer; and in his first book, *Literature and the American College*, Babbitt warned us against a double decay of the humanities—against their degenerating on the one hand into a mere dilettante appreciation of form and style, "teaching Keats and Shelley to a class of girls," and on the other hand into the pedantries of Herr Doktor Professor, the wastes of "research" without ends and specialization without princi-ples, abuses no less alien to the humane tradition.

Once the defenders of the humanities make it clear to society that they themselves are firm of purpose and high a mind, then they have some chance for regaining the ground they have lost; but while the very men who write and teach within the disciplines of literature, language, history, and philosophy are uncertain of their own rectitude, they will continue to be beaten down unmercifully. The men who love humane studies no longer can afford to wink at what a friend of mine calls "the treason of the English teacher"—that is, the betrayal of humane studies within the minds of the humanists themselves. The most common form of this betrayal is a surrender—often an unconscious capitulation—to the methods and ends of the Benthamite and sociological enemies of liberal education. When the scholar in the humanities mistakes history for a collection of "facts"; when he mistakes literature for simple amusement, or else a tool for social indoctrination; when he converts the study of languages into either the game of semantics or the utilitarian fraud of "basic conversation"; when he reduces philosophy to an arid puzzle in logic-chopping—why, then the enemy is within the gates; and it is hypocrisy to pretend to be fighting a gallant rear-guard action when, in truth, we already are hewing wood and drawing water for the conqueror.

The traditional end of human learning is something quite different from these follies and humbuggeries. As Babbitt wrote a generation ago, the end of liberal education is the disciplining of free minds, and the method is the study of "that unbroken chain of literary and intellectual tradition which extends from the ancient to the modern world." The humane disciplines do not accomplish their work by preaching, nor yet by subtle insinuation. They teach the rising generation the meaning of great literature and the nature of elevated human character, and that is sufficient. So it is that, apart from the doctrines of religion, the best minds and hearts of every generation come to understand the bonds that join them with their ancestors and their posterity. Plutarch teaches them these things, and Dante, and Montaigne, and Shakespeare, and Burke, and Ruskin. The humanist does not force his opinions upon his listeners; instead, he shows them how to form their own opinions. They learn the truths of the civil social existence, and the nobility latent in human character, equally well from Plutarch's portrait of the fanatic radical Cleomenes, or from his portrait of the indomitable

45

conservative Cato. They learn from great literature and systematic studies that they are part of a grand continuity and essence. Babbitt expresses with some power the duty of humane studies to impress upon the student the continuity of this high tradition: "The emancipation from this servitude to the present may be reckoned as one of the chief benefits to be derived from classical study." And in America, Babbitt says, we need more than any other nation to be constantly reminded that we do not live merely for the moment: "For if the fault of other countries and other times has been an excess of reverence for the past, the danger of this country today would seem rather to be an undue absorption in the present."

Ever since the disciples of John Dewey captured most of our schools, during the past four decades, and began to aspire to mastery over every department of our colleges and universities, the present has been too much with us in our educational schemes. No thinker's work, during the past century, has become more thoroughly obsolete than that of John Dewey, although he died only yesterday; for his social and educational ideas all were predicated upon the assumption, now fatally exploded, that rational and material progress is automatic and inevitable, and will lead to a benevolent universal state, equalitarian and strifeless. But an influential teacher's doctrines, however badly injured by subsequent events, often continue to govern the actions of his disciples long after they have ceased to possess any real validity. The turgid style and the unimaginative epistemology of Dewey seem to have exercised a peculiar fascination for the stubborn doctrinaires who, in any age, make up too large a part of the body of teachers; and those dull persons (true conservatives of stupidity, for they nuke the sentences of Dewey, Kilpatrick, and Counts into unalterable secular dogmas) have obtained, by virtue of the dogged and dreary lust for "administrative positions" which characterizes them, a mortal clutch upon our poor educational institutions. Professor Arthur Bestor recently described some aspects of this pedantic tyranny in his *Educational Wastelands*.

In a number of ways, the modern thinking conservative must employ some of the methods of revolutionaries, and echo the Jacobin cry of Danton, "Audacity, and again audacity, and always audacity." So it is in our abused schemes of education: a truly conservative system of learning, aimed at some restoration of the ideal of the unbought grace of life, cannot breathe until the stifling empire of the doctrinaire Deweyites is overthrown. For no one in our time is more old-fashioned than a hard-and-fast pupil of John Dewey; the weight of this being upon our schools and colleges and universities is the weight of an intellectual corpse.

Immersed in the present by the deliberate policy of the Deweyites, both the school-children and the university students nowadays are what a friend of mine, a parent, calls "bird-brained"—not that they are stupid, but that, bird-like, they cannot bear to keep at any one occupation for more than a few moments; they hurry from one amusement to another, unable really to work or to contemplate. In this respect, they have been made less than human, out of conformity to the Deweyite principle that the past is without significance for us, and that aims and values are known only through constant "creative activity"—which ordinarily must be purposeless activity, if one refuses to admit the existence of ends beyond the social modes of the hour.

These young people have been robbed of their true natural right to genuine instruction in the works of the mind, which real right Burke contrasts with the Jacobins' pretended Rights of Man. And this is only one of the several ways in which the Deweyites have converted our educational institutions into so many weapons for a concerted assault upon true Reason.

A system of education in which respect for the wisdom of our ancestors is deliberately discouraged, and an impossible future of universal beneficence taken for granted; a system in which all the wealth of myth and fable, the symbolic study of human nature, is cast aside as so much rubbish; a system in which religion is treated, at least covertly, as nothing better than exploded superstition, or at best a vague collection of moral observations; a system in which all the splendor and drama of history is discarded in favor of amorphous "social studies"; a system in which the imaginative literature of twenty-five centuries is relegated to a tiny corner of the curriculum, in favor of "adjustment"; a system in which the physical and natural sciences are huddled incoherently together, as if they formed a single discipline, and then are taught as a means to power over nature and man, not as a means to wisdom; a system in which the very tools to any sort of apprehension of systematic knowledge, spelling and grammar, mathematics and geography, are despised as boring impediments to "socialization"—why, is it possible to conceive of a system better calculated to starve the imagination, discourage the better student, and weaken Reason? In this, the thinking conservative must be a radical: he must strike at the root of this perversion of learning, for in most of our state-supported schools nowadays, and in probably the greater part of our universities and colleges, the "educational" process has become inimical to the real human person. Is it any wonder that a professor can ask Mr. Jacques Barzun what proportion of his graduate students' theses he writes at Columbia University, and be answered with a calm melancholy?

Is it any wonder that our educational administrators, to escape from the spectacle of their own failure, turn to purposeless aggrandizement, "plant," doubled and tripled and quadrupled enrollments, larger staffs, larger salaries, tougher athletic teams, as a means of concealing from the public the gigantic fraud they have put upon the nation? Here the conservative task must be one of assault and reconstruction, rather than simply one of defense.

This, too briefly expressed, is the corruption which has overtaken the individual reason, the higher imagination of the human person. But this is only half the mischief which the Deweyite oligarchy has clone to us. The other half is the terrible injury inflicted upon the disciplines which govern any just society; for despite all the dreary lecturing of the Deweyites *in re* "adjustment to society" and "democratic living," in sober fact they have been preparing the way for a soulless society to which no decent man could adjust himself in conscience, and a mass-state which is the antithesis of representative government and territorial democracy.

Dr. Gordon Chalmers, in *The Republic and the Person,* describes how the Deweyites do not really teach young people to form their own opinions, but instead drown them in social indoctrination, the repetition of equalitarian slogans and humanitarian generalizations. The disciples of Dewey, despite all their talk of "enrichment" and "freedom," are intent upon enforcing a dull conformity to the "progressive" and equalitarian prejudices they themselves happen to hold; and they try to achieve this through the totalitarian propaganda-technique of incessant repetition.

In his recent forthright little book called *Crowd Culture,* Dr. Bernard Iddings Bell describes those terrible symptoms of the triumph of the mass-mind which disgrace our news-stands and shriek from our radios and leer from our television-sets; and he says that we cannot make much progress toward a restoration of the traditional values of mind and spirit until we have commenced a reform of our American educational system. We have overwhelmed the old aristocracy of birth and wealth; now we must commence the creation of a new aristocracy, he tells us, by the educational process, so that posterity may be redeemed from the emptiness of mind and heart which impend over modern life. The great ugly tendency of American schooling ever since John Dewey's ascendancy has been to favor mediocrity and inferiority at the expense of high natural talent. If this tendency, the most dismaying aspect of the degradation of the democratic dogma—for it would be a fatal blow to progress and freedom if it endured—is to be reversed, we must act with speed and resolution to erect a new aristocracy of enterprising talents on the remains of our old aristocracy of birth and wealth. For no nation survives without a genuine aristocracy, from which comes leadership in every aspect of life. If a people repudiate true aristocracy, they will have to settle for squalid oligarchy. The Republic cannot endure without men of superior talents to sustain it, in America or anywhere else. And if we refuse to provide the sort of education which confers upon men and women some degree of the unbought grace of life, then we shall be confronted with the sort of education which breeds the commissar-mind, the unholy training of a hard and selfish elite. If we repudiate liberal education, we will be saddled with illiberal education; we will exchange a disciplining of free minds for an indoctrination of servile minds.

Emile Faguet, fifty-five years ago, in the preface to his *Politicians and Moralists of the Nineteenth Century,* wrote that an aristocracy is always emerging from the heart of the people, by a slow evolution, and that such a new aristocracy is arising in our age. He did not venture to predict the composition of that aristocracy. But whatever form this new body of leaders may take, "it will have to be persuaded, and it can be told in advance, that the life of an aristocracy depends upon the services which it renders, which is the same as saying that in order to live it must make sacrifices." Just this is the great problem of the aristocracy of intellect for which Dr. Bell hopes. "The aristocracy of tomorrow," Faguet continued, "must be made to understand now that it will commit suicide not only if it abuses its victory, but also if it takes advantage of its victory and behaves as a conqueror. This is a formidable task. It is always said that the education of Democracy is difficult. But more difficult still is the education of the successive aristocracies which are formed on the moving surface of democracies."

Now I am very much afraid that the aristocracy, or rather oligarchy, which is being trained by our Deweyites is a collection of individuals without veneration, without any apprehension of the unbought grace of life, without anything but scorn for the idea of a gentleman, without any objects but personal ambition, social efficiency, power over man and nature, and—at best—an abstract appetite for "social reform," by which they mean constant tinkering with traditional society. Far from being "education for democracy," this is training for the subversion of true democracy. The substitution of this new elite for Burke's natural aristocracy, or Jefferson's, would gradually expose the American nation—with due allowance for the different aspect which any class assumes in various nations—to the domination of a body of managers and manipulators not much superior to the Nazi or Communist elite, recruited out of conformity to official dogmas and ruthless attachment to the new order. The late George Orwell described this growing class when, in *Nineteen-Eighty-Four*, he wrote of an order of new masters, "shaped and brought together by the barren world of monopoly industry and centralized government," quite devoid of the unbought grace of life, "made up for the most part of bureaucrats, scientists, teachers, journalists, and professional politicians." Any conscientious public man, or any observant captain of industry, is aware how already this curious class of persons is tending to dominate our political and our industrial life. They are the products of "adjustment," and they are not much concerned with enduring values. Whether or not they aspire to be tyrants, they lack the high imagination which nourishes society; they have been told to conform, rather than to create. I have no taste for serving under them.

And the Deweyite contempt for traditional leadership, combining with the Deweyite love for an abstract total democracy, undermines the sources of the remaining moral and political intelligence, at the same time this new order of uninspired "adjusted" persons rises to power. In short, it ensures the triumph of mediocrity. The social theories of Dewey encourage what Mr. Arnold Toynbee calls "the imitation of the proletariat"—that is, the tendency of the upper classes in society to imitate the life and opinions of the masses, in part out of a confused sense of guilt at being different from the majority of men, in part out of a subtle fear of the political and physical power of the proletariat. Gustave Le Bon, writing only a few years before Faguet, touches upon this problem in his famous little book *The Crowd*. The opinions of crowds are propagated by contagion, he says; and this contagion presently spreads from the popular classes to the higher classes; such has been the history of socialistic ideas.

> This is the explanation of the fact that every opinion adopted by the populace always ends in implanting itself with great vigour in the highest social strata, however obvious be the absurdity of the triumphant opinion. This reaction of the lower upon the higher social classes is the more curious, owing to the circumstance that the beliefs of the crowd always have their origin to a greater or less extent in some higher idea, which has often remained without influence in the sphere in which it was evolved. Leaders and agitators, subjugated by this higher idea, take hold of it, distort it and create a sect which distorts it afresh and then propagates it amongst the masses, who carry the process of deformation still further. Become a popular truth, the idea returns, as it were, to its source and exerts an influence on the upper classes of a nation. In the long run it is intelligence that shapes the destiny of the world, but very indirectly. The philosophers who evolve ideas have long since returned to dust, when, as a result of the process I have just described, the fruit of their reflection ends by triumphing.

It might be an interesting exercise to trace thus the source of John Dewey's social collectivism, and to describe the consequent influence of Dewey's ideas upon teachers, who have been converted by Dewey to a levelling equalitarianism that (as Mr. Albert Lynd observes) would be anathema to nine-tenths of the parents and tax-payers that support our schools—if only they knew the philosophy that lies behind the verbiage of our educationists. But, as with so much else, I can only venture here to suggest a promising field of investigation for the man who retains some affection for American political liberties and American moral values.

And this process might be traced at some length in our colleges and universities, where, too often, the professor is an embodiment of Wordsworth's sigh that

> *The good die first;*
> *And they whose hearts are dry as summer dust*
> *Burn to the socket.*

Envious of the prosperity of every element in society, conscious of being neglected and contemned in a sensual age, too sunk in sloth of spirit to rise to his high duty as a guardian of the Word, this professor finds it easier to demolish than to build; and though he and his order would be the first, perhaps, to be deluged by the social and moral revolution he predicts, he surrenders to the attraction of notions beneath his real powers of intellect, the product of cold hearts and muddy understandings.

I do not mean to say that all professors participate in this charac-ter; probably a majority have not succumbed to the imitation of the proletariat, in tastes and interests, but when a very considerable part of them, in some degree, think that their duty is to level, rather than to elevate, then it seems doubtful if any educational scheme with which they are associated can give us a new aristocracy. It is at once amusing and depressing to hear some of these people try to convince themselves, and others, that modern America is dissemi-nating wisdom to greater and greater numbers of young people, instead of following in the bad old ways of European universities (of which most such American doctrinaires know nothing, actually) and educating a few persons. For these American apologists know, in their heart, that most American schools and most American col-leges, and to an increasing extent the professional and graduate schools of universities, are disseminating not wisdom, but arrogance, the presumption that comes with a trifle of ill-digested information. The graduate, who has been taught almost nothing, presumes to judge everything, secure in the splendor of his degree. Thus a class of young persons is created who are sure to be disappointed in their expectations; their opinion of themselves has been puffed up beyond any reasonable possibility of satisfaction; and, as certain experienced educators suggested in recent studies, many of these young persons will have nowhere to go. A little learning is indeed a terribly dangerous thing. Such persons were the elite of the Fascist and Nazi and Communist organizations. We are never in danger of having too many educated persons among us; but we can do ourselves great mischief by flattering the ambitions of innumerable pseudo-educated young people. What I am recommending is that we turn our attention to the arousing of liberal minds, rather than to the mass-production of "adjusted" arrogance.

The leadership we require, the leadership of honor, never can be supplied by such persons, whose principal tool is defecated intellect and whose principal motive is gratification of shabby private ambition. The aristocracy of the mind which Canon Bell commends is a very different thing from such an elite; Dr. Bell's leaders would be aware of the great realm of moral principle, always conscious of the union between the spirit of religion and the spirit of a gentleman, if they were educated according the principles of Newman. Yet I do not think we could trust even Canon Bell's rising generation, unless it should be mingled with a large class of persons accustomed to prescriptive authority in their several fields—with the ministers of religion, with successful men of practical talents, with persons of inherited wealth, with lawyers and doctors, with old families and established interests. Such a commingling of talents and disciplines keeps off *hubris,* that infatuation with one's private merit, by reminding us that the world is more than sheer intellectuality.

A leadership of pure abstracted intellect would be as mistaken, and as impermanent, as a leadership of sheer business acumen (which some people seem to desire) or a leadership of labor-union officers (which other people take for a solution to all our distresses). Besides, as Burke observes, the ascent to power and distinction ought not to be made too easy. Leadership, when a man has had to find his way upward from obscure station, ought to be the reward of labor and trial, not merely the unquestioned right of every aspirant. For a man is not qualified to lead unless he has acquired, along the road of his progress, some understanding of what honor means, and the idea of a gentleman, and the unbought grace of life. Henry Adams' novel *Democracy* shows us the self-made leader who has thought himself in too much of a hurry to bother with an abstraction like honor; and of course we do not need to go to our books to find the proof of this—the modern age is crowded with such men.

But I am anxious not to have it thought that I believe formal education useless in the endeavor to restore a general recognition of the unbought grace of life. I believe, on the contrary, that our schools and colleges and universities can do much to bring back to our consciousness the requirements for true leadership and the essence of honor. They have been negligent in these matters for a long while, in part under the influence of utilitarian ideas that emphasize the "practicality" of every study at the expense of imagination and moral instruction, in part under the influence of the positivistic notion that one "fact" is as important as any other "fact," in part under the influence of Dewey's pragmatism, which denies the whole realm of enduring values. A good many professors, however, and a good many persons in authority, are beginning to wake to the reality that the mind and the heart must be the objects of our solicitude, not merely material production and social adjustment, if we are to arrest the decay of private reason and of just leadership.

Thus we return to the natural and informal aristocracy of Burke, the mingling of inherited position with rising talents, upon the principle of honor; I do not think we ever will discover another satisfactory method for calling to leadership the men who ought to lead us. A humane intellectual discipline aids greatly in their development.

This aristocracy does not need subsidies and standardized examinations for its preservation, however; indeed, there is little enough in a positive way that we can do to aid it. This aristocracy perpetuates itself from its own power, if we simply refrain from crushing it. A natural aristocracy of leaders is among us still, and the sense of honor is not dead; and now, as a thousand years ago, that aristocracy and that sense of honor are at their finest when they are joined to a sense of religious consecration. If we desire true leadership, however, and true cultivation of the mind, we must refrain from choking the sources of this aristocracy.

We must remember that the aim of education is not to make every man like every other, but to awaken the highest talents of the best persons among us. We must recall the original unity of "honor" and "honesty." For if we acknowledge the plain fact that some men, by a kindly Providence, are made vessels for honor, then indeed we may be led with honesty; but if we adore mediocrity, our leaders are certain to be vessels for dishonor. What the zealots of Progress took for no more than windmills, now turn out to be giants in dread reality. Mr. Roy Campbell said once to me, "If you are Don Quixote, all your windmills may be giants; but all your giants will be windmills." The time is gone by when we could laugh with impunity at Don Quixote.

A number of serious observers—Mr. David Riesman, in his study *The Lonely Crowd,* eminent among them—have grown alarmed at the increasing indifference of a great part of our population to even the most urgent issues of our time. I am equally alarmed, but I am not in the least surprised. For one thing, nearly everyone is deluged daily by a mass of "fads" and opinion, heaped upon him by the newspaper press, the radio, television, and motion-pictures; he is urged to decide and act at once upon everything under the sun; and of course he cannot do anything of the kind. Thus most people, despairing of taking any intelligent part in the concerns of mankind, grow tired of hearing "wolf, wolf" cried out in frenzy every day, and sink into their own petty concerns for relief. And in the second place, the assumption that the great mass of men, once they were given formal schooling, would take an intelligent and continuing interest in the works of the mind and the affairs of nations was a nineteenth-century delusion. For a time, in truth, it seemed that an Age of Discussion had actually arrived, at least in Western Europe and North America, and that an enlightened democracy would extend its benevolent empire of reason over all the world. But this was only a transitory phenomenon; and, as Joad remarks, once the mass of men discovered that book-learning was not much to their taste when they had free access to it, they proceeded to reject book-learning and seek other diversions.

So when we hear expostulations, and expostulate ourselves, against the vulgarity of our radio and our television, the imbecility of our motion-pictures, the degeneration of our newspaper press and our popular journals, the dull conformity of most men to the life of suburbia or standardized industry, the indifference of the majority of citizens to even questions of national life and death, it is of no avail to hunger after some mysterious popular uprising against all these ills. There is no such thing as a General Will (the delusion of Rousseau) or the Virtue of the Proletariat (the delusion of Marx) or the Rational Citizen (the delusion of John Stuart Mill). No mysterious wisdom abides in the bosom of the People to which we can appeal in this hour of our need. The public is not going to protest against stupid television-programs or hysterical newspapers or the decay of our schools. The public, or the masses, have no mind or coherence, accurately speaking. In our time, the public takes what it is given. It is useless for us to form committees and draw up petitions if we act upon the fallacy of *vox populi, vox Dei*. The nineteenth-century delusion that reason and decency inevitably will triumph, if only schooling is made general and restrictive forces are abolished—the delusion of Jefferson and of Mill—now, indeed, is doing great mischief among us; it tends to restrain us, for instance, from conducting any intelligent censorship of "comic" books for children which pander to sadism and violence, and thus permits the seduction of the innocent in the name of the liberties of the mind.

The *public* is not going to save us from the decay of reason; we must save ourselves, and thereby society. The first step is to confess that any society, no matter how democratic politically, requires leaders of opinion and taste and serious thought, and that the primary purpose of any system of education is to encourage and instruct those leaders, the guardians of the Word and the unbought grace of life. The second step is to resuscitate that liberal learning which teaches men the meaning of time and duty, and which nurtures the idea of a gentleman. The third step is to impart that intellectual discipline to as many persons as can possibly benefit from it, so that we will possess a considerable class of truly educated men and women, able to be moulders of thought and arbiters of taste each in his little circle. (I do not say, with Professor Arthur Bestor, that more than nine-tenths of our population is capable of benefiting from such a discipline; but I do say that a considerable part, vastly more than the poor remnant still being liberally schooled nowadays, is capable of apprehending the principal values of the liberal disciplines.) The fourth step is to remind ourselves that the cultivation of the mind cannot be left simply to schools and the other formal instruments for learning, but must be imparted chiefly by the family, and by private reading and observation, and by the normal channels of information and amusement, and by one's daily work; this may help to emancipate us from the tyranny of the Deweyite pedant. Television programs will be better only when the people who produce them, and the people who sponsor them, and the people who watch them, have some abiding standards of reason and taste; journalism will become respectable only when it is undertaken by truly educated men, and when its public acknowledges some body of informed opinion superior to the idolized "man in the street." A distinguished botanist confided to me, recently, his conviction that our universities now are in a condition rather like that of the monasteries on the eve of the Reformation. Their original end has been forgotten; they are dominated by persons who have no real apprehension of the minds and hearts of the men who founded these great institutions; they have become shams, and abodes of hypocrites, and so will tumble like so many houses of cards, before long. Where will learning go then? Into the surviving great libraries, perhaps, or into little circles of earnest students sitting round some sport of an old-fangled professor in the evening, or into some of the study-programs of certain great industrial corporations. Now I am not myself certain that our universities will go down to dusty death in this fashion, though I often am inclined to think so; but, whatever may become of our present institutions, it is the high duty of the conservative to endeavor to redeem them from their failure, and to recall them to their true mission. Even if he does not succeed, the conservative who acts thus will have played the part for which Providence intended him.

I am well aware that I have scarcely more than touched the surface of our educational difficulties in this brief chapter. I am quite aware that the life of the modern city, for instance, puts great difficulties in the way of bringing home to the city-children the romance and nobility of the Past. I have tried to do no more than to suggest the large outlines of the problem, and the tack which intelligent conservatives probably ought to take. Some readers will object that I have not told how to solve all the difficulties of the modern mind by the uniform application of an ingenious system. I never aspired to do anything of the sort, however, in this matter or in any other. Only the doctrinaire radical thinks that the neat invention of the coffee-house philosopher can bring perfection. The conservative knows that he, personally, has no monopoly of virtue or of wisdom; he knows that the problems of men are infinitely variable; and he knows that any valuable reform in society is accomplished only through the willing cooperation of many minds and many hands, working in their particular fields. And the conservative knows that the first step toward the alleviation of any distemper is to diagnose the malady conscientiously; and that the second step is to prescribe a general course of treatment. Beyond that, particular remedies must be applied to particular persons and particular institutions. The conservative was not educated in the Academy of Lagado; he does not presume to prescribe for patients he never has seen, or (like James Mill) to write constitutions for nations he never has visited. Guided by this prudence, he endeavors to redeem the modern mind by affirming, first of all, that mind exists, and then persuading men that mind is worth possessing.

The Problem of the Heart

LIBERALS, from the days of Bentham and James Mill down to our time, never have much concerned themselves with the Heart. I do not say that liberals do not have hearts; I am sure they have; but they have long been inclined to suspect that other people have no hearts. I mean by this that the liberal has lived in the belief that a sweet reasonableness can solve the problems of society and alleviate all private troubles; think your perplexity through, and you will see the light; leave emotion out of the question if you possibly can. Now the modern liberal still is influenced by this notion, although his confidence in pure reason has been terribly shaken by Freud and Jung and the catastrophes of our century, and he has tended to borrow from the socialist some of the vocabulary of class-passion.

Somehow, the liberal still likes to tell himself, and anyone who will listen to him, a neat Plan will always do the trick for us. If something seems to be going wrong with the family in modern society, why, relax the divorce-laws, or allot subsidies to parents, or institute family councils on democratic principles. If something seems to be going wrong with the mind of industrial man, why, build more mental hospitals, or set up a program of occupational therapy, or pass a new minimum-wage law. If the number of murders and criminal assaults increases, why, build better housing, or try a new type of child-guidance, or require parole officers to have degrees in psychology. I do not mean to imply that these several measures have no value, nor that liberals often do us harm by advocating them. What I am saying, however, is that the liberal ordinarily thinks that internal and external improvement, among men, may be secured by adjustment, positive legislation, and sensible goodwill. Sometimes the liberals are right. But more often their analysis of such problems is superficial, and if they insist upon their Plan to the exclusion of more profound criticism and longer views, they may end in doing infinite harm to the very cause they would like to advance.

The thinking conservative knows that the outward signs of disorder, personal or social, very often are no more than the symptoms of an inner ravaging sickness, not to be put down by ointments and cosmetics. He is inclined to look for the real causes of our troubles in the heart of man—in our ancient proclivity toward sin, in a loneliness of spirit that conjures up devils, in twisted historical roots beneath the parched ground of modern existence, in venerable impulses of human nature which, when frustrated, make our life one long lingering death. He knows, moreover, that the task for the prudent counsellor and the prudent statesman is to make life *tolerable,* not to make it perfect; there is something in the constitution of humanity that cannot be satisfied with the poor things of earth, and so what we ought to teach ourselves is honorable resignation, not frantic indignation. He knows, with Sir Henry Maine, that in the course of history nearly everything seems to have been tried, and that nothing has ever worked really well. He recognizes, with Burke, the wisdom of the Schoolmen of the fourteenth century: for they, detecting more in man than mind, distinguished from the intellect the *heart,* or will, that complex of impulses, held together by a mysterious power that is of ourselves and yet out of ourselves, able often to overrule our intellect, whether for good or evil.

The thinking conservative perceives that pure intellect, of itself, cannot bring peace, or certitude, or love. Our passions, which are children of the heart or will, exert over us an influence which, in most men and at most times, is superior to that of the mind. To reconcile the will to right reason was the aim of the Scholastic moralist; and the conservative knows that if the heart or will is cavalierly left out of account, it will take its vengeance by perverting reason, and that harmony between reason and will which constitutes justice within the human person will be overthrown.

Ignoring the will was the folly of the rationalist in philosophy, and of the liberal in politics. The leader and governor of men who does not take into account the intricacies of their hearts will condemn a people to unhappiness. Those things which console and cherish us, after all, are products of the heart, not of the mind: love, and community, and continuity, and a sense of abiding truth. How many of us really would want to be John Stuart Mill? Who would not rather be Scott, or Hawthorne, or Disraeli, or even Byron? I do not imply that these champions of the heart were deficient in intellect; they certainly possessed reason of a very high order; but with the partial exception of Byron, they achieved that harmony of mind and heart which make a full man and a just one. Who would not rather be Coleridge than Bentham, or William Morris instead of Joseph Chamberlain? "The heart has reasons that the reason knows not," Pascal tells us; and the conservative makes this an axiom of his sociology.

I have said already that for the conservative, Love is the object of the civil social existence, and the one reality which makes life worth living. Love comes from the heart, not from the mind; even "the intellectual love of God" is too cold for most of us to embrace. To the conservative, then a social system which leaves the heart out of its reckoning must be indescribably oppressive, whatever the theoretical freedom of its mundane institutions. And at this moment, we Americans are in danger of neglecting the profound reasons of the heart, and so condemning ourselves either to the sterile existence of private aggrandizement, or to the internal and external anarchy which commonly follows dose upon the divorce of the heart from the mind.

In this nation, an expansive and complacent democracy, sensual and often bored, exhibiting great wealth and great poverty but too little of that sturdy self-sufficiency its founders designed, in which nearly everyone is schooled and almost no one educated, has become the most powerful state of the ages. As a people, we Americans are rich at present; but true leisure (a world away from idleness and "recreation") remains a scarce commodity, little commended, sometimes despised. A mature nation, however scornful of intellectual achievements and profound emotions, nevertheless cannot escape from tolerating a few men of ideas or of warm hearts. Are these men, however, to be mere captive curiosities, spared by the Vandals out of an amused contempt or a superstitious misunderstanding of their endowments? And are the masses that engulf them—preserving in the midst of the crowd these few sentient beings like so many beetles in amber—to be emptied of mind and spirit? Are the Americans of the future to be all bulls in Dr. Johnson's pasture, remarking (if ever they inquire at all) complacently, "Here is this cow, and here is this grass: what more could I ask?"

A few years ago these questions were put in a number of ways by the editors of *Partisan Review* to a number of contributors to that journal. Eighty years ago, Sir James Fitzjames Stephen inquired if the American achievement, the triumph of numbers and material production, the gratifying of "an immense number of common-place, self-satisfied, and essentially slight people is an exploit which the whole world need fall down and worship." Half the world kneels at America's feet today; but, even more acute than in Stephen's time, the question remains to be answered. Can American minds and hearts sustain the tremendous burdens that the United States have assumed in our century?

"Until little more than decade ago," the editors of *Partisan Review* commented, "America was commonly thought to be hostile to art and culture. Since then, however, the tide has begun to turn, and many writers and intellectuals now feel closer to their country and its culture. . . . America is no longer the raw and unformed land of promise from which men of superior gifts like James, Santayana, and Eliot departed, seeking in Europe what they found lacking in America. . . . For better or worse, most writers no longer accept alienation as the artist's fate in America; on the contrary, they want very much to be a part of American life." By and large, this pleases the Partisan Reviewers, but they are not unaware of certain grave dangers. "The enormous and ever increasing growth of mass culture confronts the artist and the intellectual with a new phenomenon and creates a new obstacle: the artist and intellectual who wants to be a part of American life is faced with a mass culture which makes him feel that he is still outside looking in."

The present growing indifference toward everything civilized which does not accord with popular norms; the creation and satisfaction of trifling or baneful popular appetites; the perversion of culture to the statutes of a commodity—these undeniable phenomena disturb the editors. In consequence, they ask some of their principal contributors four questions: How far have American intellectuals changed their attitudes toward American civilization? Must the American intellectual adapt himself to a mass culture? Where in American life can artist and thinker find something that will compensate for the decay of their old model European culture? In the new era of "the reaffirmation of America," can the tradition of critical non-conformity be maintained? Now these are questions difficult for anyone to answer satisfactorily, as difficult as they are ineluctable. But it must be said, in sorrow and sympathy, that the answers of the *Partisan* people (with a few heartening exceptions) are remarkably feeble or smug; and the more smug they are, the more dismaying they seem to contemplative men.

Perhaps the most smug of the contributors to this symposium is Mr. David Riesman, author of *The Lonely Crowd*. Now, being a conservative, a reactionary, what Mr. Riesman calls an "anomic," I am profoundly disturbed at the kind of complacency which Mr. Riesman radiates. Mr. Riesman, I am sure, does not call himself conservative; but he is a conservative, in the sense of taking the present drift of things for the best of all possible tendencies; and this conservatism is not far removed from what Walter Bagehot described as "the ignorant Democratic Conservatism of the masses." Smugness, even complacency at the process of change, can provoke an explosion of blind forces that revolt they hardly know why; and their rebellion brings down things infinitely more precious than the conservatism of smugness. To demolish such complacency is the duty of men who believe in a higher conservatism than mere satisfaction with being and becoming. Perhaps, as J. F. Stephen wrote, "the waters are out and no human force can turn them back"; but, with Stephen, "I do not see why as we go with the stream we need sing Hallelujah to the river god." Now Mr. Riesman, I am sorry to say—for I admire his talents as a social psychologist, worthy to be compared with those of Graham Wallas—is singing just a hymn. His title is better than his book; for though the Lonely Crowd of our desolated society is a thing of terror, and Mr. Riesman half confesses it, his remedies amount to letting the stream of human achievement splash down to a Dead Sea.

In 1952 a good word, much needed, came into our language: egghead. An egghead is the sort of person Mr. Peter Viereck, in *The Shame and Glory of the Intellectuals,* calls "Gaylord Babbitt" or "Babbitt Junior."[1] An egghead is substantially what Mr. Riesman calls "an other-directed person," or one genus of the other-directed person—instancing the swarm of commuters on the New York, New Haven, and Hartford Railroad, reading the metropolitan dailies, drawn from the salaried middle classes, empty of any true inner convictions, but desperately anxious to conform to the newer patterns of life as those patterns take shape in the kaleidoscope of American change. He is Señor Ortega y Gasset's mass-man; a mass-man who, however, thinking himself superior to the masses, aspires to be an intellectual. The egghead was a liberal during the past two decades, perceiving that his idol the intellectual was a liberal. Now, it is all too probable, the egghead is beginning to endeavor to convert himself into a conservative. Baboonlike, he imitates avidly the trick of the hour; for he has norms of his own.

I declared earlier in this book that the word "intellectual," as employed self-consciously by our *illuminati,* implies consummate snobbery, for its was long ago monopolized by a body of persons claiming to arrogate to themselves all apprehension of things mundane and divine. Yet the intellectual, unlike the egghead, is no charlatan. He may be stricken by *hubris;* indeed, I know he is but his learning, however mistakenly he may exalt the solitary intellect over conscience and authority, is genuine.

Mr. David Riesman, to judge by his several books, is an intellectual of the highest order. Defecated intellect, purged of all passion and adorned with some humor, shines out from his temperate pages. Not all intellectuals are truly educated men; but Mr. Riesman is. He has read widely, taking his books to heart; he has disciplined his method, under the influence, among others, of Tocqueville and J. S. Mill. Trained in the law, he brings to the consideration of American character the strict and valuable methods of juridical learning; an orderly touch of the legal brief lingers about *The Lonely Crowd.* Here is a man of singular intellectual penetration and synthesizing

---

1. Mr. Viereck is thinking of Sinclair Lewis' George Babbitt, not my mentor Irving Babbitt.

power, capable of drawing forth from the bewildering flood of modern life generalizations that for years to come may find their way into the thought of scholars and even novelists. "What pure reason and boundless knowledge can do, without sympathy or throb," Lord Acton once said of his friend Sir Henry Maine, "Maine can do better than any man in England." Mr. Riesman's intellect is of Maine's stamp.

Philosophically considered, Mr. Riesman is a pragmatist, immersed in the stream of becoming, with no strong historical sense, and no conviction of abiding values. He is much influenced by William James and John Dewey, and by Erich Fromm. But he transcends his sources, repeatedly asserting the strength of his independent judgement, respectful toward his teachers, but not taking them for the law and all the prophets.

Yet Mr. Riesman's studies in crowd-psychology, founded upon an improbable assumption, terminate in a dangerous fallacy. His grounds for assessing American character, or human character in general—though Mr. Riesman's chief pride is his "characterology"—are so narrow that the rigid calculus of Bentham and James Mill seems romantic emancipation beside them, and because he has no ends, but drifts in the flux of events, his remedies for the social diseases that he diagnoses so skillfully are ludicrous. How much Mr. Riesman needs a touch of poetic fancy! Lacking the Coleridgean Reason, all Mr. Riesman's prodigious skill as a social scientist, at length, leaves him whistling in a little barren room at night, lit by a single harsh fluorescent tube, while at his window crouches the stygian blackness of the Past, and at his door pants the crepuscular Future.

The improbable assumption with which Mr. Riesman begins is an abrupt application of certain demographic theories to the analysis of national character. Societies with "high growth potential," he says—that is, societies in which both birth and death rates remain high—are governed by tradition, and their members are tradition directed people. Societies with a decreased death-rate, in a condition of transitional growth, develop in their typical members "a social character whose conformity is insured by their tendency to acquire early in life an internalized set of goals." These are "inner-directed people." Last, societies in a state of incipient population decline (Mr. Riesman assuming without hesitation that our civilization now is in this state)[2] develop in their members a social character "whose conformity is insured by their tendency to be sensitized to the expectations and preferences of others. These I shall term *other-directed* people and the society in which they live one *dependent on other direction.*" The tradition-directed man lives by a set of prescriptive values, scarcely conceiving the possibility of altering the established order of things. The inner-directed man obeys a set of concepts "implanted early in life by the elders and directed toward generalized but nonetheless inescapably destined goals" (John Stuart Mill, writ large), for his society has experienced a splintering of tradition, "connected in part with the increasing division of labor and stratification of society." The other-directed man lives by no values except those of his peers, whose approval he seeks pathetically, though most of *them* have, in turn, no values but *his* approval; he comes often from the rootless salaried middle-class of modern industry and business and government; he is (my description, not Mr. Riesman's) the prosperous proletarian, the mass-man that Ortega y Gasset detests. Throughout Western society, but especially in American cities, this other-directed man is increasing in numbers and altering the whole tone of life.

This facile analysis of social change is interesting; but it is undemonstrable, and one is almost astonished that Mr. Riesman should venture to build the elaborate structure of *The Lonely Crowd* upon it. He does display a little uneasiness, it is true, remarking that Judge Jerome Frank warned him against deterministic theories. Tocqueville, whom Mr. Riesman has read with attention in some respects, seems to have had no influence upon him in this; for Tocqueville exposed with vehemence the perils of Hegelian determinism and of prophecies that work their own fulfillment. If society were so simple as this, merely trailing in the wake of population-curves, then indeed the statistical sociologist could prescribe with

---

2. It ought to be mentioned that the Report of the Royal Commission Population confirms Mr. Riesman so far as Britain is concerned, if it may be believed—which I doubt.

comparative sureness for our ills. But demographic influences, important though they are, remain only a little part of the immense complexity of human institutions. Omitting from consideration the force of ideas, of religious conviction, of political action, of human ingenuity, and even of chance, Mr. Riesman ignores nine-tenths of the consequences of social change.

The Procrustean method of Mr. Riesman really will not serve to describe our civilization, or any other civilization. And he combines with this myopic view of society an enthusiastic economic meliorism, informing us that we must teach ourselves to abandon a "scarcity psychology" (for we live in an age of boundless plenty, he is convinced) and embrace an "abundance psychology." Mr. Riesman, in fine, is the Reverend Thomas Malthus in reverse. The writings of the late Michael Roberts provide an antidote to Mr. Riesman's economic naïveté. In America especially, we live beyond our means by consuming the portion of posterity, insatiably devouring minerals and forests and the very soil, lowering the water-table, to gratify the appetites of the present tenants of the country. Burke and Tocqueville foresaw this curse of ravenous consumption that democratic societies bring upon themselves.

Yet it would be unfair to Mr. Riesman to imply that he is content with the whole present drift of things; his very titles show that he is not. The faces of the other-directed persons in his second book are not lovable. Somewhat alarmed at the dismal tendency toward a vulgar monotony and dreary imitation of other dreary people which characterize the new American society—juke-box culture— he shares Tocqueville's loathing of mediocrity, though he calls it "other-direction." He remarks the passing of the old periodicals of some intellectual distinction and respectable circulation; and though he condescends to approve the movies and the radio and television occasionally, he is somewhat perturbed about the future of American culture. (But possibly I put too much emphasis here on his fears for the other-directed man's taste, since Mr. Riesman remarks contentedly, in *America and the Intellectuals*, "The American Cultural spectrum seems more interesting and no less diverse today than at earlier times.") And especially, he apprehends the dreadful loneliness of the other-directed man, the isolated social atom with no values but radio-noise and the fads of the moment; and he hopes that the terror of this alienation from truly human existence may be moderated. Not in Mr. Riesman's pages, however, but in Canon Bell's *Crowd Culture*, do we find a succinct description of our afflictions:

> While wealth accumulates in the United States, man seems to decay. In our private lives a pervading relativism, an absence of conviction about what is the good life, a willingness to seek the easy way rather than the way of integrity, blunts the proddings of conscience, takes the zest out of living, creates a general boredom. We are not a happy people, our alleged gaiety is not spontaneous. Our boredom results not only in a reluctant morality but in shockingly bad manners. We become increasingly truculent. Our way of life, while opulent and brash and superficially friendly, is less and less conducive to peace of mind and security of soul.

If Mr. Riesman had some of Dr. Bell's strength of conviction and manliness of standards, he might become a philosopher talked of two hundred years from now. But, devoid of any end except material comfort—being in most respects, to put the matter candidly, very nearly one of his own other-directed men—Mr. Riesman seems hollow and disappointing. In his books, defecated Intellect, divorced from true Reason and Heart, rules all, and his realm is dry and withered. Compared with his intellectual descendent Mr. Riesman, Jeremy Bentham was a lusty and fanciful being.

Perceiving that "adjustment" to a world of loneliness and mediocrity is ruinous, Mr. Riesman puts his hope for the salvation of private tranquillity and general culture in "autonomy"—viz., the element of free choice that remains even in other-directed society. This Riesman autonomy is more than a little suggestive of Lucretius's atoms, inexplicably capable of deviating a trifle from their downward course. Within any society, we discern three types of individuals, crossing and transcending the division-lines of tradition-, inner-, and outer-direction. They are the "adjusted," those who reflect their society with the least distortion; the "anomic," who are maladjusted—though Mr. Riesman recognizes that in some cultures it is better to be maladjusted than adjusted; and the autonomous, who are capable of conforming to the "behavioral norms" of their society, but can freely choose whether or not to conform.[3]

The autonomous person, Mr. Riesman and his associates have discovered, is a rare bird. They have great expectation of him; but as to how he may relieve the loneliness of the crowd, they are by no means precise. He will lead, however, in the re-definition of work. Mr. Riesman is quite as anxious as was Irving Babbitt to obtain and disseminate a true definition of "work"; but he has a radically different notion from Babbitt's of what work amounts to. The autonomous ought to lead us away from strenuous endeavor, toward relaxation, we are informed. They will guide us in an Age of Play. For the future—barring stupid reaction—is to be a time of universal prosperity and idleness, and all men are to be encouraged to turn from pointless production to necessary consumption. Here we have Edward Bellamy (whom Mr. Riesman cites more than once) resurrected. We know what a truly imaginative social reformer, a man who understood the meaning of art and leisure—William Morris—thought of Bellamy's Brummagem paradise. It would be diverting to read Morris on *The Lonely Crowd*.

Mr. Riesman believes that power having trickled away from the former leaders of society until it now resides nowhere really, our present order is preserved chiefly by mere inertia. That consummate master of politics the third Marquess of Salisbury thought the same thing: power had escaped from the clutch of statesmen, he observed, "but I should be very much puzzled to know into whose hands it has passed." In the dawning age, Mr. Riesman suggests, such leadership as may be required will be drawn chiefly from the swelling mass of the other-directed: in short, by persons who have been severed from all traditional values, but whose native agility enables them to rise in a time when the fountains of the great deep are broken up, patching together out of aesthetics and the pleasure-

---

3. "Anomic" is an unfortunate term that Mr. Riesman hammers out of Durkheim's *anomique*, which (in Durkheim) signifies the ungoverned, the masterless man. Mr. Riesman expands this to signify the state of refusing to conform (or, more strictly, of being unable to conform) to the spirit of the age. One needs to be Coleridge to coin successfully words of this magnitude.

principle a trimmers' raft upon which they may keep afloat amid the waves of being and becoming. Mr. Riesman looks forward with some complacency, in short, to a time when card-sharps will be the shepherds of society.

Both Mr. Viereck and Canon Bell hope that another sort of person will provide the leadership our sick and slavishly conforming society needs: a being like Aristotle's "great-souled man," whose convictions are rooted in something more enduring than twentieth-century exigencies, and whose ends are somewhat more aspiring than Play. Mr. Viereck talks of "the inner aristocrat . . . who enforces his civilized standards from within, by cultural and ethical self-discipline," opposed to the inner plebeian, the mass-man—Mr. Riesman's other-directed individual. Dr. Bell tells us that we must have a "democratic elite," recruited by truly liberal education, not other-directed or even inner-directed, but guided in part by the wisdom of our ancestors, and in part by a power out of ourselves, Adam Smith's "invisible hand" of Providence (to which striking phrase, incidentally, Mr. Riesman refers more than once). Men of this description, Canon Bell says, are sure that we dare not ignore the voice of past ages: "They understand that both the making of their souls and also their most real service to their country depend upon their finding deliverance for themselves from pursuit of such obvious ostentatious trivialities as satisfy the masses of the moment."

Immense difficulties obstruct the forming of this democratic elite, greater even than Canon Bell suggests; but this way lies more hope for culture, and for the salvation of true humanity, than in Mr. Riesman's shadowy and ominous "autonomous" whose character brings irresistibly to mind that word beloved among eggheads, "ambivalence." Cut off by the triumph of the mass-mind and totalitarian democracy from all the unbought grace of life and even the memory of the idea of a gentleman, it is scarcely conceivable that these "autonomous individuals" could possess any greater strength of character, or means of resistance against crowd culture, than one of Mr. Evelyn Waugh's little victims in the clutch of circumstance. Men make institutions, true; but institutions also make men, as Cicero says: and with every mode of life and training swept away which used to nourish individuality and strength of mind, the "autonomous" hardly could survive by more than twenty or thirty years, at most, the collapse of a society of free choice and traditional establishments.

I have said that *The Lonely Crowd* ends in a perilous fallacy, which is this: the loneliness of the human heart, according to Mr. Riesman, may be relieved by material satisfactions and group-play. Surely we learn from history that we learn nothing from history; for here is our brilliant Mr. David Riesman, sagacious in many matters, trotting out the sorry old nag of Hedonism, which Dr. Johnson and fifty others demonstrated to us long ago to be a vicious and treacherous mount. How are we to moderate the loneliness of the twentieth-century crowd? Why, by "autonomy in play," says Mr. Riesman: which consists of "consumership" and "craftsmanship" and "taste exchanging" and being avocationally counselled. Is it for these toys that the tree of liberty has been watered with the blood of martyrs? So, at any rate, the other-directed man will think, encouraged by Mr. Riesman. Our author suggests, also, that we will find solace in release from sexual "privatization": "The autonomous . . . point the way to a new model of marriage that finds its opportunity precisely in the choices that a free-divorce, leisure society opens up. Because women are less privatized than they have traditionally been, marriage offers more for millions of people than ever before in its long history."[4] (Here the conservative interjects, "Everything but love.") Thus we arrive at *Brave New World*, with the children at their "erotic play." Well, a high degree of sexual promiscuity always has been attractive to many, as it was to the Romans of the decadence; but it has not enchanted them for long. The twentieth-century liberal, Santayana remarks, has become a regulator in all things except one: he would relax nothing except the marriage-bond.

Mr. Riesman's utopia would be too much for the stomach even of H. G. Wells: its inhabitants would look remarkably like the pretty, futile, decadent humans of *The Time Machine*. As for the physical

---

4. By "less privatized," Mr. Riesman appears to mean footloose, and he does not really mean that *marriage* offers more than ever before, but that the reduction of "marriage" to a mere declaration of cohabitation, in his opinion, makes people happier.

shape of things, that would resemble the final drawing in Mr. Osbert Lancaster's *Drayneflete Revealed,* a maze of cloverleaf intersections and traffic lanes and impersonal hives of humanity, with amid all this a forlorn scrap of venerable architecture preserved, "Cultural Monument scheduled under Town and Country Planning Act." City planners, Mr. Riesman declares in his concluding observations, "comprise perhaps the most important professional group to become reasonably weary of the cultural definitions that are systematically trotted out to rationalize the inadequacies of city life today, for the well-to-do as well as for the poor. With their imagination and bounteous approach they have become, to some extent, the guardians of our liberal and progressive political tradition, as this is increasingly displaced from state and national politics." Have we indeed come to such a pass that traffic-engineers are the best guardians of our liberal institutions?

Now in the very little book which contains Mr. Riesman's expression of satisfaction with the drift of things among us, there is a piercing criticism of Mr. Riesman's spiritless society—the contribution of Dr. Reinhold Niebuhr to *America and the Intellectuals*:

> American sanity is threatened not only by the combination of power and insecurity which has become our fate. Our culture is also threatened from within by the preoccupation of our nation with technology. The resulting crudities are much more serious than those of which our fathers were ashamed. The cultural and spiritual crudities of a civilization preoccupied with technics compare with the pastoral and rustic crudities of a frontier civilization as a neon-lighted movie palace compares with a cowbarn. Our problem is not merely the synthetic and sentimentalized art of Hollywood or the even lower depths to which television has reduced this art. It is also the problem of cheap technocratic approaches to the tragic historic drama in which we are all involved. We have wise men who think they can find a way out of our present distress by establishing clinics all over the world, which will cure children of "aggressiveness" and thus make future wars impossible. Thus life in its grandeur and misery, and history in its tragic and noble proportions, are reduced to biological lives, in order to encourage the hope that the same engineers who mas-

tered "nature" will soon achieve the mastery of this vast historical drama.

When the reader of *The Lonely Crowd* and *Facet in the Crowd* has made his way through the abstractions and the interviews of these fat books, he will find himself rewarded with nothing better than this "cheap technocratic approach." In *The Lonely Crowd*, religion is mentioned in only one connection, that being some references to "the Protestant ethic" drawn from Max Weber. Mr. Riesman is all head and no heart; and although I am sure he has an immortal soul, still he takes no cognizance of it. Tocqueville knew that this deadening and dehumanizing materialism is the corruption of democracies. "In the democracy of which you are so proud," Royer-Collard said to Tocqueville, "there will not be ten persons who will thoroughly enter into the spirit of your book." Mr. Riesman, though he quotes Tocqueville time and again, is not of the number of those percipient ten; for he ignores all the longings of the heart and all the aspirations of the spirit which Tocqueville knew to be worth more than every possible gratification of the flesh. Tocqueville describes with wonderful prescience Mr. Riesman's smug society of the other-directed, guided—if guided at all—by the autonomous:

> The first thing that strikes the observation is an innumerable multitude of men, all equal and all alike incessantly endeavoring to procure the petty and paltry pleasures with which they glut their lives. Each of them, living apart, is as a stranger to the fate of all the rest; his children and his private friends constitute for him the whole of mankind. As for the rest of his fellow citizens, he is close to them, but he does not see them; he touches them, but he does not feel them; he exists only in himself and for himself alone; and if his kindred still remain to him, he may be said at any rate to have lost his country.

This is the Lonely Crowd; and Mr. Riesman's remedy for its malaise, in substance, amounts to making alienation universal. "Things and actions are what they are, and the consequences of them will be what they will be," says Bishop Butler; "why then should we desire to be deceived?"

Yet I do not believe the future is to the other-directed, the autonomous, the arrogant intellectuals, or even the Benthamite learning of Mr. David Riesman. A prodigious ferment of things is under way, and I take it to be the work of that "invisible hand" which Mr. Riesman mistakes for nothing more than a picturesque phrase. The modern intellectual, though still sick from his smugness and conceit, is beginning to feel that he must make judgments of value, Mr. Viereck points out, "in order to sustain his own sanity and the freedom of his society. He feels he can no longer make value judgments on the basis of his former liberal dogmas: economic determinism, Deweyite pragmatism, the cultural relativism of the anthropologists he used to admire, the ethical relativism of the semanticists he used to quote." In the little essays of the Partisan Reviewers, this profound altering of conviction already may be discerned, though obscured in several writers by the vestiges of dying "liberal" and collectivistic prejudices. I think we may be standing upon the brink of the most far-reaching change in human opinions and institutions since that day when modern radicalism issued its challenge to traditional society by decorating "this hell-porch of a Hotel de Ville" with human heads on pikes. The neoterism of other-directed men and the Dinos-cult of pragmatists will not effect this mighty saving alteration: it will be worked, on the contrary, by men with a sense of high consecration, who know that the crowd's loneliness is the consequence of a flight from God.

Once upon a time, says Socrates, men would accept the truth even if it were uttered by a stick or a stone; but now they ask who you are, and what are your motives. Bowing to the modern vice of curiosity, then, I confess that I myself am a product of "the dissidence of dissent, and the Protestantism of the Protestant religion." Social conservatism, though it requires some respect for religious truth, is not the creation of a rigorous orthodoxy. But every man imbued with the spirit of veneration, acknowledging the presence of a Power superior to human will and reason, inclines in the hour of decision toward the cause of prescription. I trust that none of us shall become political Christians; but I hope that none of us shall not be afraid to infuse Christian faith into politics. A society which denies the heart its role becomes, in very short order, a heartless society.

The Problem of Social Boredom

In the first chapter of Georges Bernanos' *Diary of a Country Priest* occurs a grim description of the acedia of our times:

> My parish is bored stiff; no other word for it. Like so many others!
> We can see them being eaten up by boredom, and we can't do any-
> thing about it. Some day perhaps we shall catch it ourselves—
> become aware of the cancerous growth within us. You can keep
> going a long time with that in you.... The world is eaten up by
> boredom. To perceive this needs a little preliminary thought: you
> can't see it all at once. It is like dust. You go about and never
> notice, you breathe it in, you eat and drink it. It is sifted so fine, it
> doesn't even grit on your teeth. But stand still for an instant and
> there it is, coating your face and hands. To shake off this drizzle of
> ashes you must be forever on the go. And so people are always 'on
> the go.' Perhaps the answer would be that the world has long been
> familiar with boredom, that such is the true condition of man. No
> doubt the seed was scattered all over life, and here and there found
> fertile soil to take root; but I wonder if man has ever before experi-
> enced this contagion, this leprosy of boredom: an aborted despair,
> a shameful form of despair in some way like the fermentation of a
> Christianity in decay.

If this may be said with justice of a remote rural parish in
France, how shall we describe the condition of cosmopolis, the
sprawling and monotonous urban existence of our country? Dean
Inge once observed that the problem of boredom in society—social
ennui—never has been properly explored. It seems imperfectly
apprehended, indeed, even in its general outlines, by most social
planners and students of politics. Mass boredom seems to have
occurred from time to time in the history of civilization. We per-

ceive it in the Hellenistic world, in imperial Roman life before the triumph of Christianity, perhaps in the Byzantine era; but our knowledge of the sentiments of most men in those ages remains indistinct. The twentieth century, however, appears to exhibit alarming symptoms of social fatigue throughout nearly all the world. This malady of spirit, if it is to be remedied or ameliorated, requires painstaking analysis. I do not propose to examine it exhaustively here: the task is too enormous. But one may suggest, summarily, that an age of social boredom is characterized by the popular pursuit of material and sensual gratifications to the exclusion of other ends—Professor Sorokin's "sensate culture"—and by the terribly fleeting nature of the satisfactions even such activities afford. This plight of society is what C.E.M. Joad calls "the loss of an object"; it is true decadence.

"At the top of a high old house, a man had sat reading Russian novels until he thought he was mad." This is the first sentence of A.E. Coppard's story "Arabesque." Any man who buries himself among the statistical surveys and Benthamite studies of our present moral disquietude—volumes like Mr. Kinsey's two books on sexual behavior, or Mr. Rowntree's and Mr. Lavers' *English Life and Leisure*—sooner or later goes as mad as if he had been reading Dostoievski night and day. The quickest way to apprehend the appalling gravity of social boredom in our midst, nevertheless, is to read both the sociological reports and the Russian novels. This done, all the dismaying evidences of boredom that surround us on every hand, particularly in our great cities, fall into place, and we begin to diagnose the malady with some degree of success, even if we cannot prescribe a simple antidote. For the most dreadful picture of a bored society on the verge of the abyss, one turns to Dostoievski's *The Possessed*, wherein all things sacred and tender are made the toys of the moment, and then tossed broken upon the rubbish-heap. In the realm of the novel, however, my favorite bored devil is Mr. Jones, in Conrad's *Victory*. Boredom, sloth of spirit is a vice; and the most deadly boredom brings on the appetite for the most forbidden diversions. Mr. Jones, a person like "an insolent spectre on leave from Hades, endowed with skin and bones and a subtle power of terror," has grown so tired of life that he no longer takes much pleasure in gambling or in theft; he can be roused from his intolerable lethargy only by the prospect of murder. And so it is, or almost so, with a great part of modern society. This is no exaggeration: a mob of Mr. Joneses were the masters of the most vigorous nation in. Europe for a dozen frightful years.

More than three decades ago, the most distinguished of our living critics, Mr. T.S. Eliot, in his essay on Marie Lloyd, suggested that this dread boredom is spreading to all classes. Even the characteristic amusements of the English lower classes, like the old-fashioned music halls, are giving way rapidly before the advance of a dismal and formless apathy that denies even children the knowledge of how to play. The middle classes, he wrote, are destroying or absorbing the aristocracy from which they take their own tone, and so are becoming the instruments of their own dissolution; and even the lower classes are in imminent danger of losing their traditional strength and liveliness. "With the decay of the music-hall, with the encroachment of the cheap and rapid-breeding cinema, the lower classes will tend to drop into the same state of protoplasm as the bourgeoisie." W.H.R. Rivers, in his *Essays on the Depopulation of Melanesia,* declared that "the natives of that unfortunate archipelago are dying out principally for the reason that the 'Civilization' forced upon them has deprived them of all interest in life. They are dying from pure boredom. When every theatre has been replaced by one hundred cinemas, when every musical instrument has been replaced by one hundred gramophones, when every horse has been replaced by one hundred cheap motor-cars, when electrical ingenuity has made it possible for every child to hear its bedtime stories from a loud speaker, when applied science has done everything possible with the materials on this earth to make life as interesting as possible, it will not be surprising if the population of the entire civilized world follows the fate of the Melanesians." Eliot wrote long before the hegemony of the juke-box and the television-set.

One of the most dismaying characteristics of this social malady is that its victims, though they may be vaguely aware of a deep-seated disquiet, generally are unable to distinguish the symptoms of their affliction; indeed, they do not know the name of the affliction. Cockneys or Melanesians, they sink into a lethargy of spirit without resistance—often actually welcoming the plague as a benefit of Efficiency and Progress. It has been nearly eighty years since a man of letters whose books are read too seldom nowadays, W. H. Mallock, put into the mouth of his "Mr. Herbert," in *The New Republic*, a memorable description of the plight of the modern masses, shorn not only of the unbought grace of life, but of every prescriptive end in existence. The real significance of life must be forever indescribable in words; but today, for most men, it is not even thinkable in thought:

> The whole human race is now wandering in an accursed Wilderness, which not only shows us no hilltop whence the promised land may be seen, but which, to most of the wanderers, seems a promised land itself. And they have a God of their own too, who engages now to lead them out of it if they will only follow him: who, for visible token of his Godhead, leads them with a pillar of cloud by day, and a pillar of fire by night—the cloud being the black smoke of their factory chimneys, and the fire the red glare of their blast-furnaces. And so effectual are these modern divine guides, that if we were standing on the brink of Jordan itself, we should be utterly unable to catch, through the fire and the smoke, one single glimpse of the sunlit hills beyond.

Now it is not my opinion that industrialization is the sole cause of this weariness of mind and heart among us; nevertheless, the triumph of the machine is intimately linked with the decay of variety and individuality among the modern masses. Miss Elizabeth Wiskemann, in an essay published more than two years ago in *The Twentieth Century*, examined the spread of this apathy even in prosperous and smiling Switzerland; and she attributed the decay of culture and character to the ascendancy of mass-production.

Perhaps the most searching analysis of the influence of the machine-economy upon the human spirit is Friedrich Georg Juenger's *The Perfection of Technology* (published in the United States under the title of *The Failure of Technology*). This is a little book profoundly sombre; and the brief chapter called "The Modern Longing for Vitality and Devitalization" has a dismaying power. Intoxicated by motion, Juenger writes, mechanized man seeks insatiably after new sensations. "Mere action awakens in him the feeling of a more vigorous life; it stimulates him like a drug that creates beautiful dreams." Thinking, as Aristotle observed, involves suffering; modern man endeavors to avoid this suffering by abandoning himself to the flux of novelty and speed.

Now social boredom is indeed a kind of diabolic possession of that delicate living thing which we call human society. The deadly sin of Sloth, as the fathers of the Church and the schoolmen knew, is a spiritual malady, a listlessness of will, a surrender to a power of evil that provides mischief for idle hands. By the side of this, physical sloth is venial. The terrible punishment of sloth is boredom. And I think that if we are to make our way out of the purgatory in which we now grope—for I believe that the condition of modern society, despite many dismaying signs, still can be described as purgatorial, not infernal—we must seek the causes of that atrophy of will which ushers in sloth of spirit.

The will flags when it no longer perceives any end, any object, in existence. When the world is obsessed by means and trifles, and the ends of life have declined to no more than a faded memory in most people, then indeed we sink into sloth. Since the civil social existence began, mankind has sought certain ends, or purposes in life, which have acted as motives to integrity. The most powerful ancient motive to integrity has been religious faith; but this has ceased to be a living force among the masses of many nations. A second motive to integrity always has been emulation, or the desire for the approbation of the people who set the tone of society; but this has been much diminished by the revolution of our times. A third motive always has been the desire to provide for the welfare of one's family and heirs; but the assumption by the state of the functions of education, economic management, and responsibility even for food-supply and housing, has diminished the responsibility of the individual here, while taxation has hacked at the very foundations of the idea of bequest. A fourth motive to integrity has been simple self-advantage, the desire for worldly prosperity and improved station; but the levelling process has tended to eliminate, in much of the world, not only the "glittering prizes" of personal success, but to make even the modest rewards of thrift and diligence nearly unattainable. A fifth motive has been the desire for personal liberty, freedom from having to climb other men's stairs; but the mass-state, steadily narrowing the compass of private life, has seemed determined to supervise every individual from cradle to grave, and so has interfered with a longing that is strongest in the best and most energetic of men.

A sixth motive to integrity has been the longing for continuity, the assurance that things might be with a man as they had been with his father before him, and so might continue with his son after him; but the vertiginous passion of our age has denied the reality of the great chain of being.

When all these ends, or motives to integrity, are discarded, then truly men are but the flies of a summer, left no reason for existence except flirtation with paltry amusements. The ancient yearning of strong men to fight the battle of life manfully, to contend against adversity and evil, is dethroned in favor of a feeble infatuation with creature-comforts. Frustration brings lassitude and boredom; and out of boredom grow vice, crime, and the destructive compulsions of the mass-mind. The unbought grace of life is traded at Vanity Fair for a toy and a snigger; but the trinkets of Vanity Fair lose their glitter before morning; and there descends upon the purchasers a satiety more oppressive than the most grinding physical poverty.

I have already described Mr. David Riesman's theory, in *The Lonely Crowd*, that the character of a society may conveniently be assessed upon a statistician's curve of population-change. Societies which are experiencing both a high rate of births and a high rate of deaths tend to be what Mr. Riesman calls "tradition-directed": that is, they desire to walk in the ways their fathers have trodden. We might call them—Mr. Riesman does not employ the word—conservative. Now societies of "transitional population growth"—that is, *societies* which experience a decreased death-rate—develop "a social character whose conformity is insured by their tendency to acquire early in life an internalized set of goals." These people in the transitional era Mr. Riesman calls "inner-directed"; and what Mr. Riesman seems to have in mind here is the attitude we commonly describe as "liberal." Last, societies which "have passed through both these earlier phases and are beginning to move toward a net decrease in population are said to be in the phase of 'incipient population decline'"; these Mr. Riesman calls "other-directed" in character; and he appears to mean by this phrase what various writers describe as "the mass mind" or "collectivism."

I do not propose here to criticize the notion of employing the demographic index as an instrument for analyzing the character of an age and a people. There is something to be said for it, though I am inclined to believe that there are less treacherous methods, and that one of them (as Durkheim, in whose works Mr. Riesman is much read, suggested years ago) is the suicide-index. What I am interested just now in touching upon is the curious failure of Mr. Riesman to ask the question *Why? Why* do tradition-directed peoples generally seem to experience a high birth-rate; and *why* do inner-directed peoples generally seem to exhibit the phenomenon of a decreasing death-rate; and *why* do other-directed peoples generally seem to live in a period of incipient decline of population, if not of actual decline? Is it possible that Mr. Riesman's inferences confound cause and effect? Can it be that people have a high birth-rate *because* they are tradition-directed, and a low birth-rate *because* they are other-directed? In short, is it possible that belief brings forth the social phenomenon, rather than the social phenomenon shaping the belief? The grand question which occurs to my mind, but which Mr. Riesman never raises, is whether our place on the population-curve may not be the result of a state of mind, rather than the cause of a state of mind. States of mind, it is quite true, are influenced by external factors: industrialism, for instance, in various forms, may produce a mood of depression among the mass of men; or the prospect of new worlds to conquer may produce a mood of exultation. Yet I am inclined to believe that mind and heart, in the long run, make men what they are in any age; imagination, as Napoleon said, does indeed rule the world. "Nor is this any the less true," Coleridge observes, "because the great majority of men live like bats, but in twilight, and know and feel the philosophy of their age only by its reflections and refractions."

I tend to think, in fine, that tradition-directed people have a numerous progeny for two reasons: first, because (whatever their religion) they obey the injunction, "Multiply and replenish the earth," a tradition common to all societies; second, because they believe life is worth living; they are not bored; they believe that God is in His Heaven, whether all's right with the world or not; they find a mighty satisfaction in bringing life into the world, for life is ordained of God. "Men who do not look backward to their ancestors," Burke reminds us, "will not look forward to posterity"; and the converse is true. Tradition-directed people venerate the generations that have preceded them, and therefore are solicitous for the generations that shall succeed them. As for the high death-rate of tradition-directed societies, that is not a product of their principles, but rather of the backwardness of medical science among most traditionally-minded folk; for, by an unhappy conjunction, the advance of technical and scientific progress in the modern world generally has been paralleled by the spread of that vulgarized scientism which gnaws at the root of traditional faith, and by the triumph of that industrial standardization which breaks up the traditional structure of community. I suggest, then, that the high rate of births is a consequence, rather than a cause, of their state of mind.

Mr. Riesman, looking about for an example of the tradition-directed person, presents to us a colored charwoman from the West Indies, lost in the desolation of Harlem. I should like to suggest that respect for tradition does not exclude the appeal to reason, Burke was what Mr. Riesman calls "a tradition-directed individual"; so was Newman; so is Mr. Christopher Dawson; so is Mr. T. S. Eliot; so is Mr. Robert Frost. Tradition is comprehended in what Burke defined as "prejudice and prescription." What has been long established, whether in the minds of men or in their social institutions, obtains a just presumption in its favor, for presumably it represents the consensus of opinion and experience of many generations of thinking men, or else is implanted in the mind of the race by a power more than human. A tradition-directed man puts his trust, for the chief things of life, in Authority. Burke, in the *Reflections*, makes the most moving and convincing defense of authority and tradition ever expressed in a small compass:

> We are afraid to put men to live and trade each on his own private stack of reason; because we suspect that this stock in each man is small, and that the individuals would do better to avail themselves of the general bank and capital of nations and ages. Many of our

men of speculation, instead of exploding general prejudices, employ their sagacity to discover the latent wisdom which prevails in them. If they find what they seek, and they seldom fail, they think it more wise to continue the prejudice, with the reason involved, than to cast away the coat of prejudice, and leave nothing but the naked reason; because prejudice, with its reason, has a motive to give action to that reason, and an affection which will give it permanence.

There are other folk than Harlem scrub-women who continue to be governed by tradition in this society of ours. They are the men and women still strong in their religious convictions or still respectful of history and the intellectual legacy of the ages. They subscribe to Richard Hooker's affirmation that "The reason first why we do admire those things which are greatest, and second those things which are ancientest, is because the one are the least distant from the infinite substance, the other from the infinite continuance, of God." Often they have large families because they are not bored with life; because they see purpose in the course of human history; and because they are not shorn of hope, for themselves and their posterity.

The sort of man whom Mr. Riesman has in mind when he writes of "the inner-directed individual" is John Stuart Mill. "The source of direction for the individual is 'inner' in the sense that it is implanted early in life by the elders and directed toward generalized but nonetheless inescapably destined goals." Mr. Riesman's own references to the younger Mill, and J.S. Mill's celebrated education at the hands of his father, suggest that here Mr. Riesman is generalizing (with much justification) from a single eminent individual. Mr. Riesman also remarks that many of our national legislators are inner-directed persons of the old stamp, a vanishing generation; and that their reliance upon a residue of opinion implanted in them by their fathers, and upon the dictates of a private judgment regulated by old-fangled conscience, sets them head and shoulders above the other-directed masses whose elected "representatives" they are. Mr. Riesman is uneasy about the future of our legislative bodies, this being true; and no wonder; for the body of "inner-directed" persons is an ephemeral phenomenon, the product of the

Victorian era, the consequence of the repudiation of Authority and the substitution of Private Judgment in all things. The rise and decline of this force of "inner-directed" opinion coincides very closely with the ascendancy and decay of political Liberalism—1832 to 1914, one may say. Although the "inner-directeds," like the Mills, think that their convictions are the product of their private rationality, in truth their moral opinions and their rectitude of character are bequeathed to them by the traditional system of belief they nominally repudiate. As the traditional elements in their set of convictions weakens with the passing of the years, these persons are left irresolute and unnerved before the appetites of the masses, the crowd of the "other-directed."

The system of education which nurtured these inner-directed people being swept away, and the nineteenth-century society in which their class could flourish being almost wholly effaced in much of the world, from what sources may leaders of original opinions and secure moral fibre be obtained? That question is going to be progressively pressing, in the next decade or two. Now these inner-directed people, I think, are in considerable part the product of the same circumstances which led to a decline of the death-rate, during the past century and more; but their existence is simply parallel with that demographic change, not a consequence of it. I mean this: the modern age of scientific achievement, which brought us the improvements in medicine that reduced the death rate, also brought to many persons the opinion that the individual rationality alone can suffice for a guide in private and public affairs, without recourse to tradition and authority. This opinion was delusory; the events of the twentieth century have given it the lie; and therefore the "inner-directed" man is one of a dying breed.

The powerful current of event and opinion which refuted the philosophy of the Mills has also so quenched Victorian optimism, in nearly every social class, that now not only the death-rate, but the birth-rate too, is in decline or seems about to decline, in most of the Western world that held by optimistic rationalism. When a fatuous optimism is suffocated by the grim tendency of the time, its place is usurped by a pervasive boredom. And social boredom, being a repudiation of purpose in life, leads to a decline in the number of births—a decline in part the product of deliberate abhorrence of parenthood and deliberate measures to avoid it, in part the product of a will to annihilation which lies below the level of consciousness.

The tradition-directed person is not bored, for he feels himself to be a part of an immortal continuity and essence, and so put into this world for a purpose; and to fulfill that end—sometimes an inscrutable purpose, but an object in life, all the same—he labors habitually; it does not occur to his mind to be enduringly and consistently bored. The inner-directed person is not bored, either; for he can summon up private resources of intellect, and a sense of public duties, which are the fruit of his early training—so long as he remains confident of the rectitude of his philosophy of private judgment. But the bored masses of our age are the crowd of the other-directed; and they threaten to drown the remaining adherents of Authority and of Private Judgment in a sea of resentful mediocrity.

"As the birth rate begins to follow the death rate downward," Mr. Riesman says, "societies move toward the epoch of incipient decline of population—the prelude to the time when the birth rate will plunge below the already lowered death rate, so that the total population will decline." From such evidence as we can patch together, it seems probable that the later Roman Empire suffered from such a decline of population, out of similar causes. The traditional objects of life, the motives to integrity in private concerns and in civil social state, had withered away; boredom succeeded; and with boredom came that death-urge which spreads with a diabolical rapidity in decadent societies. The rising influence of Christian faith came too late to prevent the collapse of the structure of organized society, so that there succeeded what Gibbon called "the triumph of barbarism and Christianity." (Gibbon, like Mr. Riesman, did not always distinguish cause from effect, or parallel consequence from antecedent circumstance.)

Mr. Riesman is inclined to restrict his "other-directed individuals" to "the typical character of the 'new' middle class—the bureaucrat, the salaried employee in business, etc." But he is curiously selective here, as if it were improper to criticize adversely any group except the bourgeoisie or the upper rinses. In plain fact—though all of us are familiar with the increase of "other-directed" persons in this "new middle class" to which Mr. Riesman refers—the bulk of other-directed men and women are the modern proletariat, divorced both from tradition and from old-fashioned private judgment. Although most members of the proletariat belong to the poorer classes, economic status is not the distinguishing feature of a proletarian. One of the best discussions of the nature of the modern proletariat is contained in Professor Wilhelm Röpke's little book *The Social Crisis of Our Time.* The proletarian is a rootless man, a social atom, without traditions, without enduring convictions, without true home, without true family, without community, ignorant of the past and careless of future generations.

As Dean R. A. Nisbet reminds us in *The Quest for Community,* it is this faceless proletariat, incapable of love but eager to hate, which filled the ranks of the Nazi and Fascist and Communist parties, and which continues to constitute an immediate menace to everything old and good in our culture. A proletarian need not be poor; he may be very well fed, on the contrary; while a man who is needy in worldly goods may be rich in the life of the spirit, content in his community and family, and even endowed with the unbought grace of life. The distinguishing feature of proletarian status is the lack of roots and of principles. The proletarian is a practical nihilist. And the proletarian, by definition, is an "other-directed" man; for, lacking any traditions or private convictions of his own, he hastens to embrace the follies and schemes of whatever charlatans and demagogues affront civilized society at the moment.

Why Mr. Riesman is so careful never to mention the proletarian character of most "other-directed individuals," I cannot say; certainly the omission vitiates his book. This other-directed man, this proletarian, grows steadily greater in numbers and potential influence in a period of incipient population-decline. He is, in truth, the principal agent in the decline of the birth-rate; for, suffering from a malady which he himself cannot name, he sinks into an incurable boredom, sneers at his ancestors, lays waste the portion of posterity, and feels no impulse toward the perpetuation of his kind. Human life springs up from consummated love; but the proletarian is loveless.

In the proletarian, or other-directed man (I repeat that the proletarian is not identical with the laboring man), the death-urge triumphs over the traditional motives to integrity. It is the moral degradation of the proletariat which has made possible, and applauded, the atrocities of modern war; it is the unconscious despair of the proletariat, or mass of the other-directeds, which seems to urge humanity to commit suicide; both these phenomena are the consequence of an extreme boredom. "What is common to all other-directeds," Mr. Riesman informs us, "is that their contemporaries are the source of direction for the individual—either those known to him or those with whom he is indirectly acquainted, through friends and through the mass-media. This source is of course 'internalized' in the sense that dependence on it for guidance in life is implanted early. The goals toward which the other-directed person strives shift with that guidance; it is only the process of striving itself and the process of paying close attention to the signals from others that remain unaltered throughout life." These are the capricious and unthinking masses against whom Ortega and Marcel warn us. We see their vacant countenances in Mr. Riesman's more recent book *Faces in the Crowd*, and Mr. C. Wright Mills' *White Collar*, and Mr. Rowntree's and Lavers' *English Life and Leisure*, and Mr. Kinsey's two volumes concerned with sexual behavior, and in such novels as *The Year of the Locust*.

Now persons with all these defects never have been absent from society; but only in ages of decadence have they been able to set the tone of society. Their utter boredom, their sloth of spirit, communicates itself to the uppermost ranks of a nation, when true social decadence has triumphed. The surveys of Mr. Alfred Kinsey suggest how dangerously common, today, the type is become. Dr. Kinsey's statistical methods are shot through with error; his confusion about first principles leads inevitably to a confusion in conclusions; nevertheless, there emerges from his ponderous and humorless pages substantial proof that something is dreadfully wrong with modern society. I know of no more convincing body of evidence that boredom is near to stifling our civilization. For sexual promiscuity and perversion is one of the most immediate and common consequences of boredom. When the prescriptive ends of existence, the old motives to integrity, are forgotten by the mass of men, then the forbidden pleasures of the flesh afford a temporary refuge from the loneliness and purposelessness of life without principle and without love.

In another sense, too, Mr. Kinsey's researches are truly ominous for this nation; and they suggest boredom of a different sort, or rather boredom in another walk of life. For here we see a plodding zoologist intent upon overthrowing irreparably some of the dearest moral traditions of humanity, over a personal confusion about the several meanings of the word "law." Ignorant that there is law for man and law for thing, Mr. Kinsey mistakes scientific "law"—that is, the record of recurrent phenomena in the natural world—for moral law, and statutory law, derived from very different sources. Without entering upon the nature of this confusion, what must alarm serious observers of modern life, in Mr. Kinsey's odd performance, is the fact that here is a person endeavoring to apply the methods of a natural science, zoology, to the management of society and the realm of human morality.[1] This fallacious scientism is anything but rare among us; but Mr. Kinsey's fascination with sexual "outlets" is the most absurd of all, probably, and has had the most pernicious influence upon the opinions of the "other-directed." Now I rather think that we see here, not far below the surface of Mr. Kinsey's endeavors, yet another manifestation of boredom—the boredom of Dr. Kinsey and of professors and calculators like him. For natural science, like the other high pursuits of life, has its traditional ends; and when those ends are forgotten or denied, the natural scientist, too, is condemned to boredom.

The end of science, says Paracelsus, is to teach the fear of God, through knowledge of God's handiwork. But Bacon insists that the object of science is power; and the Baconian idea has been embraced by innumerable students of the natural and physical sciences. Power over nature and power over man gratify the *libido*

---

1. Still odder, possibly, than Dr. Kinsey's own fascination with sexual "outlets" is that he was taken seriously by the officers of the Rockefeller Foundation, who subsidized his inquiries on a vast scale, over the protest of some of their own consultants on medical matters—for this was actually represented as a contribution to medicine and public health.

dominandi of man; but something within us, for all that, cries out for knowledge that is not mere control over nature, a knowledge which is its own justification, a knowledge which reaches upward toward the source of reason. When the very possibility of this latter kind of knowledge is scorned, then the scientist indeed must content himself with the search for power; and power over nature, particularly in the zoological kingdom, does not truly satisfy; it seems to lead nowhere; it bores. A bored man of scientific disciplines almost inevitably is attracted toward the other aspect of power—control over humanity.

What better relief from boredom could there be than the demolition of the moral codes of the ages? What work more gratifying to the ego? That which a hundred generations of pious men built with immense labor and love, Faustus will explode in an instant. And will he not be rewarded with the adulation of all the other bored people who detest things established? Will he not be a king among the other-directed? "Come, I think Hell's a fable," says Faustus. "Aye," Mephistopheles replies, "think so still, till experience change thy mind." Nearly all the bored take Hell for a fable; and, to a man, they are in Hell, or on its brink. When the bored become masters of a society, then indeed, as in Germany, as in Russia, the scenes of the Inferno become terrestrial.

M. Denis de Rougemont, in *The Devil's Share*, suggests that the quantity of good and evil is approximately constant in every age, only varying in manifestation; and often I am inclined to agree with him. But we have discovered something beyond good and evil, deficient in the tragic drama of that immemorial struggle between the children of light and the children of darkness, but possessed of a deadening weight as great as that of old Sin. This peculiar possession of the modern world is Boredom, "the hunting reserve of the Demon." Boredom betrays us by weakening or altogether extinguishing the sense of a personal calling: "Let us admit that everything conspires to this end in the collectivist and rationalized era. Everything contributes to the suppression of reasons for living not foreseen by the statistics of the State. But why are we becoming collectivized, if this is something we don't really like? It must be that it somehow suits us—whatever may be the pretexts that the historians of materialist economics offer us. We seek refuge in Boredom rather than accept the challenge of an unprecedented calling—for unprecedented they all are."

Now thinking conservatives are convinced that they still have a high calling: the duty of keeping man truly human. The menace of modern collectivism, the proletarizing process, and social boredom confront us with the immediate possibility of the descent of man to a condition really less than human. (The true human person is not simply the "natural man," the tool-using animal, but a spiritual being with a mind and a heart.) One of the most pressing problems for the conservative who feels a high calling, then, is to save men from boredom. The approach of the liberal to this question ordinarily has been superficial; that of the radical, no better than a muddled endeavor to establish equal misery by compelling everyone to be bored. And since the conservative understands that we must apply our remedies to causes, rather than to passing phenomena, he seeks to exorcise the spectre of boredom by restoring among men the old objects of existence, or motives to integrity, which I touched upon a few pages earlier. I think, therefore, that if we find among the rising generation the conservators of civilization whom we need so desperately, these persons will apply their talents to the following measures of restoration:

(1) Renewing the power of religious faith, and piety, among the mass of men. I cannot enter here upon the difficulties of this undertaking; but if the task is impossible of fulfillment, then probably we are not going to be saved from boredom. Men must always be bored, if they can find nothing better in the universe than their own little mean selves; they suffer the punishment of Narcissus. I do not think that science has overthrown the empire of religion; rather, a vulgarized scientism has merely dosed the eyes of the masses to religious truth. In our day, the most superstitious persons are those who can see nothing in all creation but an old-fashioned mechanism or materialism.

(2) Reviving the concepts of honor and dignity which gave motive to honest desire for emulation—in short, reminding men that there are some persons who are more, and better, than "just

ordinary guys," and that mediocrity is not the norm for civilized beings.

(3) Returning to individuals the responsibilities which bring a, decent satisfaction, the duties of self-reliance, and the rights and actuality of private property and inheritance. The conservative is no anarchist; he knows that the just state, kept within reasonable bounds of power and function, is a force for our common betterment; but today the danger is that the state shall become all, quite as oppressive a prospect as the danger, in other times, that the state might waste away to nothing.

(4) Reaffirming the right of men to what is their own, and to whatever they can make their own without injustice to others—rewarding ability and honesty and diligence with those material satisfactions which most men always must hunger for.

(5) Reminding modern society of the truth that security, though a good thing, is not a better thing than freedom—and that, indeed, security does not long survive the extinction of prescriptive freedom. A eunuch, after all, was secure, but he was also bored.

(6) Reawakening men's minds to the eternal contract of society, which affirms that we do not live simply for ourselves, in the fleeting moment, but instead live to justify the faith and labor of our ancestors, and to transmit life and justice to our posterity.

I do not say that conservatives are sure of success in all this; the odds, in truth, are against them; but at the very least, they will have saved themselves from boredom by the attempt, even if they save no one else. The life you save may be your own. And in proportion as they make inroads upon social boredom, they will be alleviating the condition of the proletariat; for the same influences which bring boredom to every class today are the causes of the proletarizing of modern life.

The principal conservative thinkers generally have given much attention to the precise meaning of words, and with reason: "As a man speaks, so is he," Seneca wrote. They need today to examine the word "proletarian." The proletarian, in the old Latin meaning of the word, was a person who gave nothing to the commonwealth but his progeny: his sole merit was fecundity. Thus the French marshal could shrug aside the frightful price in lives paid for victory: "Paris will make good the loss in a single night." The proletarian is a person without property, without duties, without roots, without love, almost without the communion of humanity. The sober conservative, knowing that Love is the transcendent object of existence, does not hate the proletarian, as a human being; what he wants to do is to redeem the proletarian from his boredom, and bring him truly into the compass of the commonwealth. The proletarian is rootless; well, then, he must be enabled to send down roots. Ways must be found to help him to acquire property, and duties, and interests, and love. He must be restored to true humanity. The passion of Marx was to assimilate all of humanity to the proletarian condition; the object of the conservative is to lift all men up from proletarian degradation.

I am slipping into the mists of generalization, of course; one scarcely can help it, in discussing these problems, because fifty folios would be required even to commence the analysis of practical remedies for particular questions, with so huge a topic as the redemption of modern civilization from boredom. But to illustrate somewhat more definitely the mood in which conservatives ought to approach these several necessities, I am going to devote the rest of this chapter to certain suggestions *in re* Leisure. Some of the best minds of our decade have given attention to the examination of Leisure, and the topic is naturally joined to that of Boredom. We seem to have at least the potentiality of leisure for the mass of men within our grasp, nowadays; and yet we are afraid of the reality, once it has entered the realm of possibility. I think that this paradox is in part the consequence of the liberals' confusion about the true ends of life. An apprehension of the real meaning of leisure would be an important step toward emancipating us from boredom and proletarian apathy. I am not saying that the problem of leisure is the key to the whole conundrum of boredom; I am merely offering it as a specimen of that complex difficulty, and of the methods toward which conservatives ought to turn their energies.

Fifty-five years ago, Thorstein Veblen published his first book, *The Theory of the Leisure Class.* Last year, this work appeared as a cheap reprint, with an interesting introduction by Mr. C. Wright

Mills. I read this new edition recently, and found that Mr. Mills did for me, with respect to Veblen, what Eliot Vereker did for Mr. James Thurber, with respect to Proust: that is, he made Veblen seem more lucid and less important than ever before. The sub-title of Veblen's famous book is An *Economic Study of Institutions*; yet in actuality, it is nothing of that sort. Instead, *The Theory of the Leisure Class* is an exercise in heavy irony, intended to demonstrate the worthlessness of all leisure; and the spirit which animates it is the vice of envy. It is an envy highly abstract, moreover: for Veblen had no acquaintance whatever with the aristocratic mode of life he thought he was overwhelming with sarcasm, and scant acquaintance with the middle-class mode of existence; frequently, for that matter, he confounded the two in one sneer.

Dr. Thorstein Veblen was the archetype of the modern proletarian "intellectual," whose corrosive nature has done infinite harm to the West in this century. In fiction, the schoolmaster Cyrus P. Whittle, in *The Last Puritan*, bears a strong resemblance to Veblen: "He gloried in the momentum of sheer process, in the mounting wave of events; but minds and their purposes were only the foam of the breaking crest; and he took an ironical pleasure in showing how all that happened, and was credited to the efforts of great and good men, really happened against their will and expectation." Except as a writer, Veblen (as Mr. Mills reminds us) was in every respect a failure. Now to succeed as a philosopher, although failing in everything else, still is to win the crown of life. The question is, then, whether Veblen's thought was of a character which retains an enduring meaning for us. I do not think that it is; I think that *The Theory of the Leisure Class* is riddled with errors of fact and logic; and the most vitiating of these confusions is Veblen's ignorance of the meaning of the word "leisure."

For Veblen thought that leisure is simply ostentation, the arrogant luxury and display of privileged classes; it is sought simply out of a longing for selfish superiority, and indulged in as a conspicuous waste. Veblen was a disciple of Marx. Leisure, for Marx and Veblen, meant idleness. Marx rather yearns after this leisure, but his concept of its reality is curiously like a child's dream of perfect indolence. When the communist society is realized, Marx writes, then all men may be all things, and "hunt in the morning, fish in the afternoon, and make love in the evening, and criticize at dinner just as they please." In short, the leisurely communist will play Sir Epicure Mammon. Veblen was not an orthodox communist; he had no such positive program; it was his delight to undermine, not to project. But in his notion of leisure, as in much else, his master was Marx; and Marx's master was Bentham. Bentham, Marx, and Veblen, all three detesting what Burke calls "the unbought grace of life," were intent upon abolishing leisure in the interest of pure utility: for true leisure is the product of the unbought grace of life, and the justification for that unbought grace.

Mr. Mills remarks that though Veblen, the son of Norwegian immigrants, was almost a foreigner in America, nevertheless in one respect he was thoroughly American:

> Since the intelligentsia, just now, are in a conservative mood, no doubt during the nineteen-fifties Veblen, when he is not ignored, will be reinterpreted as a conservative. And, from one rather formal viewpoint, Veblen was a profoundly conservative critic of America: he wholeheartedly accepted one of the few unambiguous, all-American values: the value of efficiency, of utility, of pragmatic simplicity. His criticism of institutions and the personnel of American society was based without exception on his belief that they did not adequately fulfill this American value. If he was, as I believe, a Socratic figure, he was in his own way as American as Socrates in his was Athenian.

Mr. Mills' belief is mistaken: Veblen was not like Socrates, but like Socrates' sophistical opponents; for Socrates was a supreme moralist, and Veblen a run-of-the-mill nihilist. And since I am doubtless one of the conservative "intelligentsia" (not my word, Heaven knows) to whom Mr. Mills refers, I should like to interject that I have not the slightest intention of baptizing Veblen a conservative. He was a Jacobin, with a Jacobinical love of abstractions; and, like most pure Jacobins, he was a provincial, one of Burke's speculators of cold hearts and muddy understandings. In the sense that he had no knowledge of the world beyond the oceans, and no respect for history, truly he was a one-hundred-per-cent American of Cyrus P. Whittle's breed. But a worship of "efficiency, of utility, of pragmatic simplicity" is the antithesis of conservative belief; nor can I agree that this state of mind is characteristically American. It is undeniable that the Yankee-tinker type of American is described reasonably well by these phrases. America, however, never has suffered the misfortune of being reduced to uniformity of character. It would be ridiculous to pretend that Hawthorne, or Lincoln, or Josiah Royce, or Robert E. Lee, ever entertained such an affection for efficiency, utility, and pragmatic simplicity. Veblen stands for only one type of American; and that type is the devotee of aggrandizement whom Veblen's books denounce. There are men who kill the thing they love; there are others who become the thing they hate.

If the worship of "efficiency" were indeed an all-American value, then we would be a doomed people; for an exclusive devotion to material improvement, to the utter neglect of moral principle and the unbought grace of life, is the swiftest way to catastrophe. As yet, nevertheless, though the cult of Efficiency is powerful among us, prescriptive values still exert some check upon the lust for aggrandizement. Where the worship of Efficiency leads, a humane economist, the late William A. Orton, tells us in an enlightening book, *The Economic Role of the State:*

> Let us therefore praise the great god Efficiency. All he demands is that we make straight his path through the desert and purge the opposition.... We arrive at "justice" without mercy, "liberation" without liberty, "victory" without peace, "power" without potency—because the means we collectively employ lie on a plane so different from that of the ends we humanly desire that, the more they succeed, the more they fail. That is the nemesis of all "great powers" and of all who put their trust in them, God knows, this is not a new story.

The energumen who looks upon science simply as an instrument for procuring power over nature and man, and upon efficiency as the cardinal principle in social action, and upon leisure as mere ostentatious waste of time, or, at best mere recreation between two periods of labor—this being, in love with abstractions, possibly may become the representative American of our century. But if he does, the American hegemony will be shorter-lived than the Spartan. The cult of Efficiency is a Suicide Club, because it despises the dignity of human personality, and therefore provokes the reaction of human beings whose deepest instincts tell them that they are not meant to be machines.[2] Out of simple national self-interest, then, if nothing more, the Americans of 1954 cannot afford to indulge the abstract lust of Veblen for efficiency. We can no longer share with impunity Veblen's reckless contempt for everything that does not conform to the canons of Benthamite utility. And one of the most precious possessions of any elevated civilization is true leisure, out of which grow moral philosophy and the arts and the sciences.

This being so, it is heartening that a number of American thinkers are now giving the problem of leisure serious consideration, among them some persons much influenced by Veblen's writings. Mr. David Riesman, for instance, recently published a little book about Veblen; and in *The Lonely Crowd* and certain periodical essays, Mr. Riesman has touched upon the paradox that though we are possessed of labor-saving devices and an efficiency of production no other age dreamed of, we still do not know how to employ our leisure, and, confusedly, often try to escape from it. A writer fertile in suggestions, Mr. Riesman recognizes the gravity of the problem; yet though he has emancipated himself from the thralldom of Veblen's notion that leisure is mere ostentation, still I am inclined to believe that Mr. Riesman has not yet succeeded in arriving at first principles. For he thinks of leisure, by and large, as play, recreation, something to be used up, as if it were rather an embarrassing surplus of butter or potatoes. He still is a Benthamite at heart.

To Mr. Riesman, play (which he virtually identifies with leisure) is to become occupational therapy, the substitution of obsession with spending for obsession with getting. Spending, literally, is Mr. Riesman's favorite form of leisure activity. "Market-research" on a grand scale is one of his few positive suggestions for restoring variety and purpose to existence among the other-directed masses: "Perhaps, rather than or in addition to a world's fair, advertisers

2. The Cult of Inefficiency also is suicidal, especially in this age or immense populations that are fed and housed through the intricacies of industrial production. To the conservative, efficiency, like democracy, is a means to an end, not an end in itself.

might send out 'salesmen' whose purpose it was, not to sell but to give away goods. They would seek to discover reasons for blockages in choice, and, again like the play therapist, try to encourage the noncash 'customers' to become more free and imaginative." This plan is intended to emancipate children from "privatization"; but Mr. Riesman has similar schemes to alleviate the loneliness of adults. In an article entitled "Some Observations on Changes in Leisure Attitudes," published in a recent number of the *Antioch Review,* he writes of "discoveries being made on the frontiers of consumption" as an enriching of the possibilities of leisure. The self-service supermarket and the cookbook industry will free "the children now growing up in our demonstration suburb" of "fears, guilts, and awkwardness about food." We shall, become gourmets, to flee from the loneliness of the Crowd.

Is this, then, the appointed end of all our elaborate devices to save labor? Mr. Riesman offers scarcely any more elevated form of leisure-activity, except for a hasty reference to other "frontiers" in music, painting, literature, conversation, sports, and "the changing style of vacations." Mr. Riesman's mind, I repeat, remains wholly Benthamite. Disraeli said once that the English-speaking peoples confound creatures-comforts with civilization; certainly Mr. Riesman does. Mr. Riesman, however, is rather pleased by the apparent retreat from strenuous activity in leisure, and smiles a bit contemptuously at all old-fashioned leisure occupations, whether aristocratic, middle-class, or plebeian; he suggests that if the advocates of the old idea of "recreation" presume to oppose the great tendency of the times—like Rowntree and Lavers in their *English Life and Leisure*—all their values simply will be extirpated, with little to replace them.

Now I think that Mr. Riesman is right in doubting the efficacy of the solutions of "recreationists" like Rowntree and Lavers; for their principal remedies for the boredom of the crowd are "a well-conducted campaign in favor of chastity," "open-air entertainments," better soft-drinks, more adult-education lectures, and the encouragement of bobbies. They have no clear apprehension of the meaning of the word leisure; but, then, neither has Mr. Riesman. The decay of the proper employment of leisure, and the degeneration of the word itself in common usage, have much to do with the present social boredom that menaces even the framework of political society. If we are to approach this problem intelligently, we must begin with a better understanding of the word "leisure" and of the word "work" than Veblen or Riesman or Rowntree possesses. Two years ago, a book by Professor Josef Pieper, a German philosopher, pointed the way to a more accurate apprehension of "leisure": *Leisure, the Basis of Culture.* And thirty years ago there was published a book by an American critic which contains an admirable discussion of "work": Irving Babbitt's *Democracy and Leadership.*

Leisure, as Pieper tells us, is contemplation. "To those who live in a world of nothing but work, in what we might call the world of 'total work,' it presumably sounds immoral, as though directed at the very foundations of human society." The Benthamite and the Marxist detest the whole realm of contemplation, for contemplation refutes, by its very existence, their system of materialism. Under the regime of the Marxist planner, leisure is abolished and the man who has the capacity for thought is enrolled as a "brain-worker"—commonly at wages inferior to those of a manual laborer, as in Yugoslavia. To the masters of the total state, the contemplative is a dangerous man: for in his leisure he escapes from their surveillance, and presently his ideas may return to earth to undo the total state. Contemplation, *intellectus,* is the highest faculty in man; Aristotle suggests that it partakes of something more than human; and for this reason, too, the squalid oligarchs of the mass-state dread leisure, since they want man to be sheer animal.

True leisure is not idleness; neither is it acedia, that sloth of spirit, that boredom with the universe, which brings on the incessant but purposeless activity of the Lonely Crowd. "Metaphysically and theologically," Dr. Pieper observes, "the notion of *acedia* means that a man does not, in the last resort, give the consent of his will to his own being; that behind or beneath the dynamic activity of his existence, he is still not at once with himself, or, as the medieval writers would have said, face to face with the divine good within him; he is a prey to sadness (and that sadness is the *tristitia saeculi* of Holy Scripture)." This is our modern social boredom. It may be accompanied by extreme restless activity, even by excessive physical or

98

nervous labor; it is possible to be drunken with work, as a refuge from boredom. It is from this fate that true leisure saves men. But it is impossible to be leisurely, to find purpose in contemplation, unless one believes that there is an order more than material, a realm of mind and spirit to provide objects for contemplation. The idle man is not leisured, but only dully lacking in occupation; and one of Veblen's principal errors is his notion that people who have leisure employ it only in idleness or ostentation. Nor is leisure simply rest, intended to restore a man's nerves and body so that he may work again. A proletarian is a man who is tied to work, without the possibility of entering upon contemplation, or what M. Max Picard calls *The World of Silence.*

> Separated from the sphere of divine worship, or the cult of the divine, and from the power it radiates, leisure is as impossible as the celebration of a feast. Cut off from the worship of the divine, leisure becomes laziness, and work inhuman.
>
> That is the origin or source of all sham forms of leisure with their strong family resemblance to want of leisure and to sloth (in its old metaphysical and theological sense). The opportunity is given for the mere killing of time, and for boredom with its marked similarity to the inability to enjoy leisure; for one can be bored only if the spiritual power to enjoy leisure, or, if you prefer, to be leisurely, has died away. There is an entry in Baudelaire's *Journal Intime* that is fearful in the precision of its cynicism: "One must work, not from taste then at least from despair. For, to reduce everything to a single truth: work is less boring than pleasure."

In the preceding passage, Professor Pieper touches upon the high significance of leisure which quite escapes Veblen, Riesman, and Rowntree. It escapes then because they do not admit the transcendent importance, in this life of ours, of belief in an order that is more than human and more than natural. Veblen and Riesman are thoroughgoing secularists; Rowntree's religious faith amounts to little more than moralism. Because they ignore the sources of the idea of leisure, their whole analysis of the problem is feeble. Veblen's detestation of leisure is part of his detestation of anything that cannot be weighed and measured. Riesman's rather comic eagerness to guide us to new frontiers of "consumption" as a relief from bore-dom betrays his inability to understand that leisure is a state of spirit, not a mere busy-ness during idle hours. Rowntree's theory that improved soft-drinks will put a stop to drunkenness is suffi-cient evidence that he has not the faintest notion of what ails the modern mind, nor of the possible remedies for social boredom.

Josef Pieper, however, perceives the causes of our acedia and sug-gests, very briefly, the means of our salvation. The problem of leisure is the problem of the proletariat, the men without purpose or prin-ciple, the people who own nothing, the human beings who are tied to their work. Though ordinarily proletarians, being propertyless, are wholly dependent upon work for wages, they may not be simply the victims of economic circumstance. They may, for instance, be chained to their work by state "direction of labor." Or they may be chained to their work by an inner impoverishment of spirit; in their shrunken lives, they have lost any concept of true leisure, and turn to work as they turn to drink, for release from boredom. Such are our modern proletariat; and our society is in danger of being drowned in the proletarian sea. The proletarian professor, like Veblen, resent-ing leisure, order, and tradition, is zealous to establish an equality founded upon unremitting and inescapable work, "efficiency." Such a new society might actually be intolerable to men of Veblen's tem-per; but the last chapter of Taine's *Ancien Regime* reminds us how the abstract reformer, or rather the abstract critic, rarely realizes, until too late, that Dr. Guillotine labored for *him*.

To redeem this proletariat, rather than to confound us all in it, is the necessity now confronting the man who values civilization. Pro-fessor Pieper suggests that to "deproletarianize" we must enlarge the scope of life beyond merely servile work, and widen the sphere of servile work to the advantage of the liberal arts; and this can be attempted through three policies: "by giving the wage-earner the opportunity to save and acquire property, by limiting the powers of the state, and by overcoming the inner impoverishment of the indi-vidual." Yet these will avail only if a religious veneration guides the mind of man; as Dr. Pieper tells us, "Now, our hope is that the true sense of sacramental visibility in the celebration of the Christian *cultus* should become manifest to the extent needed for drawing the man in us, who is 'born to work,' out of himself, and should draw him out of the toil and moil of every day into the sphere of unending holiday, and should draw him out of the narrow and confined sphere of work and labor into the heart and centre of creation." The problem of leisure, like all other profound problems, leads us upward to the realm of religious faith; and today, as W. H. Mallock wrote in *The New Republic* eighty years gone, all the unbought grace of life that is purely secular, must be dust and ashes unless infused with a religious conviction that life is worth living. This is no place to enter upon the prospects and difficulties of the revival of religious convictions among the proletariat and among the men of defecated intellect; but such a book as the late Professor C. E. M. Joad's *Recovery of Belief* demonstrates that we are not yearning after the impossible.

To understand fully the value of leisure, and the necessity to society of leisured men, we need to apprehend clearly the meaning of "work." We must find our happiness in work, or not at all, Irving Babbitt told America a generation ago. But the work of which Babbitt writes does not exclude leisure; it is not total work. And the highest kind of leisure is at the same time the highest kind of work: that strenuous contemplation which demands the utmost in human powers. Aristotle declares that the end of man is an action; the most truly human action, however, is thought. Cardinal Newman remarks that "life is for action"; and what he has in mind is the action of reason and intellect. The man of liberal learning, then, the man who most deserves leisure, is the man who in actuality performs the highest kind of work. In our time, this hierarchy of work, this ethical and intellectual working, is endangered by a sullen equalitarianism which would deprive the philosopher, the poet, and the natural aristocrat of that leisure by virtue of which they are enabled to perform their own especial labors.

The fallacies involved in a definition of work purely quantitative have done much mischief during the past three generations. These illusions may be seen at work in Article 24 of the Universal Declaration of Human Rights promulgated by the United Nations Organization: "Everyone has the right to rest and leisure, including reasonable limitation of working hours and periodic holidays with pay." There is no right without its correspondent duty: so that if a man is entitled to a holiday with pay (the United Nations Organization being conspicuously a secular body, the proper phrase would have been "vacation with pay"), some other man must have the duty of paying him during his leisure. And if that other man has the duty of paying him, the person on vacation ought to have performed the antecedent duty of having labored faithfully to deserve that payment. But of these correspondent duties, there is no word in the Universal Declaration of Human Rights; and just such is the danger of these abstract declarations of rights, like the Declaration of the Rights of Man and the Citizen, implying a claim without any obligation married to it.

What nearly every man will presume, after reading this declaration, is that some central governmental body is obliged to provide him with money and leisure, whatever his peculiar deserts. The Christian concept of natural rights presumes mutual obligation; moreover, the Christian idea of such rights has the sanction of a supernatural justice to give it force; while the declarations of an amorphous political association have only the sanction of a secular humanitarianism, for what it is worth. "A liberty that is asserted as an abstract right," Babbitt says, "something anterior to the fulfilment of any definite obligation, will always, so far as the inner life is concerned, be a lazy liberty. From this point of view, all other 'natural' rights are summed up in the title of a book written by a grandson of Karl Marx: *The Right to Idleness.* We have heard asserted in our own time the abstract right of whole populations to self-determination as something anterior to their degree of moral development. To put forward a supposed right of this kind as part of a programme for world peace is to sink to the ultimate depth of humanitarian self-deception." When, in the modern state, the power of positive law is invoked to give reality to the fallacy that leisure is identical with idleness, and that a quantitative definition of work can provide us with a satisfactory scheme for apportioning leisure in society, and that all forms of leisure are equally desirable—why, then the higher forms of leisure, the leisure of contemplation, of artistic achievement, of literary endeavor, of moral reflection, of all the elements which make up the unbought grace of life, are shamefully neglected in favor of a levelling "leisure" which is mere amusement of idleness.

In any society, even in the present flushed prosperity of America, the people can afford to spend only a small portion of their collective income upon leisure; and the more of that leisure-fund is spent upon aimless amusement or in occupations actually harmful to the body social, the less will be spent upon the higher and nobler forms of leisure. Contemplation, which is the reward of ethical working, is the first to suffer, for it is necessarily the least popular form of leisure. Coleridge, in *The Constitution of Church and State*, says that in any just state a certain portion of the national wealth, which he calls the Nationalty, is set aside for the sustenance of the Clerisy, or the body of ministers of religion and teachers, the Clerks, who carry on the spiritual and cultural instruction of the people. The Nationalty, and the other economic endowments of true leisure, are being plundered today—plundered in part to defray the expenses of a state-directed material humanitarianism, in part to pay for transitory amusements. And the classes and individuals who have done the higher sorts of labor, the working of spirit and mind, are precisely the classes and individuals who, though they no longer call the tune, still are expected to pay the piper. *Their* work grows steadily more burdensome; *their* leisure steadily diminishes.

The clergyman, the magistrate, the schoolmaster, the conscientious civil servant, the industrial manager, the writer, the artist—all these are laden with increasing duties at the time their emoluments are halved, or more than halved, by the increased cost of living and by taxation; and they, who used to be rewarded for their diligence and their bleats by a leisure which many of them employed well, are now increasingly denied the hours free from labor which have become the lawful prerogative of the manual laborer. If this tendency continues, the whole quality of human achievement is sure to suffer; and everyone in society, down to the most mechanical and menial worker, will share in this suffering. A generation ago, Irving Babbitt described this grim tendency toward the maldistribution and misuse of leisure: "The laborer now has opportunities such as have never before existed to become something more. Unfortunately, as we all know, he is not using his relief from drudgery to enjoy leisure in the Aristotelian sense, but to seek amusements, in which he is almost as much subordinated to machines as he is in his working moments (automobiles, phonographs, moving pictures and the like). Perhaps the fault is not so much in the laborer himself, as in the pattern that is being offered him by the man 'higher up.'"

Leisure ought to be the reward of lofty minds and of the higher forms of work. An aristocracy, indeed, justifies itself by the work it performs; and when it fails to fulfill its high functions, then it loses its leisure and its very existence. But to condemn the very existence of a leisured class, and the concept of leisure itself, as Veblen does, is to prefer savagery to civilization. The disciples of Veblen may think that they are simply preferring the engineer to the poet; but the engineer, and the whole complicated edifice of modern industry, cannot long survive the disappearance of that leisure which elevates the human intellect and renews the ethical principles that bind together the civil social order. "Believing himself a critic of his culture," Mr. Riesman writes of Veblen, "he fell into some of its most characteristic nineteenth-century crudities and self-deceptions."

I do not think, then, that we have anything to learn nowadays from *The Theory of the Leisure Class;* nor that we have much to learn from the concepts of leisure entertained by Mr. Riesman, nor from those of Mr. Rowntree. If true leisure, as distinguished from the boredom of idleness, is to be restored to the mass of men, we must relate our opportunities for leisure to the ends of life that men have pursued since time out of mind. We must remember that the Christian idea of leisure is expressed in the holy-day. We must remind ourselves that a chief practical object of leisure is self-improvement, or emulation of the highest types of humanity. We must relate our leisure hours to the concerns of family, the welfare of our children, and the improvement of our homes. We ought to recall that one form of leisure is to turn from our accustomed work to another sort of work, equally productive, but less monotonous and employing individual skills. We might well employ our leisure to secure a greater measure of private independence and security, proportionately relieving ourselves and society of the menace of the proletariat. And we have in the new leisure of industrial society an opportunity to strengthen tradition by looking backward to our ancestors and forward to our posterity, through the study of history and the preservation of our historic heritage, and the leisurely re-examination of human needs in the light of modern conditions. To apply these general principles of serious leisure to particular circumstances is a complex task; but it is far more likely to save us from social boredom than all the schemes for instructing us in "consumership" and creating new appetites in Sybaris.

As the problem of leisure is intimately connected with the problem of social boredom, so it is joined to the problem of order in modern society. "From the point of view of civilization," Babbitt remarks, "it is of the highest moment that certain individuals should in every community be relieved from the necessity of working with their hands in order that they may engage in the higher forms of working and so qualify for leadership. If the civilization is to be genuine, it must have men of leisure in the full Aristotelian sense. Those who in any particular community are allowed to enjoy property that is not the fruit of their own outer and visible toil cannot, therefore, afford to be idlers and parasites. An aristocratic or leading class, however the aristocratic principle is conceived, must, if it hopes in the long run to preserve its property and privileges, be in some degree exemplary. . . . A leading class that has become Epicurean and self-indulgent is lost."

Our leading classes, for more than a century, have been more self-indulgent than they ought, though scarcely so profligate as Veblen thought they were. In this present iron hour, the leisure class, so far as it still survives, has very great duties and very small regards. But some classes, like some men, are ennobled by adversity; and if the men who still retain a degree of moral and political ascendancy over the masses have in them the courage to make the endeavor, it is not yet too late to preserve to posterity the unbought grace of life, and to keep at bay the squalid oligarchs who detest the world of silence and of freedom.

The Problem of Community

DESPITE the potential strength of the conservative instinct in America, American conservatives in this century have had a way of undoing themselves. I think that one of the principal errors of conservatively-inclined men has been their neglect of the need for true community. All too often they have endeavored to employ the phrases of yesterday's radicals to defend today's conservatism; and thus they have exposed themselves to ridicule from their enemies, and clouded their own understandings. Now the enlightened conservative always has stood for true community, the union of men, through love and common interest, for the common welfare. It was the liberals and radicals of the eighteenth and nineteenth centuries, not the conservatives, who did everything in their power to abolish the traditional concept of community and substitute a doctrinaire individualism, which led inevitably to collectivism, as a natural reaction. Community and collectivism are at opposite poles. Community is the product of volition; collectivism, of compulsion. Community stands for variety and intricacy; collectivism, for uniformity and arid simplicity.

The most common form of this neglect of the idea of community has been a preoccupation, in conservatively-inclined circles, with economic doctrines and the dry vocabulary of Efficiency and Success. I do not say that the economic principles of these people have been wrong; but I do say that they have emphasized economic abstractions at the expense of nearly everything else in society, and that they will fail to rouse the imagination and sympathy of the best men and women in the rising generation unless they take a different tack.

It might have been well enough, fifty or sixty years ago, to exhort the public to Free Competition and the Profit Motive and the grandeur of the Self-Made Man. But it will not do today, when men *must* have principles by which to live and die. The *reductio ad absurdum* of this school, as applied by publicists, was the injunction to American soldiers in Korea to fight and die for the American Standard of Living. There is no greater fool than the man who dies for his standard of *living*, except the man who dies for someone else's standard of living. I am of the opinion, in fine, that American conservatives ought to talk a great deal less about the laws of economics and a great deal more about the laws of justice. They ought to remember that Competition, after all, is only an instrument in Community.

That highly speculative division of knowledge which we call "economics" took shape in the eighteenth century as an instrument for attaining individual freedom. Applied at the height of the first industrial revolution to a purpose hardly more noble than the compilation of apologetics for "production," "efficiency," and "utility," and for such political ends as the establishment of tariffs in America or the abolition of tariffs in England, gradually political economy, by the beginning of our century, became a means for justifying the proposals of social planners. Many teachers and specialists in twentieth-century economics became converts to a neo-Jacobinism. Burke defined Jacobinism as "the revolt of the enterprising talents of a nation against its property."

This new Jacobinism was very like what Herbert Spencer called "new Toryism." Such doctrines of confidence in the omnicompetence of the state, W.A. Orton points out, came to predominate strongly in state universities; and F.A. Hayek has traced the theory of social engineering back to certain roots in the polytechnic colleges. Quite as eighteenth-century optimism, materialism, and humanitarianism were fitted by Marx into a system which might have surprised a good many of the *philosophes*, so nineteenth-century utilitarian and Manchesterian concepts were the ancestors (perhaps with a bend sinister) of mechanistic social planning. The old Jacobins scarcely realized that their centralizing tendencies were a faithful imitation of the policies of the Old Regime; so it is not surprising that recent humanitarian and collectivistic thinkers forget their debt to Jeremy Bentham.

Yet the abstractions of Bentham, reducing human beings to social atoms, are the principal source of modern designs for social alteration by fiat. J.M. Keynes declared, in *Two Memoirs*, that the Benthamite system produced our moral and political confusion: "I do now regard that as the worm which has been gnawing at the insides of modern civilization and is responsible for its present decay. We used to regard the Christians as the enemy, because they appeared as the representatives of tradition, convention, and hocus-pocus. In truth, it was the Benthamite calculus, based on an over-valuation of the economic criterion, which was destroying the quality of the popular ideal." Lord Keynes' little book, incidentally, is only one of several recent protests against narrow and ominous tendencies in the dominant school of political economy, with its suppositions that productive efficiency is the criterion of civilization and that state planning is the insurance of economic vigor. "What is properly called industry is not art or self-justifying activity," George Santayana wrote in 1905 (*Reason in Society*), "but on the contrary a distinctly compulsory and merely instrumental labor, which if justified at all must be justified by some ulterior advantage which it secures. In regard to such instrumental activities the question is always pertinent whether they do not produce more than is useful, or prevent the existence of something that is intrinsically good." This apotheosis of industrialism and the economists' theory of happiness has been most conspicuous in America, Santayana continued: "Occidental society has evidently run in this direction into great abuses, complicating life prodigiously without ennobling the mind.... An experimental materialism, spontaneous and divorced from reason and from everything useful, is also confused in some minds with traditional duties, and a school of popular hierophants is not lacking that turns it into a sort of idealism."

Well, Santayana made his way out of this unheeding society of "Nibelungen who toil underground over a gold they will never use" to a Roman convent; and one might have mistaken this retreat of a saddened philosopher for the final triumph of Bentham, were it not that certain signs among us suggest that political economy is recovering the broad view of Adam Smith and the easy temper of Walter Bagehot. There are even signs that political economy may be persuaded to acknowledge the suzerainty of moral and spiritual purpose.

Among the writers who have been endeavoring to effect a reform in the study of political economy are David McCord Wright, Frank Knight, F. A. Hayek, Wilhelm Röpke, and the late W. A. Orton. All these men have been devoted to freedom; all believe that liberty cannot exist in a collectivistic economy, "where the executioner has the last word." They differ very considerably among themselves, but the general tendency of their work has been to liberalize and humanize the Dismal Science. It is time we read such books; for a long time the American economy, whether dominated by conservatives or innovators, by Republicans or Democrats, has been operating without any effective intellectual principle; its operation has become correspondingly erratic, kept tolerable chiefly by preparations for war, the conduct of war, and patching up the damage of war, a condition which in nearly any time but the present would be considered perilously abnormal. If the current conservative impulse in the United States is prolonged, it will require such advice as these writers offer. But it will also require something more.

Two vocabularies express and confine the opinions of many people nowadays who talk about political economy; and both of these vocabularies are obsolete. If nothing is deader than dead politics, surely nothing is sooner superannuated than yesterday's political economy. One of these vocabularies is that of the Manchesterians, and the other is that of the socialists. They are the two sides of the coin of Utilitarianism. Both are founded upon the presumption that the real end of man, after all, is the production-consumption equation. I do not agree that man is so humble a creature. I believe that the end of man is the imitation of a Divine nature, and that this end may be attained only through freedom. Utilitarianism, in either of its forms, is servile in essence.

The Manchesterians thought of freedom as the opportunity for a man to improve his material condition through private economic action. The socialists thought of freedom as the opportunity for society to improve the material condition of the masses through collective action. We now live in an age, however—I speak of America and the industrialized Western world—in which the reality or the possibility of economic abundance already is at hand. And this abundance is produced not by ideology, but by technology. Barring social disaster, we no longer stand in danger of want in the Malthusian sense—not, at least, for some generations to come. The risk is greater, indeed, that we may become pigs in the sty of Epicurus, debauched (in the sense of true humanity) by our own creature-comforts. I think that we ought to talk less, therefore, about "efficiency" and "industrial progress" and "consumer education," and more about political economy as it is related to true freedom.

I should like to see the old phrase "political economy" restored to its former dignity. It is preferable to "economics" because "political economy" implies that the politics of a state and the economy of a state are enduringly joined. There are economics under which no real freedom is possible: communistic economies are such. There are political conditions under which no sound economy is possible: anarchy is such. Today, a good many people naively assume that we can remain free no matter how tightly the state controls or actually operates the economy. And others assume, with equal innocence, that political and personal freedom will endure, so long as we keep repeating the word "freedom," no matter how far the process of concentrating economic power in vast corporations nominally "private" is carried. Our present age of abundance offers possibilities of freedom almost unknown to earlier times. But, rather than seeking to attain that freedom, we seem to be moving unthinkingly toward a political economy characterized by the triumph of the machine, meaningless production, purposeless work and idleness instead of leisure.

At this moment, we are in a kind of transient equilibrium, in which the personal freedoms of the nineteenth century survive little diminished, and in which the material advantages of utilitarian production continue to increase. Yet I believe that this equilibrium will not long endure. As the consolidation of economic power progresses, the realm of personal freedom will diminish, whether the masters of the economy are state servants or the servants of private corporations. I do not say that this process will continue inevitably; I say only that freedom will diminish if all men become the servants of an economic structure to which there is no alternative. It still is possible, here in America, to seek means for restoring variety to economic life, purpose to work, and meaning to leisure. Nowadays, in short, we need to emphasize work for the sake of accomplishment and freedom, rather than work for the sake of quantitative production.

Just this, I venture to suggest, is a task for conservatives, in the best and broadest sense of that abused word. Conservatives generally have not been enamored of the economic science. Burke scoffed at the "sophisters, economists, and calculators" who would supplant prescriptive wisdom by their neat plans for social alteration. The dominant school of economists, from Adam Smith onward, was liberal in its assumptions, with only here and there an exception like Huskisson, After the 1880's, it is true, there occurred in political and economic thought a certain fusion of liberal and conservative opinion, predicted and exemplified by Bagehot. Yet conservatives remain in a forlorn minority today among scientific economists: the dominant schools are collectivistic, or old-fashioned Manchesterian, or new-style liberal after the manner of Keynes. Most of those economists popularly called conservative still prefer the appellation "liberal": Professor Hayek, of course, and Professor David McCord Wright, and Professor Röpke.

Nor is this simply because conservatives, in John Stuart Mill's reproachful phrase, are the stupid party. It is rather that the thinking conservative has refused to believe that economic production, whether "capitalistic" or "socialistic," is the primary concern of the individual or the state. He has tended to steer dear of the Dismal Science because he did not share the Webbs' conviction that man is principally Producer and Consumer. The conservative has been attached to traditional and rural life, resenting the excesses and injustices of the industrial system as much as did any radical socialist. Yet, that industrial system now being irrevocably established, the man of conservative impulses must teach himself to understand political economy. W. H. Mallock, sixty years ago, set himself to this task, uncongenial though it was to his character; and here in America we need such conservatives of imagination to consider the problems of our industrial age in the light of conservative principle: "conservative" as a term of principle, not simply as a term of relation. And the first duty for the conservative, in this field, is to declare what he believes and what he does not. In the popular mind, the conservative in the economic sphere is badly confused with the Manchesterian liberal. They have something in common, truly; and that is an opposition to state capitalism or state socialism; but there are differences, too.

The conservative thinks, for instance, that a great deal is wrong with our modern political economy—and that no economy ever will be wholly satisfactory. The fault is not that our economy is inefficient; it may be, indeed, *too* efficient for life on a truly human scale; rather, the economy is unsatisfactory in that, increasingly, it neglects the dignity of man. The Manchesterian dogma and the Marxist dogma treat man as a creature almost exclusively economic, and the whole unconscious tendency of the modern economic system is toward the realization of that view. (Professor von Mises really does not seem to differ much in his postulates about the nature of man from the views of modern orthodox Marxists; both are children of Bentham.) Nor is this narrowness confined to strict Manchesterians or strict Marxists. In endeavoring to atone for the atomic individualism of the last century, modern reformers are in grave danger of plunging into a materialism quite as gross, and still more hostile to true freedom.

At the moment, it is not old-fangled socialism which is the principal menace to freedom; for that is an ideology far gone in decay, even at the polls, and even the Fabians no longer have confidence in their own objectives. Old-fashioned socialism, or state capitalism, may experience a recrudescence, of course, in a time of depression, for modern man tends to hold government responsible for his material well-being, and to turn to more government when he is discontented. But just now doctrinaire socialism is in retreat generally, especially in the United States. The immediate threat to liberty, in the economic sphere, is rather one or the other of these two alternatives: first, that the great nations may become so many garrison-states, as in *1984*, with economic life, like all other aspects of human existence, directed toward concentration of power against an enemy whose ends and methods are remarkably similar; or, second, that modern civilization may sink into the condition of a culture devoted utterly to the producer-consumer equation, a universal Sybaris like *Brave New World*, in which the end of man, together with freedom, is quite forgot. In the first condition, there would be great dangers always, but no means for the individual man to fortify himself against those dangers, no place for private courage or conscience; in the second condition, there would be no dangers left to challenge man, but the destruction of competition, of the old motives to integrity, and of freedom of choice would reduce man, at the end of these centuries of civilization, to a state "as free, and as equal" (in Saintsbury's phrase), "as pigs in a sty."

For the conservative, the real end of economic production is to raise man above the savage level, to make possible the leisure which sustains civilization, and to free man from the condition of a simple drudge. When efficiency or production becomes an end in itself, then truly technology has triumphed over humanity. The Soviet experiment is only the *reductio ad absurdum* of a preoccupation with creature-comforts that sweeps away, very soon, certain things in human existence far more precious than creature-comforts, and presently—through the abolition of incentives and the deadening influence of fanatic ideology—may make even those creature-comforts scarce.

We suffer from the same disease as do the Communists, though in a milder form. Whenever we go about looking for a solution to some great social problem, we rarely recur to the first principles of human nature and society. Instead, we turn back to Benthamite dogmas. "Efficiency," "progress," and "economic security" are our god-terms, as they are those of the Soviets. When we take up our farm-problem, we phrase it in terms that imply that the farmer is simply a servant of Mammon; that his function is simply to serve the cities; and that if he is "inefficient," or in any respect less prosperous than his city-cousins, then either he ought to be shipped off to the city and fitted into the process of automation, or else he ought to be subsidized as if he were rather a disagreeable mendicant whose votes, regrettably, do count. Almost no one asks just what is going to happen to a country in which the rural population, already scarcely a seventh of the total, sinks toward extinction; or whether the rural life is not worth conserving at some cost to total efficiency;

or whether the farmer really ought to be expected to live a life, in creature-comforts and aims, precisely like that of his city-cousin. If we think of aiding the farmer at all, it is merely with the view of converting him into an agricultural capitalist. I suggest, in short, that we are suffering from a decline of social imagination, extending to—and sometimes caused by—economic theory.

Yet in criticizing the social dogmas of Bentham and of Manchester, I do not mean to deny the claims of a free economy. Without a free economy, freedom of any sort is most difficult to maintain. The reasons for this have been expounded by persons more competent to discuss them than I am. One of the best such analyses is Professor Wilhelm Röpke's *Social Crisis of Our Time*, an attack upon "the cult of the colossal." The greatest social affliction of this age, Dr. Röpke writes, is proletarianization. Capitalism may have introduced the modern proletariat, but socialism extends that class to include the whole of mankind. Our salvation, he says, lies in a "Third Way." The work of the French Revolution must be undone, not to reinstate a rule of force, but instead to venerate afresh order, coherence, authority, and hierarchy, established by prescription and consent. Society cannot be organized "in accordance with rational postulates while disregarding the need for genuine communities, for a vertical structure." The same infatuation with "rationalism" which terribly damaged communal existence also produced an unquestioning confidence in the competitive market economy and led to a heartless individualism "which in the end has proved to be a menace to society and has so discredited a fundamentally sound idea as to further the rise of the far more dangerous collectivism." In such a world, where old landmarks have been swept away, old loyalties ridiculed, and human beings reduced to economic atoms, "men finally grasp at everything that is offered to them, and here they may easily and understandably suffer the same fate as the frogs in the fable who asked for a king and got a crane."

Loathing "doctrinaire rationalism," Röpke is careful not to propound an arbitrary scheme of alteration and renovation. Yet his suggestions for deproletarizing are forthright. Family farms, farmers' co-operatives for marketing, the technical and administrative possibilities of industrial decentralization, the diminution of the average size of factories, the gradual substitution for "the old-style welfare policy" of an intelligent trend toward self-sufficiency—none of these projects is novel, but they are urged by an economist possessing both reputation and frank common sense. He sees no insuperable difficulties. To cushion society against the fluctuations of the business cycle, for instance, the better remedy is not increased centralization, a very dubious palliative, but instead the encouragement of men to get a part of their sustenance from outside the immediate realm of financial disturbance:

> The most extreme examples of this tendency are perhaps some American farmers who had become so specialized and so dependent on their current money incomes that when the crisis came they were as near starvation as the industrial worker. At the other, more fortunate, end we see the industrial worker in Switzerland who, if necessary, can find his lunch in the garden, his supper in the lake, and can earn his potato supply in the fall by helping his brother clear his land.

Humanizing of the economic structure, *a la taille de l'homme* (in the phrase of Ramuz), is the kernel of these proposals. They are not detailed, but they are cheering. In Wilhelm Röpke's pages, the political economist recollects that the art of politics has an ethical foundation, and that the purpose of industry is private contentment, not an abstract Production. And throughout Röpke's work, man is regarded as a member of a civilized community, a true person, not simply a factor in industrial output.

What is especially heartening about such books as Professor Röpke's is that doctrinaire political economy had a great deal to do with the destruction of true community among us; now, although the hour is very late, some economists are turning their hands to the task of restoration. Professor F. A. Hayek's *The Road to Serfdom*, and his *Individualism and Economic Order*, books in which the influence of Burke and other true conservative thinkers is manifest, did a good deal to remind this country of the illiberal nature of collectivism. In the history of journalism, there can have been few episodes more absurd than the wave of abuse with which certain "liberal" reviewers endeavored to overwhelm *The Road to Serfdom*, without understanding in the least what Mr. Hayek was writing about. The phrase *laissez faire* is a commination for such folk. Now it is quite true that *laissez faire* has been elevated to the condition of a secular dogma by certain other people; but here, as in the use and abuse of many other words, what we require is strict definition, not the employment of what Mr. Richard Weaver calls "god-terms" and "devil-terms."

What an elevated *laissez faire* can mean for our time, Dean R. A. Nisbet suggests in *The Quest for Community:*

> I cannot help thinking that what we need above all else in this *age* is a new philosophy of *laissez faire.* The old *laissez faire* failed because it was based on erroneous premises regarding human behavior. As a theory it failed because it mistook for ineradicable characteristics of individuals qualities that were in fact inseparable from social groups. As a policy it failed because its atomistic prop-ositions were inevitably unavailing against the reality of enlarging masses of insecure individuals. Far from proving a check upon the growth of the omnicompetent State, the old *laissez faire* actually accelerated this growth. Its indifference to every form of commu-nity and association left the State as the sole area of reform and security.... To create the conditions within which *autonomous groups* may prosper must be, I believe, the prime objective of the new *laissez faire.*
>
> I use the word create advisedly. We should not suppose that the *laissez faire* individualism of the middle nineteenth century was the simple heritage of nature, the mere untrammeled emergence of drives and motivations with which man is naturally endowed. *Laissez faire,* as the economic historian, Polanyi, among others, has emphasized, was brought into existence. It was brought into existence by the planned destruction of old customs, associations, villages, and other securities; by the force of the State throwing the weight of its fast-developing administrative system in favor of new economic elements of the population. And it was brought into existence, hardly less, by reigning systems of economic, political, and psychological thought, systems which neglected altogether the social and cultural unities and settled single-mindedly on the abstract individual as the proper unit of speculating and planning. What we need at the present time is the knowledge and adminis-trative skill to create a *laissez faire* in which the basic unit will be the social group.

The liberal values of autonomy and freedom of personal choice are indispensable to a genuinely free society, but we shall achieve and maintain these only by vesting them in the conditions in which liberal democracy will thrive—diversity of culture, plurality of association, and division of authority.

The autonomous groups to which Dr. Nisbet refers are church, family, guild or union, local community, school and university, all the complex of voluntary associations which combine freedom with love, and satisfy man's need for companionship at the same time they provide for his security. These free instruments for the welfare of men bring a psychological satisfaction, a sense of membership, that the mass-state cannot possibly, supply. But all these are continually menaced by the modern state, which seems to resent any rival to its power. The state calls itself democratic and humanitarian; in truth, these words mean nothing; for the long-run effect of consolidation and centralization must be the death of private energies and hopes. The conservative, therefore, while repudiating the doctrinaire individualism of Bentham and Spencer, contends with resolution against every endeavor of the state to encroach upon the remaining elements of free association and true community. The stifling uniformity of totalitarian democracy is not a distant prospect; it is upon us at this moment, as Professor Nisbet says boldly:

> The imperatives of war, the veneration of unity and uniformity, and the faith in historical necessity, with its corollary of irreversible historical processes—these, then, are the most powerful supports for the unitary perspective of democracy at the present time. Given these, together with the constant diminution in the significance of the nonpolitical areas of kinship, religion, and other forms of association, the task of centralization and omnicompetence is not too difficult even in the presence of liberal values. Given these conditions and perspectives, the transition from liberal democracy to totalitarianism will not seem too arduous or unpleasant. It will indeed be scarcely noticed, save by the 'utopians,' the 'reactionaries,' and similar eccentrics.

Any observant conservative must be struck by the feebleness of those organizations, in the United States, which ought to be the defenders of true community. Our chief bulwark against the total state, indeed, is today the inertia of constitutional law, not the intelligent protest of voluntary groups. The lawyers and the doctors, indeed, are reasonably vigilant; but very few other elements of the free community seem to apprehend the danger in which we stand.

Among the churches, only the Catholics have shown a consistent and intelligent appreciation of the necessity for true community, for they have a series of Papal encyclicals to afford them principle. Here and there, an isolated Protestant clergyman or congregation struggles valiantly to restore some aspect of true community; but most Protestant preaching of the "social gospel" seems quite innocent of the distinction between collectivism and community. Nor are the Catholics always able to tell the difference: an extreme naiveté as to economic facts and political institutions afflicts some zealots for Catholic Action, who come dangerously close to acting as if positive legislation and state planning could substitute adequately for private charity and voluntary association.

The free will which God bestowed upon man was the power to choose between good and evil; and if Divine wisdom was content to allow freedom of choice in this tremendous sphere, it is presumption upon the part of social reformers to deny freedom of choice in smaller matters by endorsing the compulsory humanitarianism of the state. Modern humanitarianism, as Orestes Brownson insisted, is heretical, for it is founded upon the supposition that material comfort is the supreme good. Any Christian, of whatever particular persuasion, needs often to remind himself that the great benefit of charity is not really to the recipient, but to the voluntary donor.

It might be expected that the labor unions would be a powerful expression of true community in our age; but in actuality their performance is infinitely disappointing. Professor Frank Tannenbaum, in *A Philosophy of Labor*, struggles to convince us that the unions are the great conservative force of our time; but he succeeds merely in describing what the unions *might* be, not what they seem to want to become. He looks to the unions to save us from "the evil benefits of the welfare state"; and the pensions and welfare-funds which the great unions have been obtaining in recent years are indeed a step in this direction, as some sensible and moderate annual-wage program might be. But in general, the unions, like the industrial corporations, have been obsessed with nineteenth-century economic theories, and have sought only to obtain more pay for their members, not to bring to them pride of work, variety of occupation, free association, permanence, and tranquillity.

The union leaders have risen through turbulence, and most of them rule through turbulence. The growth of "horizontal unionism" in the past twenty-five years has done infinite mischief, more than any old-fangled anti-union employer ever could have contrived, to destroy the sense of guild and dose voluntary association which characterized some of the craft unions; "horizontal" unionism partakes far more of collectivism than of community. And when one looks at labor organizations like Hoffa's Teamsters in Detroit, which is an extortionate conspiracy, one almost despairs of their salvation. The essential feature in community is *volition;* but since the passage of the Wagner Act, the union officers, with a few exceptions, have been intoxicated with their power, and have mercilessly employed both the power of inequitable law and the terror of the goon squad to make membership compulsory, so far as lies in their power, so that the great horizontal union of the automobile industry, the U.A.W., has scarcely any more element of volition in it than the most arbitrary totalitarian state.

The friends of industrial management, indeed, show more concern for the idea of community. Various corporations are doing all in their power to encourage a sense of loyalty and continuity among their employees, and books like Mr. Peter Drucker's *The New Society* explore the possibilities of reconciling freedom and security through an integration of modern industrial establishments with the local social order. But probably we ask too much if we expect the industrial corporation to make up for all the older and more tender bonds of voluntary association. It is hard to learn to love a coke-oven or an electric comptometer, and harder still to learn to love an incorporation for simple economic ends. Every development of a sense of community in the industrial system is to be received with thanksgiving, but the real task of restoration lies with the traditional agencies of community.

All these defenses against the absolute state are enfeebled; but they are not impossible to reinvigorate, if the work is commenced now, and if the thinking conservative persuades men to distinguish between free community, the product of love, and the moral isolation which Benthamites preach. In many practical measures, particularly in their opposition to state regulation of the economy, the conservative who thinks in terms of community will be at one with the old-fashioned liberal economist; but he will know that men's loyalties are to be secured only by realities less hollow than abstract economic doctrines. The error of the liberals from the beginning, as Sir Walter Scott knew, was their assumption that the world is governed by little tracts and pamphlets. This is nonsense. The world is governed by love or by hate; and if the love which is community decays, the hate which is collectivism (for whatever its pretenses to humanitarianism, in the long run collectivism turns out to be the gratification of the lust for power) grows proportionately. "Even Mormon has more votaries than Bentham," Disraeli said a century ago. Flint never will be made a decent place to live, or a safe one, by Manchesterian doctrines preached in all their rigidity; but Flint may be civilized by a restoration of community.

Community cannot be restored through any vaunting program of positive legislation; indeed, the most which conservatives can ask from the modern state is to be let alone in their labors toward the resuscitation of voluntary association. The omnicompetent state may talk the language of community, but the measures it employs are destructive of those free engagements of love and charity that constitute real community. Our national program of social security is altogether too pertinent an instance of this. Now modern industrial society has grave cause for restoring economic security—or what is really more important, the *sense* of comparative security—to the mass of men; and doubtless political government is sometimes the most convenient instrument.

The conservative wants men to feel at peace, and he looks upon government as a great power for good. But our particular program of social security, hastily drawn up and since then growing confusedly, is not a true restoration of community; it bears nearly all the marks of a remorseless collectivism. First of all, the program is centralized, divorced from local interests, differences, and affections, for the most part; the agencies of slate and local government, which should be the principal administrators, are left only minor roles. Second, the program is not voluntary, but compulsory, and its compulsory features, and the scope of its arbitrary power, have been steadily increased. Of course there are people who would not save unless they were compelled to; but it might be better for us, morally and economically, to take the risk of having to support them in their hour of need, out of pure charity, rather than to apply compulsion both to them and to ourselves. And the inclusion of the self-employed and of persons like doctors and lawyers and all the respectable professions is indefensible on moral grounds; talk about "extending the benefits" of social security to these classes is disgusting cant. They would be forced into the program because the government wants more money to spend, and for no other sensible reason.

Third, the conferring of a benefit upon the poorer classes in society, although the alleged reason for the vast social-security system, in reality is becoming only a secondary motive; the real reason why the federal government continually extends the bounds of the system is that this places at the disposal of the federal power a vast reserve of money and credit, apart from taxation. It is disguised taxation, in short, and has the advantage of meeting with less vehement protest than a new tax would. If the national government requires additional funds, these ought to be obtained through regular taxation, not through the employment of a sham. Taxation, in the English and American political tradition, is a free grant from the citizens for the general welfare; it is not extortion by a central political authority, disguised or candid. When we begin to neglect the details of our free political tradition, we are in danger of losing the essence of our liberties. Our present scheme of social security, because it ignores every element of volition and free association, is a deadening collectivism masked as liberal humanitarianism. We ought not to go back to the economic heartlessness of the Bleak Age; but neither ought we to pretend that collectivism is the only alternative.

The part which most conservatives can play in the restoration of community is a small one; but it will require constancy and discernment. I throw out here, almost at random, some suggestions as to the general line which conservatives who desire to re-establish community upon a durable foundation may take:

(1) They will endeavor to make the family function as a device for love and education and economic advantage, not simply an instrument of the feeding-and-housing-and-procreating process.

(2) They will seek to make their church and parish the means of a communion between divine love and human, and among the generations that are gone, and the generation that is living, and the generations that are yet to be; and they will express this communion in acts of charity and good fellowship. This is a great way from the Sunday-morning moralism of most clergymen and congregations.

(3) They will try to make their profession, or trade, or craft, an instrument not merely for private profit, but for satisfying their own desire to feel that somehow they matter. In professional associations, unions, dubs, and charitable organizations, they will have as their aim a meeting of minds which no uniformity imposed from above could equal.

(4) They will search for ways to turn the amorphous modern city into a series of neighborhoods, with common interests, amenities, and economic functions. They will hope to bring back political coherence and decency to the city by decentralization and the substitution of voluntary agencies for compulsory ones.

(5) They will stand for variety and independence in our schools, colleges, and universities; unlike Dr. Conant, they will detest the notion of a monotonously uniform system of public instruction, designed to propagate approved "social attitudes." They will understand that the more voluntary education we can have, and the less compulsory, the healthier our society will be.

(6) They will defend the institutions of local government against a state consolidation of power, and the rights of states against the encroachments of the federal government. For freedom and democracy—at least American democracy—are the products of local rights and true popular concurrence. They will not be deluded by the argument that local government is decayed, and ought therefore to be supplanted by a central bureaucracy; for a central bureaucracy, given the same powers, is sure to decay in its

turn, and to decay irreparably. They will turn their talents, instead, to restoring or conserving those local and prescriptive political methods which distinguish a free society from a servile society.

All this requires hard work, and infinite patience, and a sense of dedication. It is not half so exciting as sending telegrams to Congressmen or planning the industrialization of Pakistan. And when we die, the work will not be half done—no, not a quarter of it. But we shall rest easy in our consciences; for "the towering moral problem of the age," as Dean Nisbet writes, is "the problem of community lost and community regained."

The Problem of Social Justice

A FRIEND OF MINE has the misfortune of owning a number of stone cottages. I say "misfortune" because the cottages are in Scotland, and their rents are fixed at the level of 1914. The cottages were built long before 1914—some of them are eighteenth-century work, with their pantiled roofs and thick rubble walls and irregular little windows; but they are good to look upon still, with their white door-sills and their little gardens along the path to the road. The law compels my friend to keep them in tolerable repair, if they are tenanted, and to pay most of what rent he receives either to local authorities or to the Exchequer, in the form of rates and income-taxes. But the rent of each cottage amounts to a mere five shillings a week—seventy cents, at the present rate of exchange. This is not particularly depressing to my friend, for the rents of his farms are fixed at levels higher than they were during the Napoleonic wars, let alone the First World War. The cottages are a cause of expense to him, of course, rather than a source of income; but persons of his station are now resigned to being ruined, and for some of his cottages he asks no rent at all, letting them to old people who can afford to pay next to nothing. Some of his tenants, however, are better off, according to their lights, than my friend himself: they have risen in the economic scale while he has descended. His income is still much greater than theirs, but his expenses are much greater, and his responsibilities. These tenants now have better wages and shorter hours than ever they did before; they can afford their little luxuries, extending sometimes to television-sets. Some of them have come to look upon rent as a luxury— for, after all, many of their neighbors are the recipients of my friend's charity, paying nothing for their cottages. Accordingly, my friend's agent occasionally has his difficulties when he goes from door to door, on Mondays, collecting five shillings here and five shillings there. One morning the agent knocked at the door of a tenant who was in good health and employed at good wages. The tenant came to the door and announced that he had decided to pay no more rent; he could not afford it; prices were high, and he could use that five shillings himself.

"Will you be honest with me?" the agent asked.
The tenant said he would.
"Well, then," said the agent, "how much do you spend a month on cigarettes?"
"Thirty shillin's," replied the tenant, in righteous defiance, "and not a penny more."

When a man feels that he is entitled to withhold his rent, though he spends on tobacco fifty per cent more per month than he does for his cottage, his notion of Justice seems to be confused. This is not so serious a confusion, however, as the revolution of belief in nearly the whole of eastern Europe, where the possessor of property has come to be looked upon as an enemy of society, and is lucky if he escapes being driven out into the woods to die of pneumonia, or herded off to a labor-camp. My friend is in no immediate danger of such a fate, though, as things are going, the old farms that have been in his family for two hundred years will have to be sold at auction when he dies, and perhaps the roof will be taken off the big handsome house that his fathers knew before him. In Scotland, fortunately for my friend, the destruction of old institutions is gradual, not violent. But at bottom the same force which has effaced traditional life in eastern Europe is ruining my Scottish friend: a confusion about first principles. Among these principles which have sustained our civilization and our very existence ever since man rose above the brutes, the principle of Justice has been the great support of an orderly and law-abiding society.

From the time when first men began to reflect upon such matters, the nobler and more serious minds have been convinced that Justice has some source and sanction more than human and more than natural. Either Justice is ordained by some Power above us, or it is mere expediency, the power of the strong over the weak—

"... the simple plan,
That they shall take, who have the power,
And they shall keep who can."

A great part of mankind, nowadays, has succumbed to this latter concept of justice; and the consequence of that belief is plain to be seen in the violence and ruin that have overtaken most nations in this century.

Now our traditional idea of Justice comes to us from two sources: the Judaic and Christian faith in a just God whom we fear and love, and whose commandments are expressed in unmistakable language; and the teachings of classical philosophy, in particular the principles expressed in Plato's *Republic* and incorporated into Roman jurisprudence by Cicero and his successors. The concept of Justice upon earth which both these traditions inculcate is, in substance, this: the idea of Justice is implanted in our minds by a Power that is more than human; and our mundane Justice is our attempt to copy a perfect Justice that abides in a realm beyond time and space; and the general rule by which we endeavor to determine just conduct and just reward may be expressed as "To each man, the things that are his own."

Plato perceived that there are two aspects of this Justice: justice in private character, and justice in society. Personal or private justice is attained by that balance and harmony in character which shines out from those persons we call "just men"—men who cannot be swayed from the path of rectitude by private interest, and who are masters of their own passions, and who deal impartially and honestly with everyone they meet. The other aspect of justice, *social* justice, is similarly marked by harmony and balance; it is the communal equivalent of that right proportion and government of reason, will, and appetite which the just man displays in his private character. Socrates says to Glaucon, "And is not the creation of justice the institution of a natural order and government of one faculty by another in the parts of the soul? And is not the creation of injustice the production of a state of things at variance with the natural order?" The happy man, Socrates maintains, is the just man; and the happy society is the just society. It is the society in which every man minds his own business, and receives always the rewards which are his due. The division of labor is a part of this social justice; for true justice requires "the carpenter and the shoemaker and the rest of the citizens to do each his own business, and not another's." Injustice in society comes when men try to undertake roles for which they are not fitted, and claim rewards to which they are not entitled, and deny other men what really belongs to them. Quite as an unjust man is a being whose reason, will, and appetite are at war with one another, so an unjust society is a state characterized by "meddlesomeness, and interference, and the rising up of a part of the soul against the whole, an assertion of unlawful authority, which is made by a rebellious subject against a true prince, of whom be is the natural vassal—what is all this confusion and delusion but injustice, and intemperance and cowardice and ignorance, and every form of vice?"

It is perfectly true, then, both in the eyes of the religious man and the eyes of the philosopher, that there is a real meaning to the term "social justice." The Christian concepts of charity and obedience are bound up with the Christian idea of a just society; while for the Platonic and Ciceronian philosopher, no government is righteous unless it conforms to the same standards of conduct as those which the just man respects. We all have real obligations toward our fellow-men, for it was ordained by Omniscience that men should live together in charity and brotherhood. A just society, guided by these lights, will endeavor to provide that every man be free to do the work for which he is best suited, and that he receive the rewards which that work deserves, and that no one meddle with him. Thus cooperation, not strife, will be the governing influence in the state; class will not turn against class, but all men will realize, instead, that a variety of occupations, duties, and rewards is necessary to civilization and the rule of law.

As classical philosophy merged with Christian faith to form modern civilization, scholars came to distinguish between two types or applications of justice—not divine and human justice, not private and social justice, precisely, but what we call "commutative" justice and "distributive" justice. "Commutative" justice, in the words of old Jeremy Taylor, three centuries ago, is "that justice which supposes exchange of things profitable for things profitable." It is that righteous relationship by which one man gives his goods or services to another man and receives an equivalent benefit, to the betterment of both. Now "distributive" justice, again in Jeremy Taylor's words, "is commanded in this rule, 'Render to all their dues.'" Distributive justice, in short, is that arrangement in society by which each man obtains what his nature and his labor entitle him to, without oppression or evasion. Commutative justice is righteous dealing between particular individuals; distributive justice is the general system of rewarding each man according to his deserts. Both concepts of justice have been badly misunderstood in our time, but distributive justice has fared the worse.

Edmund Burke, a hundred and sixty-five years ago, perceived that radical reformers suffered from a disastrous misconception of the idea of justice. The followers of Rousseau, asserting that society is simply a compact for mutual benefit among the men and women who make up a nation, declared that therefore no man has any greater rights than his fellows, and that property is the source of all evil. Burke turned all the power of his rhetoric against this delusion. Men do indeed have natural rights, he answered; but those rights are not what Rousseau's disciples think they are. The foremost of our *true* natural rights is the right to justice and order, which the radical fancies of the French revolutionaries would abolish:

> Men have a right to the fruits of their industry, and to the means of making their industry fruitful. They have a right to the acquisitions of their parents; to the nourishment and improvement of their offspring; to instruction in life, and to consolation in death. Whatever each man can separately do, without trespassing upon others, he has a right to do for himself; and he has a right to all which society, with all its combinations of skill and force, can do in his favour. In this partnership all men have equal rights; but not to equal things. He that has but five shillings in the partnership, has as good a right to it, as he that has five hundred pounds has to his larger proportion. But he has not a right to an equal dividend in the product of the joint stock; and as to the share of power, authority, and direction which each individual ought to have in the management of the state, that I deny to be amongst the direct original rights of man in civil society; for I have in my contemplation the civil social man, and no other. It is a thing to be settled by convention.

This is the Christian and classical idea of distributive justice. Men have a right to the product of their labors, and to the benefits of good government and of the progress of civilization. But they have no right to the property and the labor of others. The sincere Christian will do everything in his power to relieve the distresses of men and women who suffer privation or injury; but the virtue of charity is a world away from the abstract *right* of equality which the French radicals claimed. The merit of charity is that it is voluntary, a gift from the man who has to the man who has not; while the radicals' claim of a *right* to appropriate the goods of their more prosperous neighbors is a vice—the vice of covetousness. True justice secures every man in the possession of what is his own, and provides that he will receive the reward of his talents; but true justice also ensures that no man shall seize the property and the rights that belong to other classes and persons, on the pretext of an abstract equality. The just man knows that men differ in strength, in intelligence, in energy, in beauty, in dexterity, in discipline, in inheritance, in particular talents; and he sets his face, therefore, against any scheme of pretended "social justice" which would treat all men alike. There could be no greater injustice to society than to give the good, the industrious, and the frugal the same rewards as the vicious, the indolent, and the spendthrift. Besides, different types of character deserve different types of reward. The best reward of the scholar is contemplative leisure; the best reward of the soldier is public honor; the best reward of the quiet man is the secure routine of domestic existence; the best reward of the statesman is just power; the best reward of the skilled craftsman is the opportunity to make fine things; the best reward of the farmer is a decent rural competence; the best reward of the industrialist is the sight of what his own industry has built; the best reward of the good wife is the goodness of her children. To reduce all these varieties of talent and aspiration, with many more, to the dull nexus of cash payment, is the act of a dull and envious mind; and then to make that cash payment the same for every individual is an act calculated to make society one everlasting frustration for the best men and women.

How was it that this traditional concept of social justice, which took into account the diversity of human needs and wishes, came to be supplanted, in the minds of many people, by the delusion that social justice consists in treating every man as if he were an identical cog in a social machine, with precisely the same qualities and hopes as his neighbor? One can trace the fallacy that justice is identical with equality of condition far back into antiquity, for human folly is as old as human wisdom. But the modern form of this notion arose late in the eighteenth century, and Burke and John Adams and other conservative thinkers foresaw that it was destined to do immense mischief in our world. Condorcet, for example, eminent among the philosophers who ushered in the French Revolution, proclaimed that "Not only equality of right, but equality of fact, is the goal of the socialist art"; he declared that the whole aim of all social institutions should be to benefit physically, intellectually, and morally the poorest classes. Now the Christian concept of charity enjoins constant endeavor to improve the lot of the poor; but the Christian faith, which Burke and Adams held in their different ways, does not command the sacrifice of the welfare of one class to that of another class; instead, Christian teaching looks upon the rich and powerful as the elder brothers of the poor and weak, given their privileges that they may help to improve the character and the condition of all humanity. Instead of abolishing class and private rights in the name of an abstract equality, Christian thinkers hope to employ commutative and distributive justice for the realization of the peculiar talents and hopes of each individual, not the confounding of all personality in one collective monotony.

Karl Marx, casting off the whole moral legacy of Christian and classical thought, carried the notion of "social justice" as pure equality further yet. Adapting Ricardo's labor theory of value to his own purposes, Marx insisted that since all value comes from "labor," all value must return to labor; and therefore all men must receive the same rewards, and live the same life. Justice, according to this view, is uniformity of existence. "In order to create equality," Marx wrote, "we must first create inequality." By this he meant that because men are *not* equal in strength, energy, intelligence, or any other natural endowment, we must take away from the superior and give to the inferior; we must depress the better to help the worse; and thus we will deliberately treat the strong, the energetic, and the intelligent unfairly, that we may make their natural inferiors their equals in condition. Now this doctrine is the callous repudiation of the classical and Christian idea of justice. "To each his own"; such was the definition of justice in which Plato and Cicero and the fathers of the Church and the Schoolmen agreed. Each man should have the right to the fruit of his own labors, and the right to freedom from being meddled with; and each man should do that work for which his nature and his inheritance best qualified him. But Marx was resolved to turn the world inside out, and a necessary preparation for this was the inversion of the idea of Justice. Marx refused to recognize that there are various kinds and degrees of labor, each deserving its peculiar reward; and he ignored the fact that there is such a thing as the postponed reward of labor, in the form of bequest and inheritance. It is not simply the manual laborer who works: the statesman works, and so does the soldier, and so does the scholar, and so does the priest, and so does the banker, and so does the landed proprietor, and so does the inventor, and so does the manufacturer, and so does the clerk. The highest and most productive forms of labor, most beneficial to humanity both in spirit and in matter, commonly are those kinds of work least menial. Only in this sense is it true that all value comes from labor.

In the history of political and economic fanaticism, there are few fallacies more nearly transparent than the central principle of Marxism. But the publication of Marx's *Capital* coincided with the decay of established opinions in the modern world, and with all the confusion which the culmination of the Industrial Revolution and the expansion of European influence had brought in their train. Thus men who had repudiated both the old liberal educational disciplines and the bulk of Christian teaching embraced Marx's theories without reflection; for men long to believe in *something*, and the declaration that everyone is entitled by the laws of social justice to the possessions of his more prosperous neighbor was calculated to excite all the power of envy. The doctrinaire socialists and communists began to preach this new theory of justice—the dogma that everything belongs of right to everyone. That idea has been one of the chief causes of our modern upheaval and despair, throughout most of the world. In its milder aspect, it has led to the difficulties of my Scottish friend in collecting his rents; in its fiercer aspect, to the dehumanization of whole peoples and the wreck of ancient civilizations.

True distributive justice, which prescribes the rights and duties that connect the state, or community, and the citizen or private person, does not mean "distribution" in the sense of employing the power of the state to redistribute property among men. Pope Pius XI, in 1931, made it clear that this was not the Christian significance of the phrase. "Of its very nature the true aim of all social activity," the Pope wrote, "should be to help individual members of the social body, but never to destroy or absorb them. The aim of social legislation must therefore be the re-establishment of vocational groups." This encyclical, in general, urges the restoration of *order*, through the encouragement or resurrection of all those voluntary associations which once interposed a barrier between the Leviathan state and the puny individual. The state ought to be an arbiter, intent upon justice, and not the servant of a particular class or interest. The late William A. Orton, in his last book, *The Economic Role of the State*, discussing commutative and distributive justice in the light of Papal encyclicals, reminds us of how sorely the concept of distributive justice has been corrupted:

> Distributive justice does not primarily refer, as does the economic theory of distribution, to the sharing-out of a given supply of goods and services, because the state has no such supply. Yet that is the conception which tends to develop in the late stages of all highly centralized societies, including our own: the notion that the masses can and ought to receive from the state goods and services beyond what they could otherwise earn for themselves. The popularity of this notion has obvious causes, ranging from genuine altruism through political expediency to undisguised class interest. It is noteworthy that, as organized labor becomes a major political force, it is no longer content—as Gompers might have been—to rely on the economic power of the trade-unions but goes on, while resisting all limits on that, to make demands for state action in the interests of wage-earners as a class. And the point is not whether those demands are justifiable as *desiderata*; quite possibly they are, since, like the king in wonder-working

days of old, we would all like everybody to have everything. The point is that this whole notion of the providential state invokes and rests upon the coercive power, regarded solely from the standpoint of the beneficiaries. Furthermore, there are practical limits to this sort of procedure; and it is less painful to recognize them in advance than to run into them head on.

And Orton proceeds to examine the necessity of reasserting moral principles in the complex economic negotiations of our time. It is impossible to determine a "fair wage," or the proper relationship between employer and union, or the aims of social security, or the boundary between a just claim and extortion, or the proper regulation of prices, or the degree of freedom of competition, without reference to certain definitions that depend upon moral sanctions. Of those definitions, "justice" is the cardinal term. The Benthamite delusion that politics and economics could be managed on considerations purely material has exposed us to a desolate individualism in which every man and every class looks upon all other men and classes as dangerous competitors, when in reality no man and no class can continue long in safety and prosperity without the bond of sympathy and the reign of justice. It is necessary to any high civilization that there be a great variety of human types and a variety of classes and functions.

A true understanding of what "social justice" means would do more than anything else to guard against that bitter resentment of superiority or differentiation which menaces the foundations of culture. We hear a good deal of talk, some of it sensible, some of it silly, about the "anti-intellectualism" of our time. But it is undeniably true that there exists among us a vague but ominous detestation of the life of the mind—apparently on the assumption that what one man has, all men must have; and if they are denied it, then they will deny it to the privileged man. The late C.E.M. Joad, a writer scarcely given to reactionary or anti-democratic opinions, noted with alarm this resentment of the masses against anything that they cannot share; and they now have it in their power, he suggested, to topple anything of which they disapprove. It is not even necessary for the masses to employ direct political action; the contagion of manners works for them: formerly a class of thinkers and artists could flourish in the midst of general ignorance, but now the mass-mind, juke-box culture, penetrates to every corner of the Western world, and the man of superior natural talents is ashamed of being different.

One could elaborate upon Joad's suggestion almost interminably. The gradual reduction of public libraries, intended for the elevation of the popular mind, to mere instruments for idle amusement at public expense; the cacophony of noise which fills almost all public places, converting even the unwilling into a part of the captive audience, so that only by spending a good deal of money and travelling some distance can one eat and drink without being oppressed by blatant vulgarity; the conversion of nominal institutions of learning to the popular ends of sociability and utilitarian training—all these things, and many others, are so many indications of the advance of the masses into the realm of culture. The nineteenth-century optimists believed that the masses would indeed make culture their own, by assimilating themselves to it; it scarcely occurred to the enthusiasts for popular schooling that the masses might assimilate culture to themselves. The magazine-rack of any drugstore in America would suffice to drive Robert Lowe or Horace Mann to distraction. Now we cannot undo the consequences of mass-schooling, even if we would; but what we can contend against is the spirit of vulgar intolerance which proclaims that if the masses cannot share in a taste, that taste shall not be suffered to exist. And this is closely bound up with the idea of social justice. If justice means uniformity, then the higher life of the mind which is confined to a few has no right to survival; but if justice means that each man has a right to his own, we ought to try to convince modern society that there is no injustice or deprivation in the fact that one man is skilled with his hands, and another with his head, or that one man enjoys baseball and another chamber music. We must go beyond the differences of taste, indeed, and remind modern society that differences of function are as necessary and beneficial as differences of opinion. That some men are richer than others, and that some have more leisure than others, and that some travel more than others, and that some inherit more than others, and that some are educated more than others, is no more unjust, in the great scheme of things, than that some undeniably are handsomer or stronger or quicker or healthier than others. This complex variety is the breath of life to society, not the triumph of injustice. Poverty, even absolute poverty, is not an evil; it is not evil to be a beggar; it is not evil to be ignorant; it is not evil to be stupid. All these things are either indifferent, or else are occasions for positive virtue, if accepted with a contrite heart. What really matters is that we should accept the station to which "a divine tactic" has appointed us with humility and a sense of consecration. Without inequality, there is no opportunity for charity, or for gratitude; without differences of mind and talent, the world would be one changeless expanse of uniformity: and precisely that is the most conspicuous feature of Hell.

I am inclined to believe, then, that the need of our time is not for greater progress toward equality of condition and distribution of wealth, but rather for the dear understanding of what commutative and distributive justice truly mean: "to each his own." It is very easy to run with the pack and howl for the attainment of absolute equality. But that equality would be the death of human liveliness, and probably the death of our economy. I know, of course, that we have all about us examples of wealth misspent and opportunities abused. In our fallen state, we cannot hope that all the members of any class will behave with perfect rectitude. But it would be no wiser to abolish classes, for that reason, than to abolish humanity. We do indeed have the duty of exhorting those who have been placed by a divine tactic in positions of responsibility to do their part with charity and humility; and, before that, we have the more pressing duty of so exhorting ourselves. There are signs, in most of the countries of the Western world, that what remains of the old leading classes are learning to conduct themselves with courage and fortitude. If they are effaced utterly, we shall not be emancipated totally from leadership, but shall find ourselves, instead, at the mercy of the commissar. The delusion that justice consists in absolute equality ends in an absolute equality beneath the weight of a man or a party to whom justice is no more than a word.

At the back of the mind of the man who declined to pay his rent, I think, was the notion that under a just domination, all things would be supplied to him out of a common fund, without the necessity of any endeavor on his part. It is easy enough to describe the genesis of such concepts; it is much more difficult to remedy them. The real victim of injustice, in this particular case, was my friend the landed proprietor—though he never thought of complaining. No one subsidizes him; his garden lies choked with weeds; he has sold his Raeburns and Constables and his ancestors' furniture to keep up his farms and pay for his children's education; he continues to serve in local office at his own expense; he labors far longer hours than his own tenants; he can indulge, nowadays, very few of his tastes for books and music, though the cottagers can gratify theirs, in comparable matters, beyond anything they dreamed of in former days. My friend endures these things—and the prospect that when he is gone, everything which his family loved will pass away with him—because of the ascendancy of the idea that justice consists in levelling, that inherited wealth and superior station are reprehensible, and that society and culture can subsist and flourish without being rooted in the past. He himself, to some extent, is influenced by this body of opinion. Thus the unbought grace of life may be extinguished by the power of positive law within a single generation.

Probably the traditional leading classes of Europe were at their worst in the Russia of the czars. But what humane and rational man can maintain that the leading classes of Soviet Russia constitute an improvement upon their predecessors? And who dares maintain that all the graces and beauties of life have been nurtured there by the doctrinaire principle of equalitarian "justice"? Man was created not for equality, but for the struggle upward from brute nature toward the world that is not terrestrial. The principle of justice, in consequence, is not enslavement to a uniform condition, but liberation from arbitrary restraints upon his right to be himself.

There is no injustice in inequality, as such; the only unjust inequality is that in which a man is denied the things for which his nature is suited in favor of a man whose claims to those things is inferior. And precisely this latter sort of inequality is what the radicals would establish, depriving a great many men of the occupations and rewards to which their nature entitles them, for the sake of a ridiculous division of all things among all men. Socialism would deprive those persons who have a legitimate expectation of inheritance of the rights of heirs, one of the most ancient rights in all systems of justice. More, socialism would deprive those persons of superior talents of the rewards which their energies and endowments deserve. On this latter topic, one cannot do better than to read the books of W. H. Mallock, particularly *A Critical Examination of Socialism* (1908) and *The Limits of Pure Democracy* (1919).

Ability is the factor which enables men to lift themselves from savagery to civilization, and which helps to distinguish the endeavors of men from the routine existence of insects. Ability is of various sorts: there are philosophical ability, mechanical ability, commercial ability, directive ability, and persuasive ability. But all these are various aspects of the special talent, produced by intelligence, which is independent of routine or of brute strength. In any age, some men possess unusual abilities, which they may employ, if they choose— or if they are persuaded—for the benefit of everyone. But these men commonly are few in number; and though it is impossible to create such Ability by state action, it is altogether too possible that state action may succeed in extirpating the Ability of a whole generation—or, indeed, of a whole people. The thing has been done before.

There is only one way to find and encourage Ability, and that is to reward it. It does no good to punish men of abilities for not doing their very best; for then they either conceal their peculiar talents, or sink into apathy. This, too, is a very old story, and a perfectly true one. And I think that invariably a principal error of the masters of the total state is their failure to provide for the reward of Ability. When that reward no longer is forthcoming, a society stagnates.

The rewards of Ability are several. There is the reward of a good conscience, brought about by duty done. There is the reward of public praise, and that of power, and that of security, and that of advantage to one's family and one's posterity; and there is the reward of material gain. This last may sound mean, but we are hypocritical if we refuse to admit that it always has been the reward most likely to attract the great mass of men—even men of talent. Edmund Burke observes that ordinary service must be secured by the rewards to ordinary integrity. If we refuse to pay for service, then we are going to be afflicted with the service of men deficient in integrity, which is worse than no service at all.

Yet the total state, and in particular the sprawling socialist state of modern times, commonly refuses to pay for economic services in proportion to the abilities required to furnish those services; therefore the modern total state soon finds itself drained of men of integrity; and the state is served, instead, by the contact-man, the charlatan, the incompetent, the brutal, and the ruthless—by anyone but the man of ordinary integrity. In any state except the most thoroughly immoral, there always remain a few persons who will serve simply out of conscience, and a few more who will serve for praise or power. But these are not enough to sustain the intricate concerns of society, if those incentives which attract common integrity are lacking. Having failed to reward Ability, the state, fatigued, descends toward the routine of insect-life. In the long run, man (not being made physically or morally or psychologically for insect-life) fails to adjust satisfactorily to this attempt at supporting the state by mere routine, and then society disintegrates.

Why do the masters of the total state, and the men who would like to convert their free society into a total state, fail to recognize the necessity for rewarding Ability? It is in part the consequence, I think, of their notion that men are interchangeable units in a social machine, and that if one unit fails to function, another unit may be thrust into the vacated place. They think in terms of the "mobile labor-force" when they ought to be thinking in terms of particular persons with particular talents. Society is not a machine; it is, rather, a delicate growth or essence; and men of ability are not cogs in a machine, but the blood or life-spirit of society.

And in part their error is consequent from their false conception of Justice. Under the influence of Marx, the doctrinaire radical has maintained that the source of all wealth and power is Labor—the physical labor of the unskilled workman, if they are pressed to a closer definition; and therefore Justice dictates that all wealth and power should return to Labor. Yet this concept is ludicrously wrong. For it is not Labor which lifts man above ant-level; it is not Labor which is responsible for the world's work; it is, not Labor which elevates a society from savagery to civilization. The real factor which accomplishes these things is Ability.

It is Ability—the ability of the statesman, the scholar, the economist, the inventor, the scientist, the industrialist—which has brought to civilized peoples justice, tranquillity, and prosperity. The savage has Labor, but his way of life prevents the development of Ability, without which Labor is mere clumsy and inefficient brute force. Men prosper in proportion as they participate in the rewards of Ability.

The advances made by men of remarkable talent are shared, in some considerable degree, by everyone in society, even by those who contribute only manual labor. As the workingman himself acquires Ability by increasing his skills and technical knowledge, he too receives the rewards of Ability. Thus the incomes of workingmen, in the past century, have increased proportionately far faster than those of any other class; and this is because the workingman, for the most part, has ceased to be a mere manual laborer, and has become a skilled participant in Ability.

An omnipotent state always can command Labor, for Labor can be exacted through force. The exercise of Ability, however, can be secured only through a system of adequate rewards. The experience of this century, particularly in Russia, has demonstrated how rapidly socialistic governments turn to force to compel labor. In England, the vaticinations of certain collectivistic writers suggest that, given the opportunity, they would be anything but reluctant to apply compulsion to labor there. When the ordinary rewards for integrity are lacking, even the commonest forms of labor can be obtained only through compulsion. But can Ability, under such conditions, be obtained at all? There is good reason to doubt that the Soviets are obtaining the Ability necessary to give their experiment vigor, even the mere vigor of material production. And any careful observer of Britain today must be alarmed for the future. The serious journals in England have awakened to the danger of suppressing or ignoring Ability, but the process already is far advanced. Taxation that even Fabian economists call "savage," death-duties that wipe out agricultural estates and family businesses, regulations and subsidies that are driving the population out of private homes and into state-built housing, a general fear that nothing a man does will endure and nothing that he saves will be worth anything to him—these influences, though moderated under the present Conservative government, continue to discourage the exertion of private abilities.

Now the rewards of Ability, as I suggested earlier, are various. The society which desires its own survival will do everything in its power to increase these rewards, not to diminish them; for Ability, given its head, pulls the whole of society upward, intellectually and materially. But Ability discouraged will decrease its efforts proportionately, to the detriment of every class and occupation. We need to respect that reward of Ability which comes from a sense of duty done, and we need to recognize that reward which consists of public honor, and we need to appreciate fairly that reward which consists of just power. But beyond these rewards, which are desired by a comparative few, we need to insure that the ordinary rewards of ordinary integrity, material rewards for material accomplishments, are not neglected; it is for such rewards, after all, that most of the material business of life is carried on. This does not mean simply a sedulous attention to profits and salaries and wages, though of course direct monetary income matters. There exist concrete rewards, however, which are not expressed simply in terms of money. One of these rewards is the ownership of private property, in its many forms; another is membership in a reputable undertaking, as distinguished from impersonal employment by the all-embracing state; another is the sense of security and permanence of possession; another is the assurance that thrift and diligence will bring some degree of decent independence, as distinguished from the uneasy condition of pensioners of the state. All these things are among the material rewards of genuine Ability, and they have been recognized as the due of able men and women for many centuries. It has remained for the arrogance of the doctrinaire socialist and the state planner, in our time, to deal contemptuously with the traditional incentives to ordinary integrity. But they will be paid back in their own coin, once Ability has been reduced to mere Labor—labor with the mind as well as the hands, dull and routine. The total state can carry on, after a fashion, so long as a reservoir of Ability is supplied by the surviving private enterprises; but in proportion as state industry increases, private industry shrinks, and with it those abilities which make possible all the material achievements of our modern life, and most of our intellectual achievements. In the total state, everything may be dedicated to Labor; but with the crushing of Ability, that dedication will result in the rapid impoverishment of Labor, too, and probably in consequences yet more grave.

To whom, precisely, would this New Order be just? In the name of Justice, as in that of Liberty, every conceivable crime has been committed. The doctrinaire radical would risk the whole fabric of society for the sake of an abstract Justice which never existed and never can exist, and which would be hateful to the radical if ever it did arrive.

And what is the conservative program where the problem of social justice is concerned? Why, to endeavor to insure that there shall be some rational relationship between endeavor and reward. Material values, not to mention moral values, are somewhat confused in a society which tolerates a barbers' association fixing the price of haircuts at two dollars, but lets its liberal-arts colleges starve to death and its judges receive the emoluments of janitors. The first step toward recovery of values is to make it clear we are not Marxists, and have no intention of making one hideous equalitarian tableland of modern life. To each man, a just society preserves the things that are his own.

The Problem of Wants

WALTER SCOTT, Writer to the Signet, the father of the novelist, was
a Scot of the old sort, frugal in the extreme, and contemptuous of
the vanities of this world. His son relates that when breakfast was
brought in, the elder Scott would taste the porridge and say to his
children, "Aye, bairns, 'tis good porridge—too good";—and then he
would pour water into it, that the porridge might conform more
nearly to Scottish virtue. Well, probably there is not a father left in
all America of precisely that degree of *severitas;* and though I am
not fond of cold water in porridge, I am rather sorry that we have
lost this extreme. For we certainly have not parted with the other
extreme, voluptuousness.

Mr. Norman Cousins informs us that "want is obsolete." I cannot
agree with him; but whatever we may say of "want" in the sense of
oppressive poverty, our wants—our desires of every sort—are
greatly multiplied in this age; and if there appears the least prospect
that we shall be denied the satisfaction of any of these cravings, an
immense popular outcry is raised in protest. Every year, we become
still more the slaves of creature-comforts and effortless amusements. Our whole economy—indeed, our very foreign policy—is
calculated to endorse and increase this appetite for material goods,
and we are urged to consume everything, at the greatest possible
rate, lest the structure of our society come tumbling down about
our ears. Writers like Mr. David Riesman would have us add Consumption to the cardinal virtues. The advertising-man whips us on;
permanence and thrift are ridiculed as obstacles to progress; and no
class is spared, certainly not the rich, so that Mr. Marshall McLuhan
suggests (in *The Mechanical Bride*) that "it may very well be that the
effect of mass production and consumption is really to bring about

a practical rather than a theoretic communism. When men and women have been transformed into replaceable parts by competitive success drives, and have become accustomed to the consumption of uniform products, it is hard to see where any individualism remains."

Tocqueville believed that a gross materialism was the greatest menace to the American democracy; and a century ago, Orestes Brownson denounced the American knack for creating new wants as an impious and ruinous passion, encouraging novel appetites that never can be truly satisfied. Our real wants, he said, are those of the spirit; but those we neglect, spending our days in a meaningless pursuit of mundane pleasure which, in the end, must betray us. And he described this avid encouragement of appetites as the essence of liberalism.

This American lust for material aggrandizement now is raised to the dignity of a social philosophy by certain publicists. We are told that the duty of the United States in this century is to lend a helping hand to a "revolution of rising expectations" throughout the world, turning the "underdeveloped" states inside out, inducing everyone to adopt the American material pattern of life, and exhorting the human race to spend its days in getting and spending. This policy, we are informed, will woo the nations away from Communism. Will it indeed? The whole end of human existence, according to Marx and Engels, is to increase the material welfare of the masses. We may promise the luxuries of Sybaris to Guatemala and Persia; but the Soviets always can beat us at that game, for promises are cheap. Now the thinking conservative, I believe, ought to contend with all his strength against this particular degradation of the American mind and heart. The conservative knows that material production and consumption are not the purpose of human existence, and that variety is better than uniformity, and that if certain ages have needed acceleration of their rate of change, nevertheless what our age requires is some check upon the speed of a material revolution which has escaped from intelligent control. The American conservative does not share the liberal's conviction that the modern pattern of Western life is the be-all and end-all of human felicity; unlike the liberal, he does not insist (in Santayana's ironic phrase) "the nun shall not remain a nun, and China shall not keep its wall."

I am quite aware that this attitude is unpopular. The great machine of modern publicity and advertising is against it; many managers of industry are against it; most labor-union officials swear by the canons of industrial expansion; even convocations of the clergy pass resolutions vaguely recommending that we put an end to "suffering and discontent" abroad by "improving the standard of living." In the middle of the twentieth century, if one is to judge by the exhortations of our political and economic leaders, covetousness has been stricken from the catalogue of mortal sins, and the art of conjuring avaricious visions has attained respectability as an electioneering device employed by every party. One scarcely can be surprised at this aspect of liberal emancipation; but certain curiously leaden and gross characteristics of the dream which the American public is urged to embrace just now, certain indications of a treacherous myopia, must disturb even the heirs of Bentham. "If men were ever to content themselves with material objects," Tocqueville remarks, "it is probable that they would lose by degrees the arts of producing them; and they would enjoy them in the end, like the brutes, without discernment and without improvement."

In the center of Michigan lies my county of Mecosta, desolate swales covered, two generations gone, with hardwoods and pines. The trees are cut now, and potatoes, cucumbers, and beans grow with difficulty among the stumps. Early one summer evening I rode along a track which ran straight as a yardstick over the sand ridges, and presently passed a farm; such a farm as one seldom sees in England or France, despite two thousand years of European tillage. This farm consisted of a few acres of rock-strewn land, encumbered with stumps still deeply rooted; a crazy shed for a cow; a sagging outhouse; and a tarpaper shanty that, what with the cracks in its walls and the sun then setting behind it, seemed translucent. Beside the house was a potato patch; a woman was hunched in the middle of it, hoeing with desperation as the daylight faded, her little boy at work beside her. Moving on, I reflected upon the pragmatic concept of prosperity and happiness which we modern Americans endorse with scarcely one misgiving.

It is doubtful whether we are a nation materially rich. The movies and the radio and television tell us we are, and so does the press. But after the movies we go home to the tiny "ranch-type" cottages of stucco that stretch (already decaying) mile on mile about Los Angeles, or to the dog-kennel shanties which house the poor of Memphis, or the interminable dreariness which rings round the core of Detroit; and we read our newspapers in houses that line the filthy old lanes of North Boston, or the mean streets off Cleveland's Euclid Avenue, or the howling South Side of Chicago. Some of us live in better places, of course; but commonly we pay a price for decency which means great sacrifice in certain other values of civilized life. A contemplative man may be inclined to think that most Americans still are as fond of magniloquent exaggeration of their resources as they were in the days of Mr. Jefferson Brick. If America is wealthy, very often her wealth is of a sort peculiar to the twentieth century and alien to the traditional standards of prosperity. We all know the new Pontiac beside the rotting cabin in the swamp, the comic-books and movie magazines strewn in the backyards of the tenements, the soda-fountain and cocktail-lounge prodigality of our time; and the television set now dominates every slum flat.

So, after all our bragging, it is not strange that we Americans desire a better life; it is not strange that successful politicians prophesy the coming of a vague plenty. Our present life, however spendthrift, is not truly prosperous—leaving happiness quite out of the question. Not only our poor are anxious for something better: our well-to-do seem to feel that an indefinable quality is lacking, that even the neat tedium of American middle-class life is growing not only expensive but somehow barren. "We are a fussical and fudgical people," John Randolph of Roanoke said once. I do not presume to weigh here the causes of our present discontent with ourselves; I am concerned just now with the remedies offered. Victorian England, oppressed by similar qualms, nevertheless rejected the diverse remedies or palliatives of Newman, Disraeli, and Ruskin. The sour dose which England swallows today may be a judgment. We Americans may sometime come off still worse, for our age boasts very few inspired theologians and statesmen and critics of society that it can reject. Only one nostrum is popular with politicians and planners in this troubled hour: more of the hair of the dog that bit us. We are invited to dispel the dreams of avarice by the specific of avarice realized.

The nominal architect of the present version of this cornucopia-theory of happiness was President Truman, with his promises of the doubting or trebling of national income, his projects to introduce the American Standard of Living to the remotest backwashes of the world (an undertaking so vague as to its motives that we have found no better name for it than Point Four), and his preference for economic enthusiasms over financial stability. But Mr. Truman was rather nostalgically reminiscent of an earlier president. He reminded one of President Coolidge: practical, blunt, average-American, utterly confident that in a nation's economy reposes its greatness and that the American economy is destined to grow and shine and swell, without limit. Swell it did, in Mr. Coolidge's administration; and presently, like most other swelling objects, it burst. It might be amusing to compare certain of Mr. Truman's prognostications and self-congratulations with parallel passages from Mr. Coolidge's addresses. Party labels make very little difference where philosophy, or the void that ought to be filled by philosophy, is uniform. Mr. Coolidge's and Mr. Truman's ideal America really is the same: an America which might be very rich in goods, but (this totally unsuspected by either gentleman) very poor in spirit. I am not writing as a partisan here. The administration of General Eisenhower has carried on this scheme of things with only the mildest of hesitations, and it was perfectly easy for the engineers of Mr. Truman's design to become the executors of Mr. Eisenhower's undertakings—Mr. Chester Bowles, for instance. We are dealing here with a confusion which transcends the rather shallow assumptions of American party platforms. And within the few years since Mr. Truman commenced his grand design, an entrenched interest of formidable proportions has developed, its very existence dependent upon the apotheosis of American materialism.

A tinge of the Wilsonian era, too, glimmers through the present national administration, as the aspirations of "Point Four" are revealed in their odd, generous, untroubled simplicity: we hear the echo of Colonel House's project for employing the restless ambitions of the great powers in a common exploitation of Africa, we glimpse the reflection of the Fourteen Points with their assumption that American principles are applicable, unmodified, universally. One feels both sympathy and fright at the spectacle of this energetic naiveté, a great, brawny, well-intentioned Innocence in a world of men whose problems are infinitely more difficult of solution than economists and engineers, *per se*, dare to admit to themselves.

A most disquieting aspect of the current readiness to treat grave problems as if they could be solved by some simple slogan or formula is the ignoring of the principle of diversity and the exalting of the principle of uniformity. This tendency was what most seriously alarmed John Stuart Mill for the future of liberal institutions; but the great majority of twentieth-century liberals embrace the tenets of standardization unhesitatingly. "We shall build up the productive capacity of under-developed nations." Some standard of beneficent industrialization is implied, but never defined; the desire of such states to be tinkered with is not investigated. The president and his advisors seem to maintain that spiritual and political and economic difficulties are soluble by reduction to a common denominator; and that denominator is The American Way. A complacency at once touching and exasperating, this sentiment is perfectly natural, for we Americans always have labored, with varying success, to reduce mysteries to popular terms—at once a virtue and a vice of our social constitution. In the present instance we contend, with an ingenuous provinciality, that all the world wants to be American. And by "American" we mean industrialized, motorized, Hollywoodized, capitalized, federalized, corporatized, synchronized, and modernized. Displaying an impatient perplexity which is wholly sincere, we decry as reactionary or conspiratorial or Russian-influenced anyone in foreign parts who dissents from The American Way. We manifest a yawning ignorance of the venerable principle that cultural form and substance cannot be transported intact from one people to another. We claim that everyone except feudal barons or Reds longs for tractors, Bob Hope, self-service laundries, direct primaries, clover-leaf intersections, high-school extra-curricular activities, two evening newspapers, Coca-Cola, and a stylish burial at Memory Grove Cemetery. The president of the United States, along with most of us, assumes that all people want happiness. He assumes that happiness is a constant quality, one and indivisible through the world. And he equates happiness with physical comfort. Austerity is Tartarus, luxury Elysium. By deduction, a man content with simplicity is ignorant and must be educated out of his apathy; a hydro-electric plant, a mechanical combine, or a carton of breakfast-food may turn the trick for him. And every successful commissar in Russia agrees with this view of life.

We have no right to be hard upon the president of the United States, whether he is Mr. Truman or Mr. Eisenhower. When he talks of soaring national income, he is speaking in a vein truly congenial to most elements in American society. If he does not see beyond the dollar-sign, neither does Mr. Walter Reuther, who hopes to drain the Serbonian bog of international suspicion by appropriating a trillion dollars for gifts unto the lesser breeds without the law. Neither does Mr. Leon Keyserling, when he assures us that "production" is the answer to Communism. Neither does Mr. Charles E. Wilson, Secretary of Defense, when he thinks that whatever is good for General Motors is good for America. Neither do the economists of the Committee for Economic Development, when they declare that the aspirations of the dawning era will be satisfied with "the doubling of real wages before 1980." This myopia is not confined to any party or order. It is a condition of an origin thus described to Dr. Faustus: "I, sir? I am Covetousness, begot by an old churl in a leathern bag." Tocqueville says that avarice is a plague to which American and all democracies are perilously susceptible; but he also observes that, forewarned, American democracy may alleviate the consequences of this passion.

Now avarice does not consist in aspiring to be decently housed and fed and clad, according to one's real needs and nature. Avarice, rather, is desiring more wealth than one's soul can support properly. Avarice sometimes produces present poverty: the miser, proverbially, is ragged and lean. And I am afraid that when our politicians and planners and sociologists talk of output and distribution and real wages, they are not so much intent upon relieving genuine poverty as upon satisfying the dreams of avarice. They are not thinking so much of a just and contented America as of a shimmering and strident America. They are not really interested in patching the tar-paper shanty in Mecosta County; they would prefer to rip down the shack, pack its inhabitants off to Detroit or Flint, put them into state-subsidized housing, find them a television set to keep them out of mischief and vagrant fancies, and set them to work upon indus-trial production. Who will miss the second-growth spruces and the little lake in the barrens, once he gets his new Ford? This, in essence, is the future which "capitalists" and "socialists" and "communists" all are arranging for us. It may be an efficient program. It is not a human program. It does not try to plumb intangible longings; it endeavors to satisfy the dreams of avarice. But avarice is insatiable. The dehumanized being with the new automobile may achieve sati-ety, but the ruling passion instilled in him will not let him rest.

We ought not to imply the existence of any intricate conspiracy to debase our poor muddled society into a collective economic undertaking with no loftier aspirations than those of an industrial corporation. However disordered at present, the social life is still an immortal compact linking the higher nature with the lower, and few of our planners have any deliberate intention of subverting the foundation of communal existence. In America, at least, almost all the partisans of calculated aggrandizement are quite unconscious of the tendency in such alterations; they seem to fancy that social and political establishments will continue precisely as they are now con-stituted, although much more prosperous. Our age, which has come near to losing the historical sense altogether, forgets that insti-tutions generally alter to suit the spiritual temper of a people. A nation that has given up Fortitude for Avarice must endure a pro-found revision of its liberties and character. If the public is told incessantly that the only important consideration is the American Standard of Living, in time the public will become oblivious to such trifles as justice, mercy, honor, and charity. An American public thus instructed will resemble closely that Russian public it despises.

The best way to understand the mind of modern Russia, I think, is to see Russian films. Not long ago the Soviet film-makers pro-duced a "documentary" about the Russian gypsies. It was admirably done, for the most part: it showed the wandering life of the steppes, the stories round the campfire, the dances, the music, the horsemanship, the strong individuality of that curious people. And then, toward the end, it dealt with the collectivization of the gypsies. A representative group of them was herded to a collective farm, where they were to spend the rest of their natural lives, and the peasants took them into raw little state-built houses, and proudly showed them the running water from real taps. The most embittered opponent of Communism could not have exposed more vindictively the *petit-bourgeois* affections of the Soviet state; but this picture was distributed, with complacent pride, by the Soviet propaganda-agency. Well, if the Russians often are their own worst apologists, we Americans, for our part, often talk as if we were so many Communist caricatures of capitalists.

One may take, for instance, an article published four years ago in *Harper's,* by Mr. Robert L. Heilbroner. America's chief problem, one gathers from this essay, is the abolition of the comparative want surviving among our ten million poorer families:

> *If* we keep on growing at our present pace—2 per cent per year— we *can* double our real earnings in our lifetimes, and before the next decade is out the average family *can* enjoy an income of $5,000. The opportunities for growth are there; the man who operates a bulldozer worked with pick and shovel yesterday, and the man behind the hoe today *can* some day sit behind a tractor. The troubling challenge is whether we will *in fact* push against our boundaries.

Mr. Heilbroner wishes us well, of course, in this proposal that we substitute for the travail of the laborer the neuroses of the machine-tender. Yet something ominous glowers behind this exhortation. One glimpses, perhaps, a countryside of the future, out of H.G. Wells or Aldous Huxley, nearly empty of inhabitants—those few who remain, submissively seated behind tractors—while in gigantic cities are concentrated multitudes of people earning their guaranteed five thousand dollars per family, or ten thousand dollars, or twenty thousand dollars, depending upon the decade. But I am not sure what these people do with their money—supposing they are permitted to dispose of their earnings according to their whims. These are the communities Mr. E.B. White suggests in "The Day It Happened" Such, at least, is the planners' society one envisions if the optimists are vindicated and matters have not gone to smash. But whenever a society fixes all attention upon earning so many thousand dollars per head of population, old devil Consequences ordinarily intervenes in short order.

Such quavers are summarily dismissed by the editors of this number of *Harper's* (June, 1950), however, who in the same issue— apropos of Mr. Heilbroner's remarks and of another article, "The Road that Food Built," by Mr. Myron Stearns—inform us:

> Such fears are meaningless in the light of the data presented by Mr. Heilbroner and Mr. Stearns. For both of these articles serve to remind us of the fundamental truth which underlies the democratic faith: that real wealth, like virtue and talent, is not a fixed total, too limited to permit everyone to have an adequate share. Neither education, nor health, nor the opportunity to use productive equipment is too good for anyone engaged in any department of productive activity. For the more of all three they have, the more real wealth they will produce.

Perhaps; although I was not previously aware that the "fundamental truth" of democracy was industrial abundance. Yet before we Americans commence distributing "productive equipment" to everyone who has, or who ought to have, a hankering for it, we might do well to inquire, on grounds purely utilitarian, just what we propose to produce. "Wealth" has disconcerting properties, as Midas found out. The following inquiries, severely practical questions, may indicate some of the difficulties to be encountered when a nation goes whole hog after a "higher standard of living."

(1) *What will the dollars buy?* An income of $5,000 in 1960 has no conspicuous advantage over an income of $500 in 1890 if it will purchase no more in goods and services. Our increase in average income during the past decade has been paralleled by a proportionate increase in prices; and during an age of manipulated and almost infinitely inflatable currencies—with a swelling population, into the bargain—I do not know what else we are to expect. The champions of an "expanding" economy inform us that they are talking about "real income," not mere nominal wages. Yet "real wages" is an elusive concept. The workingman of 1954 has a higher "real wage" than his counterpart of 1900 earned, in the sense that he is the possessor

of a gasoline engine of many horsepower; his predecessor did not have even one horse. Nevertheless, today's man may be poorer than his predecessor in terms of meat on the table, floor space in his house, durability of clothing, tranquility of environment. And the "real wages" of 1960 or 1980—supposing the aggrandizement of big government, big business, and big labor to continue at an increasing rate, as most planners conjecture—may in large part be drained off through taxation of "necessary luxuries." Without presuming to venture further into economic speculation, we ought to remind ourselves that the experience of the first half of this century indicates that augmented dollar-income tends to be offset by price increase. Certain classes and occupations have made absolute gains; but they have attained them, too often, in consequence of the diminution of the real income of certain other classes and occupations.

(2) *What aspect will society present during this contemplated age of expansion?* Epochs in which men have been devoted to "production" and "more for all" often have been intellectually and morally despicable. Usually they have conformed to either of these two social patterns: the anarchy of robber barons, or the tyranny of Five Year Plans. We have reason to expect that the state will encourage, supervise, and control many functions of such deliberate expansion; and we see already over the water—to pass by our own wartime and post-war experiences—the hectic flush and tawdry confusion of nations entering upon such arrangements. Professor W. L. Burn of the University of Durham ("The Last of the Lynskey Report," *Nineteenth Century*, March, 1949) has given us a peep into this new society:

> It is a scene in which such things as football pools, amusement machinery, and cosmetics enjoy the place of honour. . . . Wine and spirits, turkeys, sausages, suits of clothes descend upon the fortunate recipients; there are dinners at Grosvenor House, at the Garter Club, at the Garrick Hotel; hospitality is generously offered and gratefully accepted. Yet, in spite of these apparent advantages, it is not a very happy or agreeable society. Perhaps the reason is that too many people want too many things too urgently. One wants sherry casks, one wants paper; others want to float companies, to build canteens or to enlarge hotels. . . . We may imagine

the stage festooned with forms, applications for licenses, refusals of licenses, cheques that failed to command confidence and agreements that failed to produce the desired result. Music is supplied by the ringing of the telephone, the prelude to ambiguous and improbable conversations; and through this half-lit jungle, from public dinner to government department, from government department to sherry party, glides the contact-man, at once the product and the safety-valve of this grotesque civilization.

A time of rising prices, booming wages, and incalculable material alteration does not guarantee prosperity for everyone. It usually has meant privation and dismay for people with fixed or tardily-altering incomes—the thrifty, the old, pensioners, teachers, the clergy, endowed institutions, the independent shopkeeper, the small farmer, and other persons and establishments which constitute an element of stability and tradition in our civilization—precisely the classes which a just society is intended to shelter. Such a time, on the other hand, is well enough for the rough customer, the smooth operator, the rolling stone, the contact man, the gentleman who puts No. 1 first. This world-turned-upside-down excitement, this swirling flux, may seem to some people the proof of vitality in a society; however that may be, it is also the negation of intelligence in a society. In the long run, everyone comes to detest an existence so nervous and precarious, and humanity endeavors to counteract vertigo by the application of arbitrary force. Somewhere there must exist a check upon will and appetite, Burke says, and the less check there is within, the more there must be without.

(3) *What sort of people will we have become, supposing this economic expansion is accomplished?* Will we, like George Bowling in Orwell's *Coming up for Air*, revisit the scenes of our youth only to find the country which "progress" has touched an abomination of shoddy new bungalows, juke joints, concrete, billboards, and jaded faces? Too many of us already have experienced that abysmally dreary survey. Some generations of indiscriminate getting and spending are certain to develop a remarkable type of man. The automobile will be his deity, and to it he will sacrifice sometimes nearly half his annual income, his domestic comfort, his family-life, and his church. The television-set will be his preacher, and inanity

will compete with inanity for his attention, applying Gresham's Law to amusement. The state will direct his labor, and circumscribe it, and he will not protest, for he will have forgotten the nature of freedom. He will live in a vast ant-hill of a city, and he will be precisely like his neighbors, and all of them will be decadent; for decadence, I repeat, is the loss of an object in life. In the interest of efficiency, nonconformists and stragglers and dwellers in the waste will have been gathered into the city or eliminated, preferably through natural processes. And these descendants of ours never will realize that they are in the Inferno, damned for Avarice.

> The state of society now leads to such accumulations of humanity, that we cannot wonder if it ferment and reek like a compost dunghill. Nature intended that population should be diffused over the soil in proportion to its extent. We have accumulated in huge cities and smothering manufactories the numbers which should be spread over the face of a country; and what wonder that they should be corrupted?

Our planners have not yet apprehended the menace of consolidation so penetratingly expressed here—though it was 1828 when Sir Walter Scott wrote the foregoing observation in his diary.

Quite possibly I exaggerate the terror of the prospect. I have stated a few of the difficulties attendant upon the satisfaction of a national spirit of covetousness; perhaps these difficulties may be surmounted. Yet obstacles cannot be conquered until they are recognized, and it appears that our economic optimists are almost wholly unaware that any objections exist to the *ends* they propose; they are obsessed with means. Make man rich, and of course he will be good and happy—such appears to be their ingenuous premise. Doubtless it is a democratic concept; but Tocqueville takes the trouble to remind us that it is dangerously fallacious.

Confounding prosperity with strength and virtue is so perilous an error, indeed, that on most occasions it will undermine material success long before the anticipated prosperity is attained. Down comes the house of cards, and philosophies less flamboyant but more cognizant of human frailty supplant economic pragmatism. In short, I question not only the ends to which the current spirit of aggrandizement is tending, but also the efficacy of its means. A stern Providence is likely to save us from those ends by dealing with cornucopia-optimism as it dealt with Coolidge optimism, although varying its particular dispensation to suit altered circumstances. Neglect ends, and reasonably soon means are lacking too. Some instances of this cause-and-effect relationship, already experienced or about to confront us, I list here.

(1) A good many men still prefer other possessions to material wealth—or, at least, are so thoroughly imbued with tradition that the possibility of exchanging their accustomed status for an economy more actively acquisitive hardly occurs to their minds. When we recently endeavored to reform the agricultural system of Greece, our people encountered tremendous difficulty in persuading peasants to combine their fields with their neighbors' in order to make mechanization profitable; and even where we did accomplish this task, our administrators found themselves confronted with a dismaying pack of quarrels over division of rights and yields. Our agricultural advisors to Greece professed inability to understand these petty objections. But if a Greek peasant should willingly surrender sovereignty over his little plot, he would not be a peasant; and if he should refrain from quarrelling about it, he would not be a Greek. The further our planners endeavor to extend their efficiency-programs, and the more they ignore the principle of diversity, the more hostility they must encounter, not only abroad but at home. Our own farmers' repudiation of the Brannan plan is a case in point. A planner almost always leaves prejudice out of his calculations; but prejudice, the wisdom of unlettered men, sometimes rises superior to books and drafting-tables. Even when planners force through their improvements in defiance of prejudice and private preference, they often are startled to discover that an immemorial knowledge lay behind the veil of stubborn ignorance: recently in Japan, for example, where we had proposed to bolster up the economy by mechanizing agriculture, we were forced to confess that the conservative Japanese farmer was right, after all: by frugality and diligence

he had already been coaxing the maximum yield from meagre soil, and our machines could do nothing for him—the mechanical calculator against the abacus, all over again.

(2) Wealth can enervate, physically and morally. Gloss over avarice, call it efficient production, and you admit the six other mortal sins and a crowd of inferior ones. Without recommending general asceticism, still we cannot afford to forget that a man overfed, overheated, and sheltered from all the trials of the natural world soon becomes sluggish, carping, and selfish. Why, after all, should he be generous-minded? If aggrandizement is the common object of society, there remains no moral check upon the means employed to acquire wealth. Every price-gouge is justified, every exorbitant strike-demand, every judicious distribution of presents to public servants. And presently the material production of such a society commences to decline, from causes both too numerous and too obvious for us to trace here. As that society becomes physically indolent and spiritually slothful, its mind begins to fail—for even an era of violent conflict is more stimulating to the intelligence of a people than the torpor of materialism. The imaginative man feels crushed, despised, and lets the world go hang. Now our industrial economy, of all systems man ever created, is that most delicately dependent upon public energy, private virtue, and fertility of imagination. If we continue to tell ourselves that prosperity is all, we shall find ourselves remarkably unprosperous.

I do not mean to infer that most of the people who want "planned production" are hedonists personally. Doubtless they go to church, instill altruistic sentiments in their children, and are generous with the time and money they devote to the community. We are speaking, rather, of the tone a society is liable to assume as the popular sentiments consequent upon these planners' principles filter into the public consciousness. Suppose these forecasts turn out to be inaccurate, now; suppose (for national economies are distractingly erratic) that general income fails to increase as prophesied, or even shrinks; what will the public do and say in such an event? The public will have been told pontifically, for a considerable period, that it has a right to steady economic betterment, and the virtual certitude of it. Almost certainly, then a shocked people will conclude that they have been the victims of a conspiracy, that someone has absconded with the cash; and it will be a very ugly public. However benevolent the intentions of our optimistic planners, the popularization of their ideas exposes us to the risk of a nasty social upheaval.

(3) We Americans are not alone in this world. While we are intent upon getting, other nations will be pursuing other objects—or, at least, pursuing what is ours. The demonstration of this truth has been performed so often by history that mentioning it is almost embarrassing.

A fanatic confidence in planned production is not going to deter the Communists. For a long time they have been denouncing and ridiculing American materialism, to their considerable advantage among the peoples of Europe and Asia. We are held in contempt to an increasing degree as boors who think that dollars can conquer ideas, and we find ourselves suffering from the unpleasant paradox of being represented by the arch-materialists of the Soviets as gluttonous dullards. Our own curious reluctance to confess that we Americans do have values of spirit and mind has helped the Communists incalculably. We have thought it a display of manliness to assert that we are interested only in "practical," dollars-and-cents concepts; and now we have found that our audience has adjudged us not virile, but puerile. The suspicion with which even the British are coming to view American civilization, the positive loathing of Americanism expressed (from a knowledge sometimes too scanty, perhaps) by conservative and intellectually-eminent Continental circles, should be warning sufficient.

Very few, not even the poorest of the poor, are sufficiently aroused by a call to the standard of "production" to give their lives for butter. Some ideal man must have; and if we offer him none, he will accept the crude and brutal ideal of Communism, rather than wander in a vacuum. The Soviet policy of starving this generation that future generations may surfeit, however unjust a course, offers *something* to the desperate imagination of modern man; and "production," as it is advocated by our planners, seems to forget that humanity has anything to feed except a body. If we continue in our present intellectual sterility, we shall lose the adherence of the rising generation not only abroad but at home. When our system affronts enterprising talent with nothing but an expression of sluggish vacuity, our darling "production" is liable to be conducted, before long, under wholly different supervision.

We need not go far to seek ideals and imaginative concepts to oppose Communism. Christian morality, national freedom, natural law, dignity and justice—in the long run these (supposing we manifest a genuine belief in them) will vanquish the dreary professions of Marxism. But if the world decides that these concepts are mere words with us, and that our only real god is our belly, we may as well give up military resistance to Communism. No matter what the volume of its steel production, the nation which has disavowed principle is vanquished.

The odds are that we may be saved from ourselves. We probably shall not be permitted to dedicate our hearts to the routine of production and consumption: the Communists, the peril of national atrophy which often becomes apparent as materialism increases, and the stubborn prejudices of ordinary humanity are likely to prevent us from dehumanizing ourselves. We shall be forced to think of objectives less concrete, but no less real, than steaks and thermostats and radio-shows. A merciful Providence, rather than knocking down our Tower of Babel, condescends merely to forbid us to build it. All the rest of this century will be a time of alarms and battles. Such an age is a bitter and destructive lesson, but it is preferable to the degradation of humanity through avarice. Mankind, in the era that is opening, will be shamefully corrupt, as men always are in varying degree; but Men are not going to be reduced to the level of Things, as for a time it seemed they would. Mind and spirit will not be extirpated.

Yes, the projects of our efficiency experts and professional planners and utopian sociologists are going to be abandoned, as man is compelled by the necessities of a dangerous time to resurrect old simplicities and old virtues. But the danger remains that by the time we Americans realize the folly of materialism unalloyed, our planned-production people will have involved us so deeply in their arrangements that extrication will be excruciatingly painful. The public consciousness needs rousing now. More dreams of avarice will only make the waking harsher.

Is it so difficult, after all, to convince men that simplicity may be preferable to complexity, modest contentment to unrestrained sensation, decent frugality to torpid satiety? The first set of sentiments never has been wholly dormant in America. When I have occasion to discuss means for reinvigorating the traditional character of man, I sometimes borrow from the sociologists and the psychologists their methods of culture-analysis and case-history. These useful types of demonstration, a good deal discredited by certain ends to which neo-positivists have employed them, deserve rescue. Possibly they need re-designation, too. In any event, I have found them serviceable in analyzing the aggrandizement-doctrine of human happiness.

First, the culture-survey. Ever since the anthropological tail began to wag the sociological dog, professors of the social sciences have been embarking for the islands of the antipodes and returning with blazing revelations for our enlightenment, such as the disclosure that marriage rites in Papua differ from those in Springfield, Illinois; and the surprise that political structure in Yap is not very similar to political structure in Birmingham. Being properly impressed by these marvels of scientific observation, some time ago I, too, made my way to a remote and simple island—Eigg, in the Small Isles of the Hebrides—and there I spent more than a month among Hebrideans, who have the advantage of being more intelligible than New Hebrideans. The scenery is desolately noble, the people are interestingly Gaelic and Papist, and the island has little more connection with progressive civilization than if it were in the South Pacific.

Most of the hundred people of Eigg are crofters, dwelling in whitewashed cottages of rubble, cultivating patches of ground four or five acres in extent, fishing a bit for mackerel or lobster, keeping a cow or two, feeding ducks and chickens, living very frugally indeed. Over every corner of Eigg broods the high, black, volcanic Sgurr, mists veiling its peak; and the crofts look upon the treacherous currents of the Sound of Rum. Probably the average cash income here is not more than a third of the thousand dollars which Mr. Heil-broner considers poverty for an American rural family. These islanders have a priest and a Church of Scotland missionary and a doctor and a shop and an English laird who makes his appearance in summer. Their old communal spirit is much atrophied; and their fuel and some of their food is imported. But they retain the placid-ity of people in whom traditional standards dominate will and appetite: no automobiles, no movies, no novelties, few radios, few ambitions—a condition of status. A rabbit shot in the morning, an egg or two, watercress from the brook, vegetables from the croft, porridge, some pickled mackerel—there is no complaint at this diet. When the young men of Eigg came back from the war, they had small desire to escape into the progressive world; on the con-trary, they tried to find niches for themselves in Eigg, which is a dif-ficult thing to contrive in a shrinking economy that does not fit snugly into the pattern social planners have drawn up for the new Britain. The people of Eigg have the pleasures of affectionate fami-lies and quiet life, the consolations of religion, the security of those who do not expect efficient production. They need no police-force; there is no drunkenness; and one sees a great many smiles. I do not suggest that we can impose the social pattern of a little Hebridean island upon America, any more than we ought to think that New Hebridean mores justify American slips from conjugal virtue; but I do suggest that the production-and-consumption view of society is neither the universal nor the traditional belief.

Now for the case-history. Years ago, on a June morning, there came up to me a tall, stooped old man wearing a straw sailor hat and a black suit—my employer. He knew my face, but, like many other people, he did not know my name; while, I, like many other people, had the advantage of him in this particular: it was Mr. Henry Ford. He took me into the little brick shed where he had con-structed his first automobile and told me of those days in 1893—told me with obvious satisfaction, yet satisfaction tinged with anxi-ety, as if he wished to be sure of the approbation of the young. "It don't seem long since I built it." He glanced out the window at his enormous museum of a dead America, Greenfield Village, which encompassed us—and then stared across the wooded acres of his estate to the stacks of the Rouge Plant, hemmed about by the hideous streets of East Dearborn and Melvindale and River Rouge. He had been a farm lad in those flatlands once; and now he had obliterated, without willing it, the country that he knew as a child, except for this lifeless sanctuary within brick walls; and there was doubt in his heart.[1] When men or nations sweep away their past in the process of aggrandizement, presently the dream of avarice gives way to a forlorn longing after things beyond recall.

Well, many of us Americans are poor, and abject physical poverty can be unhealthy for mind and heart, too, depending upon particular circumstances and the spirit in which it is received. If, in this time of troubles, we find that we have social energy to spare, we shall do well to help the people who cling to the tarpaper shanties in the barrens and the people who live by old trades and old ways at the risk of poverty. But the attainment of a general luxuriousness would be of dubious benefit, and the sacrifice of personality and independence for "production" would be a pitifully ineffectual way of defying the collectivists, though it might turn out to be a means of joining the Communists. Our planners, intent upon consolidation, efficiency, standardization, and innovation, seem to have ceased to ask themselves what they are designing. Whatever they include in their present plans, they exclude contentment.

For a generation it has been fashionable to plan for the attainment of this interesting condition of society. Possibly our tormented era will employ guides endowed with imagination of a quality different from that of the Utilitarian planner. The conservative thinker does not believe that men are made happy by creating

---

1. I choose Henry Ford as an instance of an entrepreneur with some sense of community and some respect for old values, not as the archetype of innovation. He undertook several experiments at great expense toward reconciling the old rural order with the new urban life, such as the purchase and restoration of little water-powered mills in small towns, where the millhands might obtain part of their sustenance from gardening, and retain their old character, rather than sink into a proletarian condition. All this was abandoned at Ford's death, and the Ford Foundation which inherited most of his millions has been conducted upon the principles of "disintegrated liberalism," with none of the sound, if eccentric, common sense of its founder.

and stimulating new wants, he does not believe that men are made happy by attempts to satisfy to repletion every physical craving. He believes, instead, that the best way to bring contentment to humanity is to strengthen and restore those old ends of existence, those old motives to integrity, which I have described earlier in this book. Stability instead of velocity, community instead of reckless self-expression, satisfying work instead of novel amusement, a decent competence instead of an incessant pursuit of luxuries—these are the ways to the peace which passes all understanding.

At home, the American conservative will endeavor to exert some intelligent check upon material will and appetite. If, indeed, as the economic optimists declare, we are in an age of plenty, then we ought to begin to employ these material endowments after a fashion which will bring our wants into conformity with truly human needs. We ought to stand for decentralization of industry, craftsmanship rather than mass-production, making our homes durable and our communities beautiful rather than pouring our money and our publicity-facilities into a frantic lust for immediate consumption of luxuries. People who fret about business-cycles ought to turn some of their attention to the encouragement of an economy founded upon an enduring demand for the commodities of permanence, instead of the markets of frippery and speed and rapid decay. Our industrial system, quite possibly, has given us the leisure and the margin of security which can make practicable a general provision for the fundamental wants of everyone in these United States; if this is true, then we ought to use our reason to employ the mechanism of industrial production for conservative, rather than revolutionary, economic ends. American industrial genius, rather than running to waste in domestic luxuries and extravagant donations to the whole world, can now be diverted to the humanizing of trade and manufacture, and the restoration of community. For this purpose, centralized planning is not merely unnecessary, but positively baneful: what we require is the moving of men's minds—the minds of the captains of industry and the leaders of labor, the minds of the journalist and the economist—toward a reasoned material conservatism which comes from private and local beneficence, and toward an appreciation of varied tastes and varied skills, rather than industrial uniformity. In a sentence, what we ought to have in prospect is not an America covered from coast to coast with speedways, over which we roar incessantly in an endeavor to forget our lost heritage, but an America of beauty and purpose in which we do not need to run away from home. And, turning away from the furious depletion of natural resources, we ought to employ our techniques of efficiency in the interest of posterity, voluntarily conserving our land and our minerals and our forests and our water and our old towns and our countryside for the future partners in our contract of eternal society.

Abroad, we Americans ought to hearten and help everyone who stands for traditional rights and the wisdom of their ancestors, not to talk of "a revolution of rising expectations" and of imposing the American Standard of Living on the Bedouia and the Javanese villager. We ought to respect and enjoy the differences which distinguish other cultures from our own. We ought not to swagger insolently among the nations, bullying or bribing them into a sterile conformity with our particular pleasures. And the worst manifestation of American hubris, I think, has been our determination that all peoples ought to think as we do. Even old Herodotus, at the dawn of Western civilization, knew better than that. We made many blunders, with the best of intentions, during and shortly after the late war; but the silliest of them was to endeavor to "re-educate" our vanquished adversaries. We authorized a horde of our pedagogues to descend upon Germany and Japan, to wash the brains of the lesser breeds without the law; it never seemed to occur to the makers of American policy that although things may have been gravely wrong with education in Germany and Japan, those faults were precisely what our Deweyite pedagogues admired, and the surviving virtues were what we hoped to eradicate. We failed, after doing considerable mischief, and now, for the most part, the schools and universities of Germany and Japan are going their own way once more. But we did succeed in awakening an enduring resentment against our meddlesomeness. What we were asserting, in effect, was our right to remake the world in our own image. "Surrender to us, and we will annihilate your personality, and mould you afresh upon our perfect model." The wants of other nations are not necessarily

American wants, and the means to wisdom are not monopolized by American techniques.

Long ago, after having knocked about the world more than a little, I determined to make the motto of John Randolph of Roanoke my own: *nil admirari*. Yet wonder, like cheerfulness, will keep breaking in; and though I thought I had become incapable of amazement at the presumption of those Americans who are intolerably smug, smugger far than George P. Babbitt, in their creed of superiority to all other ages and peoples, three years ago the arrogance of one American of this stamp succeeded in exasperating me. The gentleman in question was a Mr. David Williams, director of research for the Political Action Committee of the Congress of Industrial Organizations, whose article "The New American Revolution" was printed in the *Twentieth Century* for August, 1951. The Americans, in Mr. Williams' radical opinion, ought to spend their time carrying on a perpetual revolution, at home and abroad, organic change for its own sake. Now Mr. Williams is not a Marxist, but a simon-pure "capitalist," though a servant of the great labor unions; and what he desires to bestow upon Europe is mass-production and the abolition of all traditional classes, and upon Asia, thoroughgoing industrialization and Western modes of thought and amusement. The following passage—though not the most presumptuous in his essay—may indicate sufficiently the Benthamite materialism of his program:

> The result of all these factors was that the 'second Industrial Revolution'—the transformation of industry to mass production for mass markets—had, in comparison to America, hardly begun in Europe. Handicraft production, or small-scale production in old-fashioned family-owned firms, prevailed to an astonishing degree. Moreover, there was stubborn resistance to change. Many Europeans preferred the old ways of doing things. They seem to like the very 'chains' in which Jefferson had seen them bound over a century earlier.... History is something of an ironist. The early Marxists saw the need for completing the bourgeois revolution, as an essential step toward socialism. When they had the chance in Russia, they shirked the task and took the easier road to totalitarianism. Would they have ever dreamed that, almost against its will and even without itself consciously realizing it, the United States

has dedicated a great share of its energy and resources to carrying through the bourgeois revolution all over the world?

It is Mr. Williams' opinion, in brief, that we ought to contend against the Soviets by making the whole world into one proletarian paradise of creature-comforts, outbidding Marx, and annihilating every form of variety and national character which conflicts with an intolerant Americanism. But I think we have too much sound sense left in us to do anything of the sort. This new imperialism, more insidious than the old, is enthusiastically applauded by many of the very persons who would denounce nineteenth-century methods of Western aggrandizement—Mr. Norman Thomas, for example. But if it is pursued, it will make a hatred of America, and an envy, more virulent, and more excusable, than the present wave of anti-Western emotion in Asia and Africa. And it will not bring peace to the nations; for stimulated desire cannot rest. What provokes violent revolution in Asia and Africa is not physical want, but the sense of social insecurity, the loss of community, which has come with the introduction of Western techniques and badly-apprehended Western political ideas. The mass of the people of China and India and Egypt always have been poor, but they have not ordinarily been revolutionary. They scream and destroy insensately today precisely because persons like old James Mill, or young David C. Williams, have encouraged in their hearts the lust for wants which never can be satisfied.

Fortunately, we have a body of opinion in this country at the antipodes from that which Mr. Williams represents. I cannot do better, here, than to quote from the remarks of Dr. Harry D. Gideonse, president of Brooklyn College, on "citizenship education" (published in the proceedings of the *Middle States Council for the Social Studies*, Volume 50). Freedom, he says, "is not a by-product of the conveyor belt and the advertising business"; and one of the cardinal errors of many American conservatives has been to maintain this position.

"Materialism—where philosophically explicit or implicit—is poison to a free society, and the fact that we are aware of its role in Soviet ideology or propaganda does not diminish our responsibility to define it properly in its American version. Purely economic views of the nature of man on the part of some of our conservatives can be as subversive of freedom as the optimistic theories about the nature

of man advocated—or implicitly assumed—by some of our liberals." And we have been at our worst in endeavoring to thrust these
views of wants and desires and satisfactions upon older societies:

> The weakness of the exclusively economic view of "freedom" is best
> illustrated by a glance at our difficulties in "selling the American
> way" to such a country as modern India. When we diagnose the
> needs of India, we speak of her need for free markets, capital invest-
> ment, industrialization, higher material productivity—and we take
> the moral pre-suppositions of such a prescription for granted.
> From the standpoint of millions of Indians, the moral pre-suppo-
> sitions are the real problem. If you believe in the spiritual virtue
> and physical "renunciation"—and specifically if you believe in
> accordance with the teachings of the Hindu classic, the Bhagavad
> Gita, that "freedom is the absence of desire," then the whole philos-
> ophy of recasting Indian motivation on the model of the psycho-
> logical assumptions of a modern American advertising agency will
> appear to be directly subversive of a classical Indian conception of
> freedom itself. To the traditional Hindu view a reduction of mate-
> rial wants will make all the concern about free markets, industrial-
> ization, and even sanitation, essentially irrelevant "busy work"
> which restricts freedom because it limits the higher range of choice
> which is the spiritual core of his deepest faith.

For the sake of this ideal of renunciation, for an effective protest
against the arrogance of Western materialism, the Indian people
threw all their strength to the cause of Gandhi; this was the driving
impulse behind their twentieth-century revolution, not any idea of
an American "revolution of rising expectations." I could think of no
better way in which to make Americans detested in Asia, and in
most of the rest of the uneasy world, than to represent them as the
champions of a gross materialism, the enemies of moral tradition,
the devotees of incessant change. American conservatives ought to
see that their nation turns another face to her potential friends. We
cannot escape our duties in the community of nations, nor should
we want to; but it is our high obligation to play the part of conservators of justice and order, not the agents of the universal industrial
proletarianization which Marx prophesied. Government is a contrivance to satisfy human wants; and the greatest of mundane wants
is the surety of enduring values and enduring forms.

The Problem of Order

LAW AND ORDER, though they are connected intimately, are not identical. Order, in society, is the harmonious arrangement of classes and functions which guards justice and gives willing consent to law and ensures that we all shall be safe together. "Orders and degrees," Milton says, "jar not with liberty, but well consist." Order also signifies the honor or dignity of a rank in society; and it signifies some particular profession or class; and it signifies those established usages which deserve veneration. "Without order," old Richard Hooker writes, "there is no living in public society, because the want thereof is the mother of confusion." it appears nowadays that the decay of the sense of community among modern men has brought on a corresponding decay of order, inner and outer, so that truly, in most nations, "every thing includes itself in power, power into will, will into appetite." When no man feels settled into an order, then the individual has no dread of censure, but is restrained in his appetites only by the threat of force: the policeman supplants, so far as he is able, the old influence of emulation and the soft but effectual controls of good repute. Almost no one is afraid of "public disapproval" in the abstract; what we fear is the loss of good repute within the little platoon we belong to in society, the reproaches of our parish, our club, our neighborhood, our partners, our guild or union. The proletarian, the man who belongs to nothing, has lost the very concept of order, as he has lost community; he is a social atom, and thus, often, he is shameless; and force is employed to make him conform reluctantly to the conventions which once men obeyed out of a longing for good repute. Force, however, has its limitations; the more it is exercised, the less efficacious does any particular application of it become; and as the imitation of the proletariat

creeps ever higher in a decadent society, and as the process of material proletarianization goes on apace, the number of persons who
believe intelligently in the preservation of any regular system of law
and order grows steadily smaller—until, perhaps, we arrive at that
triumph of squalid oligarchs who promise to save the state from
anarchy, but exact the price of abject servitude.

Now disorder, in the common sense of that word, is increasing
most ominously in modern society; and I think that one of the
principal causes of this disorder is the enervation of the idea of
order in its traditional sense—that is, the spirit of class, duty, and
honor, the sense of responsibility and common interest within
long-established social groups, which is closely bound up with
Burke's "unbought grace of life." The evidences of this disintegra-
tion of obedience to established customs and of the prescriptive
framework of the civil social existence are all about us. In Britain,
where for a great while the reign of law and order was established
more securely than in any other principal state, the annual number
of indictable offenses has more than doubled in the past fifteen
years. In the United States, the increase in the number of crimes of
violence has been even greater. As the old agencies for the enforce-
ment of law find themselves unable to deal with this collapse of the
moral sanctions for integrity, every state tends to resort to centralized and arbitrary methods for preserving some sort of social discipline. Thus private liberties, and the prescriptive operation of equal
justice, retreat before the advance of the total state. We do well to
view with suspicion the steady increase of the powers and range of
legislative investigatory committees; but we are silly if we think that
this ominous growth of inquisitorial authority is without cause; it is
the logical consequence of a terrible decay of mutual trust and of
private responsibility. The less control survives within private life
and local community, the more control will be exerted by the centralized state, out of necessity. When true order crumbles, then a
tolerable simulacrum of order is imposed upon society by men who
love power, if they love nothing else.

The decay of respect for law is only the most obvious proof of the
decline of order in our age. It extends to the universities, where—
with a few exceptions—the whole concept of a hierarchy of values is

forgotten, being supplanted by the cafeteria-style curriculum. It is quite possible to find in a university catalog more courses listed in fly-casting than in Greek. One man is as good as another, or maybe a little better, most university administrators presume; and, similarly, all studies are considered equal in value, except, perhaps, that those most newly devised are given pride of place over traditional disciplines. This, too, is the consequence of the decay of order: the decline of belief that an orderly mind is disciplined by a certain order of studies.

And disorder is spreading rapidly to all the works of the mind. The average student, like the average sensual man, detecting this, is never satisfied to dwell long on any particular topic, but moves eternally restless, impelled by a vague and shallow curiosity, bored with the slightest delay or difficulty, treating everything in heaven and earth alike, upon the assumption that all objects and topics possess equal value, all things holy or profane, and that they exist simply to engage, for a moment or two, the impatient interest of the rising generation. All creation, then, is very like the contents of one of our picture-magazines, to the majority of young people: a jumble of political exhortation, exhibitionism, appeals to concupiscence, reproductions of works of sacred art, representations of murder and rapine, advertisements for creature-comforts, denunciation of our opponents abroad, and adulation of motion-picture actresses. This, I think, brings on a disorder of the mind which is a preparation for disorder of the spirit and of civil society.

Though the problems of leadership and of order are closely related, they are not identical. The problem of leadership is the great question of how we may obtain and encourage the men of probity and courage and loftiness of spirit that our age requires; the problem of order is the great question of how we may persuade men that they are not sufficient unto themselves, but require membership in an order—and that a number of orders, with distinct functions and responsibilities, is a benefit to society, rather than a violation of free institutions. The ministry of religion is an order; the body of scholars and teachers is an order; a guild or union of skilled craftsmen is an order; the multitude of small farmers, taken collectively, is an order; the profession of medicine, or of law, is an order; the management of industry is an order; the class of shop-keepers is an order. When men recognize their membership in a decent and responsible order, when they are not mere flies of a summer, then that sense of membership and duty is reflected in a respect for law and far social decency. I am not suggesting that we create new orders, or that we invent any new pattern of politics to favor one order or another; I am simply endeavoring to say that the sense of order, of honorable membership, is a great force for good, and ought to be encouraged. We need to undertake what Dean Nisbet calls "the quest for community," if we are to escape from the menace of universal proletarianization.

Nor is membership in an order what educationists in the tradition of Dewey and Kilpatrick call "adjustment to the group." The age of chivalry and of Scholasticism, when order attained its most complex development, was eminently an age of proud independence and great variety of talents. It is the proletarian, not the member of a coherent order, who conforms, sheep-like, to the group. This proletarian conformity, this intolerant passion for levelling all orders and confounding all persons in one amorphous social mass, with identical tastes and identical talents, has been erected into something that resembles a system of ideas by the disciples of John Dewey.

The member of an *order* is a person, an individual, proud of his status, but quick to defend his dignity of mind and independence of action; while the conformist to the group, the mass-man, accepts his vague status without hope or pride, and dreads any necessity for the exercise of private resolution or intelligence.

But a man who feels himself dignified and protected by being a member of an old and valuable order does not envy the possessions of another order; he is conscious of an end in life, and therefore does not experience that galling resentment against whatever is not his own. But when orders are abolished, and the whole population is reduced to a uniform proletariat, then anything possessed by men of superior diligence or intelligence or taste will be coveted by the masses; and if it cannot be divided, it will be destroyed. The Jacobin and the Benthamite have this in common, that they arouse (as Burke reminds us) in men destined to walk in the obscure ways of life expectations that cannot be gratified without destruction of the moral order to which we are made.

This dull envy of the proletarian heart oppresses every modern state—the United States of America less than other nations, perhaps, because here, as yet, an abundance of creature-comforts has mollified the mass mind—and will grow quite as menacing as Joad suggests, unless thinking men begin to set about the redemption of the proletariat.

To some extent, Mr. David Riesman, in *The Lonely Crowd*, recognizes the gravity of the problem confronting modern society, in which the decay of order leaves the mass of men without principle or leadership, prey to every vagrant whim. Power no longer really is joined to wealth, or to numbers, or even to strength; what power remains within the control of particular individuals often is manipulated by the contact-man, who represents little but his own private interest.

It is Mr. Riesman's hope that this order in society— or, at least, some leadership in society—may be maintained by persons whom he describes as "the Autonomous." But he suggests that it is harder than ever before, nowadays, to develop autonomy of character; "In what sphere does autonomy exist today, when the older barriers have crumbled and can serve neither as defenses nor as obstacles for a lifelong agenda of attack?"

Mr. Riesman's answer is somewhat disappointing. He suggests that the autonomous might struggle against the prevailing prestige of work, in favor of leisure, or rather in favor of play. He might seek to diminish "the privatization of women," or study "consumership," or engage in "avocational counseling." It may occur to some of us that these activities scarcely will suffice to give order to a society on the verge of violent dissolution. Mr. Riesman would like the autonomous to lead us toward utopia—that is, his Utopia of Consumption—but he is rather afraid that, the autonomous tending to be feeble in numbers and in will, "parties and authoritarian movements will force people toward goals which are neither commonsensical nor utopian but merely regressive." Not all of us are likely to share Mr. Riesman's sighs of longing for the Utopia of Consumption.

Such, in substance, are my sentiments concerning Mr. Riesman's brummagem Utopia and Mr. Riesman's autonomous individuals. The summit of their ambition would be to lead us to a New Era of Consumption; and, in a time when we live quite literally beneath Damocles' sword, and suffer in a dread waste of spiritual desolation, the autonomous other-directed men in whom Mr. Riesman places his trust at considerable length in *The Lonely Crowd* are no more competent to give us order than they are to bail out the Atlantic with a sieve. Politics is scarcely the consummation of human reason; yet without some order in politics, we are unlikely to attain much order in higher things; and Mr. Riesman's autonomous individuals seem incompetent even to influence our politics in any appreciable degree. They are rootless, the dilettantes of taste and feeling, the people whom Gissing calls "the unclassed"; and they cannot lead us to any principle of order because they themselves know no order of spirit or mind. They are unable to repair to any standard of reason and duty. Men without principle must become, in time, unprincipled men. Mr. Riesman himself recognizes the political pusillanimity of his other-directed but autonomous individuals:

> In any case, the autonomous, insignificant in numbers, play a minor and scarcely discernible role in our politics. One might expect, *a priori*, that the autonomous in character would, in their political style, go beyond the intellectual limitations of the moralizer and beyond the moral limitations (and hence the intellectual ones) of the inside-dopester and would become genuinely involved with politics, intelligent about it, and emotionally committed to it. But this is not always what we end. Many people who are clearly autonomous in character are sometimes political indifferents. Other autonomous people, less adequate in politics than in other life spheres, are indignants and sometimes inside-dopsters. Conversely, some people may manage to be productive in their political roles who are anomic or adjusted in character: politics may be their most creative sphere. On reflection, this is perhaps what we should expect if we remind ourselves that such words as autonomy and adjustment are constructions, not real people.

This last sentence of Mr. Riesman's, like a great many of his conclusions, is what the defecated intellectual of our time likes to call "ambivalent"—that is, after having at great length described the type of human being whom Mr. Riesman calls "autonomous," the author of that word himself casts it into the winds of doctrine and disavows any further responsibility for it. Yet I think that indeed we may very well remind ourselves that this abstraction "the autonomous individual" is quite as treacherous as those Jacobin abstractions which Burke stripped naked. And to put any trust in such "autonomous" persons for the restoration of order among us would be an act of folly quite as disastrous as Rousseau's trust in the Natural Man. I think that the reason why the "autonomous" individual can accomplish nothing in politics or in any other significant realm of endeavor is simply this: only the moralizer can bring order into the formlessness of a confused society or a confused mind. Now Mr. Riesman employs the word "moralizer" in a peculiar fashion, rather as a term of smiling denigration, after the style of the positivist with the word "moralist." But morals have been creeping back into good repute, in many quarters, recently; therefore it is become no longer especially witty to sneer at "moralists"; it is shrewder to eschew the word "moralist" and substitute the term "moralizer"; and then, by a subtle association, the critic of traditional morality may succeed in bringing any system of morals into doubt by his especial usage of the useful term "moralizer." Now we cannot know the heart; therefore I do not presume to say here whether Mr. Riesman's espousal of the word "moralizer" is the result of deliberate policy or of unconscious association; but I think I perceive that the suffix "-izer" carries with it an appreciable connotation of mingled charlatanry and stupidity. Mr. Riesman's typical "moralizer" is an old-fangled statesman, like Gladstone or Wilson, who injects irritating moral dogmas into the pleasant play of politics:

> The typical style of the inner-directed person in nineteenth-century American politics is that of the moralizer. Since the inner-directed man is work driven and work oriented, his profoundest feelings wrapped up in work and the competence with which work is done, when he turns to politics he sees it as a field of work—and judges it accordingly. Presented with a political message, he sees a task in it, far from seeking to demonstrate his knowledge of personalities by explaining its meaning, he responds

with emotional directness and often naïveté. While this, however, does not mean that all inner-directed people are responsive to politics and are moralizers, one sees in America of the nineteenth century a powerful tendency to moralize the well-defined interests of the self and hence to respond to political attack by political indignation. Therefore, moralizing becomes a virtually uniform political style for the inner-directed.

I myself happen to prefer Benjamin Disraeli to William Ewart Gladstone, and William Howard Taft to Woodrow Wilson. Yet I should be very sorry to exchange the nineteenth-century liberal statesman for the "autonomous" politician who has no standard of reason and duty to which he can relate his decisions of the hour. Mr. Riesman suggests that we cannot yet be sure that we are forever emancipated from the influence of the political moralizer: "In view of the indeterminacies of history, it would be rash to predict that the moralizing style is doomed and that no revival in America is possible. Indeed, if influential others become moralizers, the other-directeds, because they are other-directed, will try to be moralizers, too."

Has this not always been so? The mass of men, after all, in any age have taken their morals, like their taste and their manners and their very dress, from the people whom Mr. Riesman calls "others"—that is, the natural leaders in every order of society. It cannot be otherwise, for most men cannot possibly govern their lives according to the scanty stock of private reason which is theirs. I think that a principal hope for our enduring manfully this present winter of our discontents is the revival of moralizing among those persons that have been formed by character and by association for the leadership of their fellows. But this moral leadership is not likely to be recognized by the mass of men unless there is restored among us a general consciousness of order upon some such system of principles as that implicit in Burke's writings and speeches. "The awful Author of our being," says Burke, "is the author of our place in the order of existence." God, "having disposed and marshalled us by a divine tactic, not according to our will, but according to His, He has, in and by that disposition, virtually subjected us to act the part which belongs to the part assigned to us." Men are not identical in beauty, or in strength, or in cunning, or in wisdom, or in skill of hand, or in the physical senses, or in the qualities of emotion. It is for the betterment of all men that a "divine tactic" has established among us Order, through which the strong are the guardians of the weak, and the old are the preceptors of the young. When order is overthrown, then truly the qualities in man which most nearly approach the supernatural are crushed by those qualities which are most nearly brutish.

When men think themselves able to be all things, then order is broken, and presently men find themselves slaves to the merciless forces of nature. Before we can restore law to this broken world of ours, we must bring back to men's mind the idea of order, which teaches that men are not identical and unitary, but very different persons, with different characteristics and tastes and abilities, and intended for very different functions in the civil social existence. Not all men can be masters; but it is no disgrace or privation not to be a master; for the master, like Dionysius and like Damocles, lives with the sword swaying above his head. We are made for cooperation, not for strife; and order is not a corruption of the natural equality of man, but instead the realization of the providential design which made us one another's keepers. To understand the necessity for order, and the rightness of order, men must apprehend the idea of justice. Justice and order, like all other abiding realities, are moral ideas; therefore it must be the moralizers, and not the autonomous, who will lead us back to order, if ever we will consent to be led.

Sometimes I think that the most urgent need of our time is for Don Quixotes to lead us. In Don Quixote, we see the spirit of a gentleman, and the age of chivalry, and the idea of honor, and the unbought grace of life, at their most fantastic; yet the great soul of the last knight-errant rises superior to his madness and his misfortunes; and the spirit of his age, and the petty figures of the creatures who conform to that spirit, are shamed by Don Quixote's courage and charity. We are perishing for lack of Don Quixotes to attack the windmills of our modern servility and our modern boredom; this is sober fact, and no mere rhapsody of our imagination. A good many of our ancestors thought, about 1790, that they were putting an end to order and honor simultaneously. Well, we have been tolerably successful in burying the idea of honor; but leadership always rises dreadful in its winding-sheet, metamorphosed; and the face of the new leadership, in much of the world, is the face of Don Quixote's ogre.

> Let us now praise famous men, and our fathers that begat us. The Lord hath wrought great glory by them, through his great power from the beginning. Such as did bear rule in their kingdoms, men renowned for their power, giving counsel by their understanding, and declaring prophesies, leaders of the people by their counsels, and by their knowledge of learning meet for the people, wise and eloquent in their instructions. Such as found out musical tunes, and recited verses in writing. Rich men furnished with ability, living peaceably in their habitations. All these were honored in their generations, and the glory of their times. There be of them that have left a name behind them, that their praises might be reported. And some there be, which have no memorial, who are perished as though they had never been, and are become as though they had never been born, and their children after them. But these were merciful men, whose righteousness hath not been forgotten. With their seed shall continually remain a good inheritance, and their children are within the covenant. Their seed stands fast, and their children for their sakes. Their seed shall remain forever, and their glory shall not be blotted out, Their bodies are buried in peace, but their name liveth for evermore. The people will tell of their wisdom, and the congregation will shew forth their praise.

So says Ecclesiasticus. Leaders who are honored in their generations tend to become honorable leaders; we are what people think us, and what we think ourselves. But if a society sneers at the whole idea of order, then the leaders of that age will assume the character which public opinion thrusts upon them, ruling by power or fear, love and honor lacking. So it is that order and honor are connected; and so it was with the old Romans. Cicero, in his *Offices*, describes this high old Roman virtue at length. In the first book, defining the sources of moral goodness, or honesty, he plays upon the dual meaning of the Latin word *honestum*, which could signify either moral rectitude, or honor. From the elements of beauty, consistency, and order, Cicero says, "that moral goodness which we seek is forged—that honesty which, though it be untitled, still is honorable; so that we say truly, even when it goes unpraised, that its very nature makes it praiseworthy." This high rectitude, independent of worldly station, gave the Romans their great dignity and strength of purpose, men fit to lead and to judge; and it had four aspects: the use of reason to ascertain Truth; the conserving of society, to give every man his due and to enforce contracts; the expression of a high-minded and intrepid spirit; and the realization of a noble order and balance in character, modest and temperate. When the Romans began to neglect these principles of *honestum*, then honesty and honor both withered, and the leader of the old order, Cicero, was butchered by the leader of the new order, Antony. Leaders every age must have; and when the unbought grace of life is derided, then, as sure as fire will burn, some new Antony will gloat over the dead face and the dead hands of some fallen Cicero. By 1918, our society had managed to discard most of its old leaders; by 1956, our society, throughout most of the world, has come to writhe in the clutch of men still worse than Antony.

> "Be thou lowely and honest
> To riche and pouere, in worde and dede,
> And then thy name to worshyp shall sprede,"

says the Booke of Precedence. When the leader of men, or the master of men, ceases to recognize these high duties of the unbought grace of life—when he ceases to care whether his name to worship shall spread—then honor is gone, and honesty is gone, and right and wrong and justice lose their names, and everything includes itself in power.

One of the most penetrating and heartening endeavors in this reexamination of first principles is a recent book by M. Gabriel Marcel, *Man Against Mass Society*. And a short but important chapter in this book is called "The Reintegration of Honor." "It is important to notice that everything seems to be in alliance today to destroy this notion of human honor, as to destroy all other notions that reflect an aristocratic morality," M. Marcel observes, "People affect to believe that an aristocracy can be only a caste and that the caste-system as such is a mode of existence condemned by history. Now, while we may readily agree that a closed caste-system appears to us today as something indefensible, on the other hand we must utterly deny that the idea of aristocracy implies any system of this sort." M. Marcel was awakened, one night, to a renewed consciousness of honor, "the assurance that it is an honor to be a man," by listening to a Bach concert. There can be an aristocracy without wealth and without noble ancestry, he tells us; an aristocracy of true honor, pride in rectitude of character, scorn of flattery, loathing of equivocation, courage and candor in every act of life. This is a proper pride in being a man, not the *hubris* of presumption. With such a man, his word is himself. Honor appears to be closely joined to a noble and generous simplicity in the fundamental human relationships. But these are the very bonds between man and man that are tending to disappear in a world where individuals, reduced to their abstract elements, are more and more merely juxtaposed, and where the only hierarchies that remain are founded either on money or on educational qualifications whose human significance is practically nil."

M. Marcel does not mean by aristocracy a political oligarchy; what he has in mind, instead, is John Adams' definition of an aristocrat—"By aristocracy, I understand all those men who can command, influence, or procure more than an average of votes; by an aristocrat, every man who can and will influence one man to vote besides himself." Marcel defends the idea of a gentleman of which Burke spoke, and which Fenimore Cooper defined thus: "The word 'gentleman' has a positive and limited signification. It means one elevated above the mass of society by his birth, manners, attainments, character, and social condition. As no civilized society can exist without these social differences, nothing is gained by denying the use of the term." Such an aristocracy, founded upon local associations, a sense of honor, prescriptive ideas, and natural talents, constitutes a true order, and it is the strongest barrier to the menace of the total state, the world oligarchy of the technocrats.

Mr. T. S. Eliot has the same concept of order in mind when, in his *Notes Toward the Definition of Culture*, he remarks that if we are to avoid the tyranny of a rootless elite (like that proposed by Karl Mannheim), we need to shore up the idea and reality of true class. Class is not the same thing as an elite, nor is it the same thing as caste. Class is the loose association of persons whose talents and

accomplishments, wealth and station, bring them together naturally, for their common benefit and the benefit of society in general.
Here in America, a considerable hostility toward the word "class"
persists. But I think it is a hostility of ignorance. We ought to
remind ourselves that it was Marx, not Jefferson, who yearned after
the classless society. When class is eradicated, then no barrier
remains to the power of the mass-state, and no check upon the
arrogance of an elite freed from all the compulsions of honor which
membership in an ancient class puts upon them. Mr. Eliot expresses
this truth succinctly and courageously:

> The case for a society with a class structure, the affirmation that it is,
> in some sense, the "natural" society, is prejudiced if we allow our-
> selves to be hypnotised by the two contrasted terms *aristocracy* and
> *democracy*. The whole problem is falsified if we use these terms anti-
> thetically. What I have advanced is not a "defense of aristocracy"—
> an emphasis upon the importance of one organ of society. Rather it
> is a plea on behalf of a form of society in which an aristocracy
> should have a peculiar and essential function, as peculiar and essen-
> tial as the function of any other part of society. What is important is
> a structure of society in which there will be, from "top" to "bottom,"
> a continuous gradation of cultural levels: it is important to remem-
> ber that we should not consider the upper levels as possessing *more*
> culture than the lower, but as representing a more conscious culture
> and a greater specialisation of culture. I incline to believe that no
> true democracy can maintain itself unless it contains these different
> levels of culture. The levels of culture may also be seen as levels of
> power, to the extent that a smaller group at the higher level will have
> equal power with a larger group at a lower level; for it may be argued
> that complete equality means universal irresponsibility; and in such
> a society as I envisage, each individual would inherit greater or less
> responsibility towards the commonwealth, according to the posi-
> tion in society which he inherited—each class would have some-
> what different responsibilities. A democracy in which everybody
> had an equal responsibility in everything would be oppressive for
> the conscientious and licentious for the rest.

Class, or order, thus defined, is not extinct in America. We have,
for instance, a body of lawyers of integrity and strong respect for
prescription, which class Tocqueville describes as an aristocracy in

the midst of democracy; we have men of old family and inherited wealth who are today taking a greater part in our public affairs than they have done for a long while; we have men of business of strong practical talents and some attainment of mind; we have a clergy more earnest and perceptive than we have any right to except; we have professors of arts and sciences worthy of their high calling; I hope that we shall find presently within the labor unions, now that their position in the nation is assured, a leadership sober and liber-ally-minded. We have, moreover, a political order; we are not a totalitarian or plebiscitary democracy. The Congress of the United States is an order, and the members of the several state legislatures constitute an order; the upper officials of administrative depart-ments constitute an order; the county and township supervisors are an order. Conscious of a special position and special duties, such groups as these preserve us from arbitrary executive power and popular confusion; they keep our practical politics *orderly*.

Samuel Johnson and Edmund Burke, though they were agreed upon much, differed in more than party labels. For Johnson thought that political institutions are superficial: what preserves or destroys justice and freedom is the moral temper of a people. Burke, however, though awake to the power of the moral climate of opin-ion, believed that the particular system of social organization under which a people exist helps to shape their moral character, and there-fore must receive the most sedulous attention. In this chapter, I have been rather Johnsonian, preaching a respect for the idea of order, but saying very little about any practical application of orders in the United States of America. I do not mean to ignore this latter point; but I think we will do well simply to recognize and preserve our present orders, rather than to attempt to shape some New Order.

In the course of a nation's history, there may come a time when conservatism, in its narrower sense, is obsolete: when the traditional beliefs and the prescriptive establishments have so decayed that they cannot be restored; when the love which gives coherence to a national community is altogether lost; when social orders have lost their meaning, and external order is swallowed up in violence. Some people say that France has now arrived in that condition, and so must be reconstituted wholly, that the welter of ancient animosities may be washed clean away. It may be so, in France; I do not know. But I do not think it is so in America. I do not think it is so here, despite the disorder which makes our city streets more dangerous than the jungle, and turns our universities into diploma-factories. I do not think that the constituent elements of our national order are injured beyond possibility of recovery. Therefore I would sweep away none of them, but would endeavor to repair them all. And I would employ for this purpose no ingenious novel devices, but simply the agencies for restoration which are accessible to us all—the church, the political caucus, the union, the club, the college, the newspaper, the publishing firm, the business establishment.

We Americans, by fits and starts of mistaken zeal for pure democracy, have often injured the reality of order among us. I believe, for instance, that we injured our political order by adopting universal suffrage, direct primaries, popular election of senators, and other measures calculated to substitute direct democracy for representative government. Yet I do not recommend that we try to reverse these measures; instead, we ought to adopt them to the concept of order. The conservative, knowing that radical backward-looking alteration is quite as perilous as radical forward-looking alteration, accepts certain things as given in history, and reconciles irrevocable change to certain unchanging values. In this particular instance, the conservative has the task of preventing abuse of the devices of direct democracy which might injure order far more than the architects of these devices ever intended. The advocates of universal suffrage, direct primaries, and popular election of senators confidently expected that these measures would bring about a vast public interest in politics; and their opponents, most of them, believed this quite as thoroughly, but feared the probability. In plain fact, nothing of the sort has happened. The task of having to decide on every candidate and every issue, with the gigantic ballots which are the consequence, has bored the average citizen, so that either he does not vote at all, or else his vote is scarcely better than chance. We are menaced by indifference, not by partisan passion. Now the conservative, understanding this paradox, will endeavor to apply the principle of order to elections, encouraging in every community those coherent elements which make up a body of reasoned opinion by which the mass of men and women may be guided; and he will try to restore among the mass of men and women a respect for the idea of order, so that their votes are cast with some deference to the opinions of their natural leaders, not at random, or in obedience to this editorial or that radio-broadcast. In short, the conservative will seek to utilize and improve the orders which already exist in our nation, not to impose an exotic pattern of abstract hierarchy.

By and large, the conservative will accept American institutions as they exist today; he will not dabble with experiments in the corporate state, drawn from the works of Pareto, or endeavor to force upon American politics the views and methods of European social-democrats. He knows that constitutional structure, like a country's literature, is the product of long and intricate national experience, not to be improved upon by indiscriminate borrowing from foreign patterns. The orders he hopes to support are the orders which have existed in American society from the inception of the Republic. His energies ought to be engaged in reminding people of the importance of such orders, and in awakening these orders themselves to their responsibilities.

Neither will the conservative expect to create a new elite, after the design of Professor Mannheim, nor to behold the development of some such "saving remnant" by a quasi-automatic process out of the decay of old orders. He will doubt that we need any such new-modelled body of persons. Mr. David Riesman, in his latest book, *Individualism Reconsidered,* maintains that our culture can be redeemed from mass-sterility only through such a development: "One requirement is a type of character structure that can tolerate freedom, even on it; I call persons of this type 'autonomous,' since they are capable of conscious self-direction. The very conditions that produce other-direction on the part of the majority today, who are heteronomous—that is, who are guided by voices other than their own—may also produce a 'saving remnant' who are increasingly autonomous, and who find strength in the face of their minority position in the modern world of power." Now the conservative suspects that such hopes are idle fancies; for he knows that people cannot be "autonomous" without roots or principles, some sanction for their self-confidence and some regular discipline of their intellect. He

182

knows that true freedom of the mind and of action is the prerogative of men and women rooted in an order, with an historical tradition and sense of continuity, who defend their rights because they
would be ashamed to betray their legacy. The most "autonomous"
persons who ever existed, the Christian gentlemen whom Burke
eulogizes, were free because they felt themselves to be secure in an
order, attached to which were very high privileges and very great
duties.

I do not give us up for lost; I think we retain the energy to bring
back true order to our society. But the task will require ten times as
much intelligence as we have displayed in recent years. Not long
ago, I am told, a very rich man in New York gave several hundred
thousand dollars to an advertising-agency to publicize the virtues of
"free enterprise." It was all money down the drain, of course, for the
American public is so soaked in advertising and slogan-propaganda
that a new deluge means that much water off a duck's back. I rather
doubt if this donor had any idea that he was a member of an order.
Yet he *was*, all the same; and if he had spent his money upon the
restoration of order, and community, and continuity, he might have
accomplished something. The process would have been infinitely
slower than the advertising-agency's campaign, it is true, and infinitely more subtle; but it would have made its mark in the Republic,
and the advertising campaign was forgotten the week it ended.

If men of wealth constitute a valid order in the nation, at least
they do not seem to have resolution enough even to stand by their
own order: for while (despite the present bad repute of the Soviets)
it is still possible to obtain nearly any sum of money to finance
some social-planning survey or some radical journal, it is next to
impossible to raise a penny for any truly conservative program. A
businessman will spend fifty thousand dollars on a neon sign, but
will be unable to see the point of spending fifty dollars to save the
Republic. That is a symptom of the decay of order nearly as alarming as the symptom which I described at the beginning of this chapter; but we may contrive to save such people, in spite of themselves.
Money, and most respectable media of communication, still are on
the side of the liberals and radicals; but the key to order is in the
possession of the conservatives.

The Problem of Power

POWER, generally defined, is such an absence of external restriction and limitation that only the inward determination of the subject causes the subject to act or to refrain from action. Now the conservative of reflection always has been sedulous to seek out the precise meaning of words; for the ability to apprehend and employ words accurately is the chief instrument of true reason, and it is through the knowledge of words that we are able to link generation with generation, so that the minds of Aristotle and of Shakespeare are not alien to us. Well, power, in short, is freedom from restrictions and counterbalancing farces. Power over men is the ability to do as one likes, whether other men like that course of action or not. Intelligent conservatives, from Burke and Adams to our time, have looked upon power as a most dangerous thing; for though unchecked power means complete freedom for the powerful man, it means abject servitude for his neighbors; and where power is triumphant, justice cannot abide, since justice promises to each man the things that are his own.

Thus the conservative, reading the lessons of history, has sought to hedge about power with strong restrictions, and to divide authority among many groups and institutions, that concentrated power may reside nowhere. History convinces the conservative that wherever these walls and barriers to restrain power are cleared away in the interest of "efficiency" or "simplicity" or "modernization," power proceeds to make short work of all the elaborate structure of private and public rights which have been developed, through compromise and experience, in the course of history. The conservative knows the proclivity of human nature toward sin; and he knows that the form of sin to which the stronger natures are prone is the lust after power. For the past two centuries, a variety of amusing endeavors have been undertaken by liberal thinkers to demonstrate that men really are benevolent in impulse, but are corrupted by institutions and environment. Sweep away restrictive political institutions, old prejudices, obsolete moral codes, the liberals have said: then the natural healthiness of human character will be brought to the surface, and men will be joined in amity, emancipated from silly old conventions; every impulse will be gratified, and every form of selfishness will vanish.

Such theories were immensely popular throughout the Enlightenment, and were given literary expression by writers of great talents, like Rousseau and Condorcet. Burke and Adams thundered against these illusions, for their view of human nature was derived from Christian thought; but, after a partial eclipse, these optimistic doctrines regained their popularity in the nineteenth century, especially in the form of Positivism, which pretended to "scientific" proofs of the goodness of natural man, the supreme Positivist, Comte, maintaining that the brain contains an "organ of benevolence." The material progress of the nineteenth century, and the spread of democracy and liberalism, seemed to confirm both the idea of progress and the idea of natural benevolence.

These concepts became an inextricable part of socialist thought, and whole schools of philosophy and psychology embraced them almost without question. In America, they were woven into the system of John Dewey, and thus made virtually official doctrine in the educational system of this century. Experimental psychologists and sociologists proclaimed to the world that their researches into child-character and group-behavior confirmed the belief that man's natural impulse is benevolent, and that the old theory of a lust after power, *pleonexia*, was an exploded superstition. The theories of Freud were employed by some critics of human nature and society to demonstrate that all men want, after all, is sexual satisfaction, and that, therefore, a desire for power *per se* cannot exist.

As this optimism grew in intensity, it produced a momentous alteration of liberal political opinions. Liberals of the old school (many of them strongly influenced by Burke) had been quite as suspicious of concentrated power as were the conservatives—if not always for precisely the same reasons. Jefferson or Samuel Adams in America, Acton or Bagehot in Victorian England, had dreaded every form of consolidated authority, and in the interest of liberty had sought to confine power within the strongest constitutional limitations. But as the twentieth century opened, the newer liberals—in America, in Britain, and on the Continent—let this policy fall into desuetude. After all, they maintained, did the problem of power exist any longer? Even John Stuart Mill, despite his misgivings for variety and private liberties in the dawning era, had insisted that Force, as a factor in politics, had faded out of the modern world, and that henceforth all nations would be governed by Discussion. What would Power matter in the new age? Reasonable debate would replace primitive appeals to naked strength. And besides, the liberals told themselves, power was now in safe hands. The old-school liberals had feared power because power, until the Age of Discussion, had tended to slip into the hands of the church establishment, the monarch, and the aristocracy. But with the ascendancy of popular sovereignty, representative government, and equalitarian ideas, power might now be safely entrusted to the People. Surely the People would not abuse power, for that could only be to their own disadvantage; the selfishness of prelates, kings, and barons had no counterpart in the warm hearts of the masses.

Conservative thinkers like Stephen, Maine, and Lecky, when this optimism was approaching its height in the 1870's, retorted that the new means of power being developed in the modern age would be employed far more unjustly and far more violently by the mass-state than by the old-style aristocratic society; but the liberals would not listen to these vaticinations. By the turn of the century, probably a clear majority of men and women who thought at all on such topics were firm in the conviction that Power had become only a question for the schools. They were ready to employ the concentrated power of the modern state, of modern industry, and of modern means of communication to advance the material interests of the masses. The Liberal Party in Britain, and liberally-minded people in America, abandoned their old dread of power and adopted in its place a happy confidence that through democratic methods power could be employed with no necessity for outmoded restraints. Social welfare surely transcended any legalistic attachment to political forms; the conservatives were frightened at mere shadows of the past.

Now the First World War gave these liberals a very rude shock: Discussion, after all, had not wholly subdued Force; and certainly some persons involved in that unfortunate affair had seemed to love power for its own sake. But the liberals comforted themselves with the explanation that this struggle, when all was said, had been merely the last futile upheaval of the Bad Old Order, and that open covenants openly arrived at, universal democracy, and the League of Nations would proceed to make a humanitarian end of the institutions which had permitted power to be employed for violent ends. Somehow, nevertheless, the world refused to settle down; the open covenants lived no longer than Wilson; the democracies set up throughout Europe began to fall apart as soon as they were constructed; and the League of Nations found itself quite impotent. Then came the Second World War, and that was the quietus to the liberal notion that unchecked power is no menace, in modern times. I am quite aware that some persons go on talking as if we still were living in 1895, and pretending that psychiatric clinics could cleanse evil (or rather the maladjustment called Sin) from every human heart; but it is mere force of habit which enables these people to take themselves seriously. They, who pride themselves on their candor, are obdurately defiant of recent history. They are the most old-fashioned people alive, for all their talk of Progress. For what we saw at work between 1936 and 1945 was naked power, power unrestricted either by moral principle or by political devices. Lord Acton was vindicated, and all power was revealed in its tendency to corrupt, and absolute power was displayed in its utter corruption. The desire for power, the catastrophes of a decade proved beyond argument, is the most devouring of passions, a lust beyond the lusts of the flesh.

"To them, the will, the wish, the want, the liberty, the toil, the blood of individuals is nothing," Burke wrote of the Jacobins. "Individuality is left out of their scheme of government. The state is all in all. Everything is referred to the production of force; afterwards, everything is trusted to the use of it. It is military in its principle, in its maxims, in its spirit, and in all its movements. The state has dominion and conquest for its sole objects; dominion over minds by proselytism, over bodies by arms." Hitler, and the whole corps of scoundrels who, with him, lusted after pure power, demonstrated to the twentieth-century liberals the terrible truth of Burke's words; yet some of these liberals still endeavored to argue that if only the aim of the total state should be materialistic humanitarianism, as in Russia, power would be no problem. The conduct of the Soviets during and after the war made mincemeat of this delusion; all the liberals could manage to say, in the face of Soviet imperialism, was that somehow Bad Men had got into the Kremlin, and this was "Stalinism," not the natural consequence of concentrating authority in the centralized state. The liberals sought for some new hero, flirting with Marshal Tito and anyone else they could discover; but somehow every man invested with absolute power turned out to be corrupted absolutely; and so it has come to pass that one might as well hire a blind old woman for a policeman in Hell's Kitchen as employ a representative twentieth-century liberal for a guide to political realities.

The conservative, on the contrary, now as formerly, knows the peril of power, and the practical means for restraining power. To John Adams and James Madison in the United States, to Burke and Disraeli in England, we can turn for guidance. The thinking conservative has consistently sought to keep power from the appetite of any man or any class, through respect for prescriptive constitutions, attention to state and local (as distinguished from central) government, checking and balancing of the executive and the legislative and the judicial divisions of political authority, and prudent confinement of the state's sphere of action to a few well-defined objects. Just this conservative policy of restraining power by constitutional arrangements has been the chief attainment of American political philosophy, from the colonial thinkers and the framers of the Constitution, through Calhoun and Webster, to our own day; and just this search after a just balance of authority has been the great practical success and lesson of the American political experiment, ensuring to us a high degree of freedom and right for three centuries.

This end was the reason for which the most influential work of all our political literature, the *Federalist Papers,* was written. The renewed attention which that series of essays is receiving nowadays suggests how the minds of most serious students of American society are being turned to the problem of power. Madison, Hamilton, and Jay, statesmen severely aware of the frailty of human nature, understood that tyrants and mobs are restrained from overthrowing justice and liberty more by wise constitutions than by any wisdom innate in "the People"; and, drawing from the political experience and tradition of the colonies and of England, they convinced their new nation of the prudence of a federal system of government, founded not upon abstract concepts, but upon historical experience and juridical precedent. John Adams during the same period, in his *Defence of the Constitutions,* drew up a gigantic brief for the division of political authority, in the light of European history from the sixth century before Christ to the contemporary system of England and the Swiss cantons.

The system of checks and balances in government, the decentralization of authority, and the several other Constitutional devices to restrain power were designed, in short, by the leaders of both the Northern and the Southern states, to conserve the justice and the freedom which Americans had long enjoyed; and thinking conservatives have adhered to this system for hedging and confining powers ever since then. Mr. Crosskey's recent work, and certain other curious endeavors to prove that the authors of the Federal Constitution really had something like the welfare state in mind, are historically worthless, however interesting they may be to the student of psychology. We cannot remake history by rewriting it to suit our fancies, however much we may contrive to confuse people for a little space: the intention of the founders of the American Republic is perfectly clear, and it was substantially a conservative intention, quite as Burke's struggle against the unitary designs of George III and his friends was conservative. The conservative political leader in America, from President Adams and President Madison to Senator Byrd and Senator Taft, has detested consolidation of power. The inclinations of Alexander Hamilton sometimes are adduced—especially by enemies of conservatism—as evidence to the contrary: but Hamilton, though his suspicion of popular sovereignty and his affection for the rights of property certainly are characteristics of conservatism, was not really a conservator of old ways, but a planner of a new order: the industrial and consolidated America which he intended to create truly was a more radical vision than any of Jefferson's, and a public suspicion that Hamilton was somehow alien to the political tradition of America barred him from the presidency. The liberal is mistaken, and the conservative ill-advised, if they try to make Hamilton into the founder of our conservative politics. In *The Federalist*, surely, Hamilton writes as a conservative of reflection; but this tone, for him, was compromise with the popular prejudice, and not his heart's desire. The truer conservatism of John Adams expresses the conservatives' view of consolidation with admirable brevity: "My opinion is, and always has been, that absolute power intoxicates alike despots, monarchs, aristocrats, and democrats, and jacobins, and *sans culottes*."

When, then, Dr. Harry D. Gideonse approvingly calls certain political thinkers of the rising generation "the New Federalists," he is accurate. The American conservative is truly a federalist, a balancer of authority, a restrainer of power—not a consolidator, and not an anarchist. With Lincoln, the conservative takes a middle path between such extremes, not out of any misconceived attachment to the "excluded middle," but because he does not believe that security and justice can be found in any fanatic scheme of absolute sovereignty or absolute liberty. And, possessing this tradition of political commonsense and practical experience, American conservatives may hope to deal prudently with the problem of power which confronts the United States in our time.

That problem, in this grim hour, has two principal aspects: the necessity for restraining power within this country, or of preventing the establishment of a unitary state; and the necessity for restraining power in the affairs of nations, both the power of the Soviet states and the power of our own country. In considering these matters, the American conservative needs to remind himself that power is held in check by two influences: moral authority, or the dictates of conscience; and political authority, or the barrier of good laws. I write here of the internal problem of power, first, and then conclude this chapter with some remarks on the role of the United States in a time of what is called (rather loosely) "power politics."

A great many people, in both major political parties, including most professors and most journalists, seem to be aware in some degree that American society is not secure from the menace of political totalitarianism; and since the first step toward remedying a malady is to recognize its symptoms, this is all to the good. Almost no one in the United States desires the coming of the total state: conservatives, and liberals old-style, and liberals new-style, and even most radicals, are unanimous in denouncing such a new order. But I am disquieted by the babel of their voices. Some of them think that the terror is being brought about by unscrupulous Congressmen, and others by planners in the Pentagon, and others by the Communist underground, and others by a cabal of industrialists, and others by the trade-union leaders, and yet others by Lord knows what clique or interest. For my part, I distrust all these theories; indeed, I distrust the Conspiracy Theory in general. I know that there has been at least one serious grand conspiracy in the United States, within this century, and that is the Communist conspiracy. But of itself, the Communist design accomplished very little: its only considerable success was the partial influencing of American foreign policy, during the late war and in the confusion which followed the war; and that business, I trust, has been given the quietus, though the consequences of the mischief done will plague us for a great while. Well, I distrust the Conspiracy Theory of politics because I know how easily such a notion is perverted into some such vicious nonsense as the pretended Protocols of Zion, and because I do not think that any considerable historical movement has had its real source in deliberate and artificial conspiracy.

Conspiracies, rather than creating events, result from events. Hysteria over conspiracies commonly is the mark of a shaken and violence-infatuated society: of such an origin was the Roman hysteria about the Christian Conspiracy, and the post-Reformation hysteria about the Witchcraft Conspiracy, and the Restoration hysteria about the Popish Plot, and the German hysteria about the Jewish Conspiracy. This is not to say that there were no Christians who hated the imperial government, or no witches,[1] or no Catholics

---

1. It may be worth while to remark here that, in the heat of all the current talk about "witch-hunting," most of our liberals forget that there really were plenty of witches in the sixteenth and seventeenth centuries—this is, persons who pretended

who disliked the English establishment, or no Jews who opposed the Nazis. What I am saying is that these several elements neither did form an effective conspiracy against the existing order, nor could have. This inability is equally true of the several elements accused of conspiring against American institutions, with the exception of the Communists; and even our Communists would be ineffectual except for especially propitious circumstances. To rant about a Grand Conspiracy is in itself exciting, and saves people the trouble of serious thought or sober action; but ordinarily it induces, rather than repels, the thing dreaded.

So I believe that we ought to give much less consideration to the Conspiracy Theory of the total state, in its various forms, and more to the actual process by which such a state is developed; for its growth results in considerable measure from the confusion of the minds and hearts of the very people who detest it; indeed, like the Roman and the British empires, it is created in a fit of absence of mind. The late George Orwell, though he described so truly the dreadful features of the New Order (particularly the love of pure power which inspires its masters, as represented by O'Brien), prob-ably blundered in suggesting that the total state is the produce of a deliberate or quasi-deliberate desire upon the part of a circle of men with an unholy appetite for power. Most of us have an unholy appe-tite for power; but if we recognize that appetite for what it is, at least in the earlier stages of the process, we are able to shrink back aghast at its hideousness. The heart is hardened only by degrees, where the average sensual man is concerned: some komsomols who were sent to liquidate the kulaks, in 1930, wept as they thrust peasants out of their cottages; but I doubt if many tears flow nowadays, even croco-dile tears, in the camps of the Siberian Arctic.

In America, then, I do not think that there is much clear and

---

to be adept in the necromantic art, and often sincerely believed in their own powers. Since then, as Dr. Johnson said, "Witches have not ceased to exist; they have merely ceased to be prosecuted." I think incidentally, that some of the people who are most wrathy about "witch-hunting" run the risk themselves of forming a notion of a Witch-Hunters' Conspiracy. And as a final little digression here, I ask to be allowed to observe, for the record, that (newspaper columnists to the contrary) no witches ever were burnt in Massachusetts or anywhere else in America: they were hanged.

present danger of our traditional society being overthrown by any concerted effort of fanatic zealots for the total state; even most of the people whose lust for power would be gratified under a new order do not yet recognize that vice in themselves, and would not yet tolerate it in others. What we have to dread is that our complex structure of sentiment and political institutions, which shelters justice and order and freedom, will be reduced piecemeal, gradually, often with the very best of intentions. Social planners, in colleges or out of them, are very fond just now of laughing at the late Senator Taft's phrase "creeping socialism," There is more than one sort of laughter; whether or not the damned cry, I am sure they laugh; and it is altogether possible that some of these humorists may laugh in a different key, thirty years from now, I certainly hope not, for people of my cast of thought would almost certainly have been exterminated by that time, in the course of events.

There *is* such a thing as "creeping socialism"; and the worst of it is that socialism never ceases to creep until it becomes totalitarianism, nor can it, in its nature. Though I do not agree with Herbert Spencer in many things, he knew whereof he spoke when he wrote, "Socialism is slavery, and the slavery will not be mild." Most socialists today are gentle and benevolent people, with less than the normal share of the lust for power. But it is not men of this breed who manage the New Order, when it arrives in all its fullness: they are lucky, indeed, if they are merely ignored; ordinarily they are among the first to be marked out for elimination. Their function has been to undermine every political and economic element of the old order, always with the best humanitarian intentions; that done, O'Brien and his associates take office.

This, therefore, is the process which is liable to make an end of American society as we know it, unless intelligent conservatives begin to oppose it effectually. Power will be released from its bonds by the decay of the old moral and institutional barriers to *pleonexia.* Religious faith, which through its inculcation of humility and resignation has made men ashamed of their appetite for power, may degenerate among us into mere humanitarianism, devoid of any spiritual sanction; and the pure humanitarian is no better than a man halfway down the road to pure egoism. Private property and ability may be so weakened by the fiscal requirements of the humanitarian state that the burden becomes unbearable, and the state has to assume control of the whole system of production. Constitutional provisions for the checking and balancing of political authority may be so nullified by judicial decisions and legislative infringements that we are left with a simple "plebiscitary democracy," in which the executive of a unitary state (preserving, it may be, some superficial vestiges of local governments and representative assemblies), elected nominally by the masses but actually brought to office and kept there by the publicist and the manipulator, is compelled to make all the decisions for everyone—and must, in the circumstances, make most decisions imprudently.

All this accomplished, the picture of the Republic will indeed be faded nearly out of recognition, and the men who used to be nurtured by the Republic no longer will be found; and power will be the prerogative of the new elite, the planners and managers and police-officials. These planners and managers and police-officials will not be the same mild-tempered persons most of them are now; for power intoxicates; and the public servant of a constitutional republic is a very different man from the public master of a total state. If you have happened to observe in action some stupid and callous policeman on one of our metropolitan forces—such policemen, providentially, are still in the minority, of course—accustomed to deal with ignorant or criminal people, you will have a notion of this new elite.

And all of this will have come to pass in a public fit of absence of mind, in which nearly everyone who had any part in the process acted with the best of intentions. It will not have been the Conspirators who will have done the mischief; it will have been the Humanitarians, who will have gone about their business with such phrases as the Dignity of Man (a purely secular Dignity, naturally) and the Inviolability of Civil Rights forever in their mouths.

A conservative may very well be in favor of a great variety of forms of local paternalism, and I hope that most conservatives are. But let me italicize the word *local*. The further charity is removed from the donors, the less charitable it becomes; the further authority is removed from local communities, the less democratic it becomes;

the further the constitutional delimitation of powers is ignored, the more menacing the centralized state becomes. If for want of a nail the shoe was lost, and the horse, and the battle, it is quite as true that a minor program of the kindliest designs may open the way to a regime of altogether another complexion. I am aware that I run the risk here of sinking ignominiously into bathos. But I am fortified by a remark of Unamuno's in *The Tragic Sense of Life:*

> The greatest height of heroism to which an individual, like a people, can attain is to know how to face ridicule; better still to know how to make oneself ridiculous and not to shrink from the ridicule.... For it was by making himself ridiculous that Don Quixote achieved his immortality.... Cournot said, "It is best not to speak to either princes or people of the probabilities of death; princes will punish this temerity with disgrace; the public will revenge itself with ridicule." True, and therefore it is said that we must live as the age lives. *Corrumpere et corrumpi saeculum vocatur.*

It is my hope that conservatives will not be afraid of the public's ridicule, for the public's sake. The conservative, in our time, must be prepared for the role of Don Quixote. Surely it will seem impossibly old-fashioned to talk of checks and balances; surely the phrase "states' rights" will summon up roars of laughter; surely any objection to consolidation will be met with jovial references to "horse-and-buggy days." But just as surely, if the conservatives do not have the hardihood to endure such ridicule, the time will come—and that perhaps within a single generation—when it will be not only ridiculous, but quite futile, to talk of "personal freedom," "the rule of law," and "the dignity of the human person." I think, in plain words, that the conservatives of the present decade, and the next, and the next after that, must stand firm against centralization, specious legislation that offers to substitute a passing "security" for a prescriptive liberty, and the conversion of representative government into plebiscitary absolutism.

And now a few words concerning power among the nations. It is ours already; and we have done with it what men always have done with pure power: we have employed it abominably. I do not say that the Nazis or the Japanese militarists would have employed it to better advantage, or that the Communists would use it mercifully; on the contrary, I am certain that, to the best of their ability, they would have striven to accomplish still greater mischief. But that does not excuse us. The learning of physical science, and the perfection of technology, instead of being put to the improvement of Reason, have been applied by modern man to achieve mastery over nature and humanity; and that mastery has been brutal. We Americans happened to be first in the race for the acquisition of the tools of mass-slaughter, and we used those tools as the Roman used his sword and his catapult against Carthage.

We might like to forget the circumstances of our triumph over Japan, as doubtless there were Romans who, once the heat of the fight was past, would have preferred to forget the storm of the citadel. But in the history of nations, as in the lives of men, there are things done that cannot be forgot. Penance may be undertaken, and, by the grace of God, true contrition may be experienced; yet the recollection will not fade, and, though others may forgive us, we cannot forgive ourselves. The act *per se,* even the instant obliteration of great cities, though shocking enough, is not so unforgivable as the motive. What was our motive at Hiroshima and Nagasaki, in a country already pleading to surrender? We try to tell ourselves it was to "save American lives"; but in our hearts we know that if our primary concern really had been for American lives, we would not have prolonged the war in Germany by our insistence upon unconditional surrender; perhaps, after all, our primary concern ought not to be for our own lives, but for justice and mercy under God. If our primary concern had been for our own lives, we would not have gone to war at all.

In plain fact, our motives for destroying Hiroshima and Nagasaki were mixed, but chief among them seem to have been these three: a desire, based upon sheer expediency, to overawe the Russians; an unhallowed appetite for vengeance; and the ferocious intoxication of pure power. I say these things not out of any desire to revive dead grudges, but to emphasize that we Americans now are face to face with the problem of power; we are looking upon the stony countenance of Medusa. After all our humanitarian bragging, in the course of the war, we behaved precisely as we accused our enemies of behaving. I am afraid that we must confess, now, that Americans have no peculiar exemption from Sin, as a people, and that pure power, in our hands, is as dreadful as pure power in the hands of any other nation.

As to what can be done to hedge about this new form of power with restrictions, the conservatives cannot possibly offer any easy answers. We are not going to find ourselves led, of a sudden, by philosopher-kings, and I should not trust even Marcus Aurelius or Alfred the Great with pure power—they, indeed, would have been horrified at having such a trust forced upon them. What the conservative can do is to seek for means to prevent the employment of this power by any tight little circle of men who might judge it expedient to annihilate some obdurate opponents, the end justifying the means. A handful of individuals, some of them quite unused to moral responsibilities on such a scale, made it their business to extirpate the populations of Nagasaki and Hiroshima; we must make it our business to curtail the possibility of such snap decisions, taken simply on the assumptions of worldly wisdom.[2] And the conservative can urge upon his nation a policy of patience and prudence. A "preventive" war, whether or not it might be successful in the field—and that is a question much in doubt—would be morally ruinous to us. There are circumstances under which it is not only more honorable to lose than to win, but quite truly less harmful, in the ultimate providence of God.

Probably it is a disguised blessing that we no longer have the awful sole responsibility for attempting to confine this new means of pure power we have unchained. In the whole realm of our relations with the Soviets, with which subject the problem of external power is now inseparably joined, conservatives ought to summon up their old acquaintance with real human character, as distinguished from radical abstractions of human nature, and accordingly remind the nation that Russians, like all other human beings, are interested in self-preservation, and that the fanaticism of early revolutionary

---

2. The target originally selected for the first atomic bomb, I am told, was Kyoto, a city of no military significance, but artistically to Japan what Florence and Venice combined are to Italy, and the seat of Japanese traditional learning. The chances of the weather caused the designation, instead, of two industrial cities. Probably nothing could suggest better than this the hostility of pure power to all the arts of civilization.

aspiration ordinarily is much moderated after four decades, and may be made to see reason, if reason is backed by quiet strength.

In working for a concert of the nations, the conservative in America ought to bear in mind the principles of liberty under law that are his own peculiar heritage, and the tactics of prudence which are his inherited method. He will look upon the United Nations Organization, for instance, as an opportunity for reasonable consultation and for applying some ethical standard to the conduct of international affairs; but he will not entertain extravagant hopes of a wisdom more than mundane issuing from the collective deliberations of that body. He will not be over-impressed by talk of a supranational authority administering impartial justice and establishing the terrestrial paradise; for he knows that the whole is no greater than the sum of its parts, and if no nation has yet achieved perfect justice and security and freedom within its boundaries, no new-born world state is going to do anything of the sort.

Improvement in nations, as in men, must come from within, for the greater part. He will not be led into fallacious comparisons of a projected world-federation with the federal union of the thirteen original states, for he knows that the American system was the product of a common history, common interests, common language, and common political and social institutions, not of sudden abstract inspiration. And he will take care not to sacrifice the present very real rights of Americans for some airily speculative future rights of Man, as expressed in that fantastic document called the Universal Declaration of Human Rights.

It is Shakespeare who tells us that when order is dethroned, "then everything includes itself in power, power into will, will into appetite." The conservative, believing that not goodwill unaided can put a check upon power, defends that just order in society which puts laws above men and prescriptive rights above present expediency. At present, this problem of power is not merely a question of social well-being, but unmistakably a question of the survival of civilization, or even the survival of human life as a whole. The conservative, however oppressed by this responsibility, brings to it a cast of mind far better suited for the task than the disintegrating optimism of liberals and radicals.

The Problem of Loyalty

A FAITHFUL MAN is not of necessity a loyal one. To produce loyalty, love must be added to fidelity. In some sense, then, the insistence upon "loyalty oaths" and fervent professions of patriotism is a part of that degradation of words which constitutes so dismaying a manifestation of the confusion of our times. Loyalty cannot be forced, any more than love. The patriotism which is the product of fear or of self-interest is truly the last refuge of a scoundrel. We may prosecute a man who, having sworn fidelity to the state, breaks his oath; but positive law cannot create loyalty. Most of the eagerness of legislatures and boards of regents in America to exact pledges of conformity from civil servants and professors and teachers is so much lost endeavor. It is simply one aspect of that tendency toward democratic despotism which Tocqueville describes with candor.

The menace of democratic despotism—the silent tyranny of the majority at any given time—never is absent from American life; the complex of defenses against the popular prejudice of the hour which still survive in Britain, for instance, scarcely exist here in the United States. In England, the influence of class distinctions and interests, the remnants of private income, the existence of autonomous bodies like the universities, the discipline of the public schools, and other vestiges of an aristocratic order, continue to exert a check upon popular will which is not felt in America. In democracies, Tocqueville observed, public opinion is like a great wave, sweeping everything before it; and then, rushing back, it demolishes parties and prejudices it had favored before, Democratic opinion is constant only in its passion for conformity. What the masses detest is dissent, rather than any particular system of opinions. Having grown accustomed to the flattery that the people always do right, democracies endanger themselves by their glowering hostility toward that criticism and that lively protest of minorities which keep any nation from stagnation.

I am somewhat amused, accordingly, at the current professions of terror, in many quarters, at "inquisitorial methods" and "witch-hunting" by legislative committees. We are even told that such committees are "undemocratic"; yet nothing could be more democratic, for good or evil, than the proclivity toward searching the consciences of one's neighbors. It is an old American custom. I never happened to relish it; but I find it difficult to accept unquestioningly the sincerity of many of the persons who now cry up the dangers to the Fifth Amendment of a Constitution which formerly they derided as an obsolete eighteenth-century scrap of paper. Committees of Congress and of the state legislatures have been busy for many a year prying into the opinions and conduct of various minorities; but not until the Communists and their sympathizers began to be annoyed by these committees was such a wail of protest raised. I am afraid that much as a part of the present talk about "academic freedom" means no more than freedom for the disciples of John Dewey, so a good deal of the present solicitude for civil liberties means no more than friendliness toward the rights of people who deny the very existence of prescriptive rights. It is well that we should guard jealously our prescriptive liberties; but we ought to guard them consistently, if our motives are to be above reproach. And I am not in the least afraid that the structure of the American republic is seriously endangered by legislative investigations, however badly conducted. Considering the burdens that the United States have assumed in recent years, and the menace of modern warfare, it is a matter for congratulation that the American people and American legislators have been so moderate as they remain today.

No small part of the present commotion about the menace of inquisitorial procedures, indeed, is the product of boredom and of our relish for snatching fearful joys. A great many of us rather like to fancy ourselves bullied, spied upon, and generally menaced. The notion of the Great Conspiracy, so potent for harm among the modern masses, is not confined to the people who dread Communism: it dominates equally, though in a different garb, the imagination of the humanitarian liberal, the "other-directed individual" of some education, a man unconsciously eager to convince himself that he *matters* by crying out that someone is trying to snatch away his rights. Like Humpty Dumpty, he flatters himself with the notion that people are listening at keyholes and peering around corners, sedulous to catch him in some act of noncomformity. Many of the people who talk most glibly about "witch-hunting" conjure up their own witches, really, in an endeavor to forget their private insignificance. Thus in some degree the controversy about loyalty is a symptom of a collective neurosis: something indeed is gravely wrong, but the malady is confounded with the superficial symptom. I think that by far the greater part of what is said and written about loyalty, these days, is the product of hysteria, of special interest, or of a passion for self-assertion. Yet the problem of loyalty, in its more serious aspects, urgently requires rational examination in our present hour of wrath.

Toryism, said Cardinal Newman, is loyalty to persons. What are democrats and liberals loyal to? To the state? To abstract ideas? To the United Nations Organization? Josiah Royce, nearly half a century ago, in *The Philosophy of Loyalty*, endeavored to construct some system of values to which men of the modern age might be loyal; but, as Mr. Daniel Boorstin observes in his recent *Genius of American Politics*, "While his philosophy of loyalty provided an absolutist strongbox for American values, when one opened the box, one found it contained almost nothing; he urged his readers to be loyal to the principle of loyalty." Now in a state professedly Christian, loyalty to the Christian religion might be expected; but the United States have no establishment of religion. Americans do not look up with awe to kings, or with respect to nobility. We talk of loyalty to "Americanism" or "the American way of life"; but those phrases are meaningless, or positively baneful, unless they are attached to particulars. I have not the slightest idea of what "the American way of life," in the abstract, may be. Toward what, then, are American legislative committees, and the bulk of the American people, anxious to secure loyalty?

The opponent of things established in America, or the doctrinaire collectivist, will say that this solicitude for loyalty is no more

than a slogan designed to secure the rich in their present possessions, and the reactionary in their prejudices; but such critics will be
wrong. The concern for loyalty is heart-felt among Americans,
though often its expression may be confused and misdirected.

A conservative impulse, in short, is the power that sustains the
present demand for loyalty. Conservation of what? Not of "democracy," *per se.* What the Americans are zealous to safeguard is a complex of rights and laws far less abstract than idealized democracy.
They demand loyalty, first of all, to the Federal Constitution and the
state constitutions; then they seek to exact fidelity to certain prescriptive institutions and habits which they apprehend with reasonable clarity: private property, liberty under law, freedom of worship,
a just distribution of political power, and a respect for individual
personality. I do not mean that many Americans can state this concept of loyalty; of course they cannot; no people are generally glib at
expounding their own first principles. But they know well enough,
for all that, what they dread in collectivistic designs for social alteration, and to what ethical and social standards they would have us
repair in our present discontents. The great majority of Americans
have very little understanding of, or sympathy with, the Universal
Declaration of Human Rights of the United Nations; it is not loyalty
toward abstractions which they seek; they are zealous, rather, for
loyalty toward the prescriptive values of American society.

This is not a loyalty to be derided. If this loyalty is denied, indeed,
the impulse behind it will become a dangerous power; for loyalty
lives upon love; and as love, perverted, becomes lust, so loyalty,
frustrated, becomes fierce intolerance. If already certain ugly and
ominous tendencies may be discerned in the American insistence
upon "loyalty," I suspect that these are the consequence of the
mocking of loyalty, among many of the illuminati, for some years
past, and of a growing realization that many persons endowed by
the public with high responsibilities had lost all idea of what loyalty
to a nation's traditions really amounts to. A popular impression
exists that a national leadership which could entrust Mr. Alger Hiss
with state secrets, and make Mr. Owen Lattimore its unofficial con-
sultant upon Oriental policy, was badly confused as to the nature of
loyalty; and a great part of the American public is inclined to

believe, also, that many persons still influential in the conduct of national affairs have not succeeded wholly in clarifying their understanding of such matters. Both these popular opinions have ample justification.

Any ordered society has a right to protect its own existence; and, if the choice must be made, that right of society transcends the lesser right of individuals to follow their own humor or to tamper with existing institutions after some predilection of their own. A people have the right, in consequence, to expect that their officers shall obey the established laws of the land, and that their professors and teachers shall not preach subversion, and that liberty of expression shall not be allowed to degenerate into license. A nation so "liberal" that it cannot bring itself to repress the fanatic and the energumen, under any circumstances, soon will be reduced to a condition thoroughly illiberal. A nation unable to formulate any principle of loyalty, or unable to distinguish valuable criticism from irresponsible sedition, is thoroughly decadent. There is truly a reality in national loyalty; men long to be loyal to something greater than themselves; and if we refuse to admit the very principle and necessity of loyalty, very soon we shall be confronted by anarchy or tyranny. The question before thinking men is not whether loyalty ought to be expected of the citizen, but rather of how loyalty may be defined, and of how a reasonable degree of loyal acquiescence may be distinguished from the corruption of servile conformity to democratic despotism. It is pointless to ask whether legislatures have a *right* to inquire into the loyalty of public servants and even private persons; of course they have such a right. The real realm of discussion ought to be the definition of what true loyalty is, and the delimitation of the bounds within which legislative committees may prudently take action.

We are silly if we expect loyalty to a nation's traditions to be the product of untutored feelings. More than most other crimes, treason is the consequence of a failure of understanding, rather than of a heart consummately evil. Some people refused to believe in the guilt of Mr. Alger Hiss because he was happily married, and had decent manners; Lord Jowitt even thought that his responsible position was *per se* proof that he could not be disloyal. The mind and heart of a traitor are not ordinarily the mind and heart of a pickpocket, however. In some considerable part, surely, Hiss' failing was a failure of reason, the belief (not uncommon among sentimental humanitarians) that loyalty toward some new world order transcends all traditional loyalties. We ought neither to confound the crime of treason with the crime of violence, nor to refrain from punishing disloyalty when it is committed by "nice" people. Burke, in his "Letter to the Sheriffs of Bristol" (1777), touched upon the danger of confounding treason with piracy; this is "confounding, not only the natural distinction of things, but the order of crimes, which, whether by putting them from a higher part of the scale to the lower, or from the lower to the higher, is never done without dangerously disordering the whole frame of jurisprudence." Loyalty is not determined by whether men "meant well," or by the degree of disinterestedness of the men in question. Here, as in so many other respects, the urgent necessity for Americans is to define their terms. The greatest and most dangerous traitor may be an abstracted visionary, nearly selfless.

Now Americans usually have been sufficiently broad-minded about the matter of loyalty; we are not accustomed to compulsory oaths and test acts. It is the peril of the present hour, when betrayal of scientific and military secrets may mean national destruction, which has brought us face to face with the grim nature of the problem of loyalty. The zealots for absolute freedom of opinion and action (by which they commonly mean absolute freedom for "liberals" of their own kind) might do well to remind themselves that there is something even more precious than absolute liberty, and that is absolute survival. Congress and the state legislatures, as the representatives of popular sovereignty, have not only the right of inquiring into the loyalty of persons in high or responsible station, but the absolute duty of concerning themselves with such matters. Often such investigations by legislative committees have been badly conducted; and that is scarcely surprising, for the responsibilities of legislators are so numerous, nowadays that they have time to do nothing really well. For all that, anyone who believes in popular government cannot logically deny the authority of such committees to function. Sometimes such investigations have exceeded their lawful scope, and sometimes the language and conduct of investigators has exceeded the bounds of decorum and even justice. Yet though we ought to be jealous of our liberties, and of the honor of our legislative bodies, nevertheless we ought to guard with equal vigilance against irresponsible abuse of legislatures and fatuous remonstrance about matters we know only through newspaper headlines and gossip columns.

"To make us to love our country," Burke says, "our country ought to be lovely." The triumph of a true loyalty, after all, will not be decided by the activities of Congressional committees; if loyalty loses ground in men's hearts, all the positive law in the world will not save a nation. Loyalty, I repeat, is the product of love. We cannot be loyal to a thing that is morally ugly or unjust. The disloyalty which all the Western nations experienced to their cost during the past generation, that disloyalty which grew out of the defecated intellectuals' defection to a god that failed, can be atoned for only by a tender attention to the qualities which make a society lovable. The effective conservatives of the rising generation, then, must be the poet and the philosopher, the artist and the builder; that loyalty of spirit which nurtures patriotism will be revived, if revived at all, not in government offices, but among men of spirit and intellect. The present interlude of "loyalty checks" we ought to look upon as a mere interim, however distasteful, between an era of doubt and an era of renewed faith. And I think, with Burke, that before we can love humanity, or even the nation, we must "learn to love the little platoon we belong to in society." Loyalty grows out of the family and out of local associations; it is no abstraction of ideology. Men who would sever society from its traditional roots, out of a lust for abstract efficiency or equality, destroy the sources of that loyalty which, teaching us a principle superior to self-gratification, keeps the knife from our throat.

"There ought to be a system of manners in every nation which a well-formed mind would be disposed to relish": this sentence Burke prefaces to his observations on the love of country. Well, the traditional system of manners is much decayed nowadays throughout Western society, and particularly in America; and as for loveliness, Western civilization, since Burke's age, seems to have been intent upon one of the principal studies in the curriculum of Alice's Mock

Turtle, Uglification. "I have always been of the mind that in a democracy manners are the only effective weapon against the Bowie-knife," James Russell Lowell observes in one of his letters, "the only thing that will save us from barbarism." Manners, and the visible loveliness of a society in which taste and feeling have their due, are a cement of loyalty.

Now it would be laborious and painful to recite here a catalog of the incivility of our age; nor would it be useful, for we see all about us, every day, that disheartening contempt for station, and age, and sex, and character, which is a degradation of the democratic dogma. We see it in the Capitol at Washington, and we see it on every city bus. "One man is as good as another, or maybe a little better": this presumption, induced by the decay of liberal education, the gutter press, and the diminished influence of the religious concepts of hierarchy and veneration, ultimately may overthrow both republican government and the complex technological achievement of modern civilization. Instead of endeavoring to make most men into gentlemen, we have been intent upon reducing any surviving gentlemen to the condition and manners of proletarians. Dr. Johnson did not recognize the word "civilization" as legitimate English: "civility," he told Boswell, was the proper term to describe a high civil social order. In its traditional usage, "civility" imports both the idea of citizenship and the state of being civilized, as well as good breeding and courtesy. Once the kind of civility represented by manners is cast aside, the responsibilities of citizenship and the very foundation of civilized existence are in peril. Similarly, the words "generosity" and "generation" come from the same root; and when a society has treated with contempt the chivalric idea of high breeding, then the very life of that society, the process of its generation, is threatened.

> "I know the Table Round, my friends of old;
> All brave, and many generous, and some chaste."

Mannerless nations, incivil societies, end in servility to some strong brute who does not require the trappings of a moral imagination; and peoples without respect for generous hearts presently lose even the love for giving life to the next generation, and make some Alfred Kinsey the dreary keeper of their conscience.

The beauty of manners which a well-informed mind is disposed to cherish—this is a form of beauty which is withering even as we describe it; and as it withers, the higher loyalty to our country is correspondingly weakened. And I believe that the other chief visible sign of a country's loveliness—its physical being, its scenery, architecture, art, and pattern of town and country—is desperately sick among us. The triumph of the mass-mind in the realm of art is in part the consequence of certain powerful causes which also crushed or distorted the traditional framework of society; and the revolt of the masses is in part itself the cause of the degradation of a country's beauty. The industrial revolution, for instance, created the modern industrial masses; it also overwhelmed those established artistic skills and handicrafts which were joined to traditional art, and substituted new patterns of life and new methods of design for the prescriptive framework of the arts. These causes and consequences are too intricate for any adequate description here. To put the matter briefly, I think that since Burke wrote we have seen a progressive degeneration of the arts and the very physical aspect of most modern states.

One may see the process being completed by the wreckers' bulldozers almost anywhere in Britain, nowadays; and as for America, the spectacle of the devastation of our country's loveliness is so gigantic as almost to defy description. I find it curious to reflect that Harriet Martineau once remarked that Milton must have been thinking of southern Michigan when he wrote the garden parts of *Paradise Lost.* In southern Michigan (where I was born) the process of alteration now rushes on at vertiginous speed. We sweep away our trees, our hills, our very churches, out of our passion for unchecked motion. An infatuation with haste is one of the marks of a profound social boredom; and this is stamped upon our character. No consideration prevails against the lust for speed. We are about to embellish the Upper Peninsula of Michigan with mile on mile of hot-dog stands and motels, so effacing the very reason why people used to come to the Upper Peninsula—that is, for the unspoilt character of the country. The endeavors of our recently-founded National Trust to preserve our old buildings are insignificant in comparison with the furious energy of the traffic engineer and the tasteless entrepreneur. No people in all history have been so insensitive to ugliness as are we Americans today, making our roads hideous with billboards and our magazines hideous with vulgarity. There has been some improvement of domestic architecture among us, if we compare our present standards with those of 1910 or 1920; but this amelioration has been offset by the spreading blight of jerry-built little houses thrusting into the countryside from every town, as if we were determined to realize one of Karl Marx's fondest dreams, that town and country should merge in one amorphous blur. One of the dreariest experiences a man of some taste can have is to drive along a road in Michigan, say, or Tennessee, dotted with grotesque shacks and juke-joints and motels, blotting out the natural charm of what once was handsome country; and nothing is better calculated to stimulate reflections on how the decay of taste and the decay of the traditional framework of society are joined.

Nor is vulgarity confined to the classes vulgar in the old sense, in our society. A glance at the architecture of most American universities ought to suggest to any reasonable observer that taste is nearly dead at the top of our society, as well as at the bottom. Most recent building at our institutions of higher learning is monstrous; it is not "modern," and not "traditional"; certainly it almost never is "functional." The university may have a well-endowed school of architecture, with a complex hierarchy of professors; but the proof of the pudding is in the buildings the university erects; and, with a very few exceptions, that proof informs us that our professors of architecture are quacks: they have neither taste nor technical skill. "Administration" buildings look like factories, but are less efficient than the most decrepit little office tucked away in some Oxford quadrangle; classroom buildings have corridors too narrow to let the students into their rooms without interminable queuing, and the rooms themselves are cursed with bad proportions and overheating; chapels look as if they were designed by the League of Militant Atheists, to make a mockery of religion. I touch upon these matters because they suggest how thoroughly the decay of taste and skill has worked its way upward among us, as well as downward. The only considerable accomplishment of the modern age in building is in steel-and-concrete construction; but that is the work of the engineer, really, not of the architect; and ordinarily it is quite indifferent to beauty.

Probably it is not possible—to employ a phrase of Chesterton's—to "rouse a great wild forest passion in a little Cockney heart." Though the average countryman and the average townsman in our time suffer from a pronounced degradation of taste, still the average man never has had much of an eye for beauty. In former times, however, the average man felt some degree of respect for fine buildings and scenes because he endeavored to copy the taste of his superiors; he deferred to their aesthetic judgment. Now he has lost the quality of deference, or perhaps has lost any true superiors. Sir Osbert Sitwell tells us that there is no such thing as folk-art, and no such thing as folk-costume: these are simply imitations, commonly delayed in time, of the art and dress of the upper classes. Lord Raglan insists that there really is no such thing as folklore: the traditional tales of a people are simply the popularized versions of stories which had their origin among the aristocracy. So it is with the sense of beauty. We are foolish if we expect to summon forth a native and untutored love of beautiful things from the vulgar heart; appreciation of natural and artistic beauty is the fruit of long study and discipline; and if the classes which encouraged that study and that discipline are depressed, or if they neglect their old function of forming the taste of a nation, then surely the mass of the people will be indifferent, or perhaps hostile, to the charm of nature and the charm of art.

Tocqueville, in the second part of *Democracy in America*, predicts that in a classless society, dedicated to economic equalitarianism, and indifferent to traditional freedom, the arts must perish, as much else perishes under democratic despotism:

> Not only would a democratic people of this kind show neither aptitude nor taste for science, literature, or art, but it would probably never arrive at the possession of them. The law of descent would of itself provide for the destruction of large fortunes at each succeeding generation, and no new fortunes would be acquired. The poor man, without either knowledge or freedom, would not so much as conceive the idea of raising himself to wealth; and the rich man would allow himself to be degraded to poverty, without a

notion of self-defense. Between these two members of the community complete and invincible equality would soon be established. No one would then have time or taste to devote himself to the pursuits or pleasures of the intellect, but all men would remain paralyzed in a state of common ignorance and equal servitude.

When I conceive a democratic society of this kind, I fancy myself in one of those low, dose, and gloomy abodes where the light which breaks in from without soon faints and fades away. A sudden heaviness overpowers me, and I grope through the surrounding darkness to find an opening that will restore me to the air and the light of day.

Tocqueville proceeds to point out that the only security against the coming of such a regime, the death of all art, is the preservation of the rights of property, the rights of bequest and inheritance, and the traditional liberties of persons, in democratic society—in short, the exertion of constitutional and moral checks upon the leveling appetite. He also observes that a number of very large fortunes is more beneficial to the arts and the welfare of a community generally than is a greater number of modest fortunes; for the millionaire can afford to patronize the arts on a large scale, or to undertake enterprises of an enduring and noble character, while the Man with only modest wealth does not have sufficient surplus to achieve any work of much beauty or permanence.

Now I think that in the English-speaking nations we have come very close to the classless and tasteless society which Tocqueville dreaded, and that chiefly within the present century. We still have men of wealth; but their prospect of conveying their fortunes to their descendants is terribly diminished; and, as their consideration and influence have been injured by the levelling temper of the time, they have lost proportionately their own sense of duty toward the arts and a high culture.

Privilege, in any society, is the reward of duties performed; and the guardianship of culture being one of the chief duties of any leading class, it is not surprising that when rich men cease to be patrons of arts and letters, presently they cease to be rich. Yet in our time, perhaps, the leading classes have been as much deprived of their responsibilities as they have been derelict in their fulfillment.

A society intent upon employing the power of positive law to force existence down to an equalitarian Dead Sea will destroy beauty as it destroys inequality. Some friends of the planned economy talk hopefully of a future in which state subsidies, or the surviving funds of great impersonal foundations, will undertake the patronage of arts and letters. I am unable to share their optimism: the record of the state and the foundation as patrons, thus far, is not heartening; the millionaires themselves did better.

I suggest, therefore, that if we love beauty, we will be wise not to destroy those classes, and that pattern of society, which support the unbought grace of life. The rich man often has failed to do what he ought for the life of art and the life of the mind; yet the failure of the commissar would be infinitely more lamentable. To recur to my example of architecture and town-planning, the outward aspect of life under a collectivistic state, devoid of all the complexity and variety of traditional existence, would be a hideous monotony. In the monolithic hive-building of Le Corbusier at Marseilles, in the lofty wastes of Stuyvesant Town, in the dreary streets of the British New Towns, in the cartoon by Mr. Osbert Lancaster called "The Drayneflete of the Future," we behold the hulk of this architecture, and the spirit which would brood over the unfortunate beings condemned to inhabit these barracks. If Gothic architecture was the highest achievement of man in the arts, surely this architecture of the future (despite all the perfection of technology which it represents) is the lowest, lower than the log-cabin or the igloo or the hogan; and the men and women who submitted to this new order would have forgotten altogether the unbought grace of life.

All this may seem remote from the problem of loyalty; but it is not. Loyalty to a nation comes in part from the appreciation of intangible values: equal justice under law, security of life and property, a common religious faith, a common literature of elevation, the knowledge of a great history. These things, I believe, are even more important than manners and beauty. But these intangibles commonly are taken for granted by most people; only a small minority really are aware that justice and freedom and order are not the gifts of nature, like sun and rain, but are the product of tradition and of the strenuous effort of our ancestors. Wrong though they may be, most people tend to judge their society not by its intangible qualities, but by its immediate influence upon their own temper. I have chosen, therefore, to emphasize the qualities of loveliness which encourage loyalty to a nation, because almost no one else is saying anything about these, and because they more directly influence popular opinion, even though the people who are so influenced may be unaware of the source of their prejudices.

"To make us love our country, our country ought to be lovely." Is it possible to love the gritty squalor of the Black Belt of Chicago, or Main Street in Los Angeles? Conceivably; but it is wiser not to put that strain upon loyalty. The better natures among us, surely, will be hard put to it to love America if it becomes a nation wholly mannerless, an incivil society, in which "tough-mindedness" is praised as a cardinal virtue, in which generosity and charity are scorned as weakness, in which all great literature, and the whole stock of a moral imagination, is rejected out of a lust for the gratification of carnal appetites and a taste for second-hand narrations of violence and concupiscence. The conservative of reflection will not be afraid to defend the manners and the tastes of a gentle and generous nature, in this industrial age.

With similar resolution, the thinking conservative will struggle to preserve the face of his country from disfigurement, and the character of his cities from proletarian hideousness. Whenever a project for material change is put forward, he will ask first of all not the question, "Is there money in it for us?", but "Will it make men love their country?" He knows that money is made for men, not men for money; he knows that men work and fight for a country which appeals to their hearts, rather than their pocketbooks. In reconciling necessary change with the elements that hold men's loyalties, he will put the considerations that pertain to traditional living first, and the considerations that pertain to material aggrandizement second. Such choices will arise with great frequency in the next few years, and it is time conservatives began to face them frankly. One instance: I am told that the authorities of the Port of Detroit, by way of preparation for the coming of the St. Lawrence Seaway, have requested that the whole American side of the Detroit River, from Toledo up to Detroit, be devoted to docks and warehouses and factories and railway yards, and that the appropriate political agencies condemn a wide strip the entire length of the river, accordingly. This is the pure Utilitarian mind at work. Production is the only important task of life, and Profit the only important end. The conservative thinks otherwise. When the conservative turns planner, his impulse is not to drive men out of their accustomed ways of life, but to reconcile economic change with all the amenities and decencies of traditional existence; and when he is told that some great new development is underway, he does not exult, "How rich we shall get!" but inquires, "Can money pay for this break with beauty and tradition?"

For that reason, the conservative distrusts the typical social planner, trained in Benthamite methods, blind to individuality and true order, intent only upon Efficiency and Simplicity. Our cities and the whole face of our country urgently require restoration and improvement, and the conservative is going to have to undertake that duty, unless he is ready to let it go to the Utilitarian by default. But when he turns his hand to prudent reform, the conservative remembers that the reform ought to be the voluntary work of the people concerned in it; that it ought to be a local undertaking, so far as possible, not a centralized Grand Design; that its object is to keep men human, not to make them into units for efficient industrial production; that individuality, not collectivism, ought to govern the architectural and social features of such a reform. The face of any civilized country comes to resemble the minds of the people who inhabit it; the country dominated by avarice and compulsion will tend to be ugly, but the country inspired by charity and love will tend to be beautiful.

To put the whole matter with the greatest possible conciseness, loyalty toward the nation, like the love of man for woman, cannot be forced. When we find disloyalty widespread, we must suppress it for the time being, of course; but suppression alone will not suffice. On the face of things, we will do well to suspect that there is something ailing with the heart of a society in which loyalty-investigations are a recurring phenomenon; and conservatives will seek to make the nation lovable for all the better natures, in ways tangible and intangible, in the equal administration of the laws and in the physical pattern of life. We will not baffle the Soviets by imitating them, either in security-methods or in the conversion of society into a machine for production. All the strength of Russia was insufficient to subdue little Finland, for the Finns loved their country. Such a love is not bought by high wages and chromium gadgets; it grows out of loyalties to a nation's traditions, and contentment with a nation's present.

The Problem of Tradition

Everyone seems to have a hankering after tradition nowadays—
especially the people who denounce most things established in
moral and politics. These gentlemen sometimes cry up the "real
American tradition," which they take to be composed of a biting
secularism, a carping egalitarianism, and a Rousseauistic notion of
democracy. I disagree. I think that America has room aplenty for a
variety of traditions; diversity and freedom of choice, indeed, are
real American traditions. And I do not think that there is anything
like a Marxist tradition embedded in American hearts and ways.
Therefore I think it worth the trouble to write something here
about what the word "tradition" means.

Formerly the word meant *oral* communication, as distinguished
from books or documents; in the twentieth century, however, "tradition" is widely employed to signify, also, prescriptive wisdom
expressed in literature. The Latin verb *tradere*, meaning to "hand
down" or "hand over" is the root of our word. In common usage,
tradition implies the spiritual and cultural inheritance which the
existing generation has received from earlier generations. It implies
acceptance, preservation, and passing on. Tradition gives permanence to customs and ideas; it confers upon change the element of
continuity, keeping the alteration of society in a regular train. Everything which the living possess has roots in the spiritual and intellectual achievements of the past. Everything man has—his body, his
mind, his social order—is in very large part an inheritance from
men long dead. The passage of time brings into existence new
acquisitions; but unless men know the past, they are unable to
understand the distinction between what is permanent and what is
transient in their lives. Man is always beset by questions, of which

215

the greatest is the question of his own existence. He cannot even begin to think about his existence and lesser questions until he has acquired the command of means that come to him from the past, such as the names which people customarily use with reference to modes of being and acting. Man inherits a physical world, a biological world, and a cultural world. Tradition is principally concerned with his cultural world—which, nevertheless, is closely joined to his physical and biological worlds. Tradition is the means by which man comes to understand the principles of his own nature and of society; it joins the individual with the generations which are dead and the generations which are yet to be born, the unity which Burke called "the contract of external society." Tradition, in short, is a way of preserving the wisdom of our ancestors and a means by which we can give some significance and application to our own private reason.

The importance of tradition to the individual and society has been recognized by philosophers in every age. Cicero, in his *Republic* and his *Offices*, shows how the Roman commonwealth was dependent upon custom and inherited belief for justice, order, and freedom. Fulbert of Chartres, in the eleventh century, observed that "We are dwarfs mounted upon the shoulders of giants," able to see so far only because of the stature of the wise men who have preceded us in the development of civilization. The present, in the eyes of the man attached to tradition, is merely a film upon the deep well of the past, an illusory line of demarcation between history and futurity. It is upon the past that the future must be built. Continuity of civilization and human intelligence can be maintained only if the past is conserved through living tradition. The man who respects tradition, then, is not a reckless reformer who would alter society and human nature upon some utopian design, but a thinker who tries to reconcile the best in tradition with the constant necessity for change. Burke said that his model of a statesman was one who combined the disposition to preserve with the ability to reform. A healthy society, he suggested elsewhere, is never wholly old or wholly new, but, like any living thing, is forever casting off its old fabric and acquiring new tissue. Prescription, or tradition, is the means by which this healthy society preserves the wisdom of our ancestors and applies that wisdom to the new problems which it faces.

The Problem of Tradition

The process of growth always involves the process of reform—the process by which the acorn becomes the oak. This process is always at work in human affairs. The problem which thinking men always face is the necessity of distinguishing between necessary and desirable alteration, and unnecessary and undesirable destruction. Tradition is a guide to the permanent qualities in society and thought and private life which need to be preserved, in one form or another, throughout the process of inevitable change.

True progress, improvement, is unthinkable without tradition, as Vazquez de Melia suggests, because progress rests upon addition, not subtraction. Change without reference to tradition runs the risk of aimless alteration for alteration's sake, terminating in anarchy or nihilism. Real progress apparently consists in improvement of private and public morality, private and public intelligence, the increase of justice, order, and freedom, and of those material conditions which contribute to human happiness. It is scarcely possible to judge of what humanity wants, or of what measures are calculated to make men better or happier, without knowledge of what benefits have been gained in the past, and of what mistakes have been made. Tradition is the means by which humanity filters out its mistakes from its progressive discoveries. Every great institution among civilized men seems to have tried to recapture or preserve the values of the past. This is especially true of the Christian Church, sifting the pre-Christian inheritance of Western culture and "baptizing" whatever might be adapted to Christianity.

Tradition works in the sciences, also. The essence of tradition is the preservation of continuity in the midst of change. The modern physical sciences rely continuously on certain abiding principles, despite the fact that modern science is always reviewing, and sometimes revising, those principles in the light of newly-acquired knowledge or theory. A.N. Whitehead, in the first chapter of *Science and the Modern World*, makes some observations on this theme. It is often argued that the essential characteristic of the physical sciences is dependence on weighing, measuring, counting, and the like. Whitehead, however, sees that the essential characteristic is the idea of oneness, of unity, which is a view not far removed from that of the medieval Scholastics. The medieval age was a period of practice in

217

the use of Aristotelian logic, examining its relation to the idea that the truth about the universe is necessarily one truth. The principle upon which Aristotelian logic depends, the principle that Aristotle named as the principle of greatest certainty—the law of contradiction—is the central principle in physical science. This principle, unlike the weighing, counting, and measuring that frequently are regarded as most important in the physical sciences, is basic to all knowledge. It illustrates the idea of identity in continuity, and is dearly joined to the idea of one God, one truth. Thus tradition—the preservation of continuity, the retaining of unifying principle despite the acquisition of new knowledge—operates in the sciences.

Yet there can be error in tradition, and even a tradition made up of errors. Man always is compelled to choose among conflicting traditions, and to sort out from the mass of inherited precept the maxims and customs which truly apply to his present situation in the world. This is a problem which cannot be solved by any hard-and-fast rule. There would be no problem of tradition if men were not in some important senses free. When men let their moral and intellectual freedom sink altogether into desuetude, and rely uncritically upon pure tradition, their society is liable to pass into decay, or at least find itself unable to resist the pressure of livelier societies: such appears to have been a condition in the civilization of ancient Egypt and of Peru. Routine without change, and change without routine, appear to be almost equally perilous.

Yet it does not follow that all traditions are evanescent. At the core of the body of traditions of any society is to be found a number of customs and precepts, described by some as natural law formulated into traditions, which that society ignores at its peril. And, far from being peculiar to a savage or barbarian condition of society, this seems to be especially true of complex civilizations, which are the more dependent upon certain underlying assumptions about man and society, the more complicated their activities become. Some of these traditions appear to be almost universal in essence, although they are formulated in various ways. The Decalogue expresses some of the more important of these, in the Judeo-Christian culture. The distinctions between good acts and evil acts; the duties within the family; the duties toward other men; the relationship between God and man; these concepts ordinarily are defined and maintained in any society by the force of ancient traditions, accepted almost without question from time out of mind. And when they are doubted or denied by the doctrinaire skeptic, any society is in peril of losing these moral sanctions which make the civil social order possible. Whether regarded as revealed truths or as necessary fictions (Polybius, in the Hellenistic world, took the latter view, as have various cultural relativists since his time), the traditions which govern private and social morality are set too close about the heart of a civilization to bear much tampering with. Skeptics like Hume, and rationalists like Voltaire, have acknowledged the necessity for conventions and traditions to make life in society tolerable.

The religious and ethical conviction which, however weakened in some quarters, still governs Western civilization in large part, is composed of Jewish, Greek, Roman, and Christian elements; and it is sanctioned and sheltered by a complex body of traditions. Shorn of tradition, our modern attitude toward the meaning of life would be meagre and feeble. The Christian attitude toward the importance of tradition is suggested in the second epistle of Paul to Timothy, Chapters III and IV: "But continue thou in the things which thou has learned and hast been assured of, knowing of whom thou has learned them. . . . For the time will come when they will not endure sound doctrine; but after their own lusts shall heap to themselves teachers, having itching ears. And they shall turn away their ears from the truth, and shall be turned unto fables." To the Christian, conformity to religious tradition is not superstition, but the part of wisdom; it is the doctrines of presumptuous private rationality and interest that are fables. Tradition, in short, to the religious man, is transcendent truth expressed in the filtered opinions of our ancestors.

The part which revelation has had in the formation of tradition is variously interpreted, according to the credal or philosophical views of various authors and expositors; but it may be remarked here that all great religious traditions have laid claim to divine inspiration for the origin of their system. The Old Testament, in considerable part, is the record of a system of morality being gradually revealed by divine authority to an erring people; from that revelation, tradition took form, so that the lessons of revelation would not be lost with the passing of a generation or two. In the eyes of most Christians, at least until recent years, the hand of Providence at work in the world constituted a continuing revelation, and therefore was refreshing and reaffirming tradition. The cosmogonical and ethical principles of Gautama and of Mohammed, similarly, claimed the authority of special revelation for the establishment of tradition. Nor is the claim that revelation inspired tradition to be dismissed simply upon rational or logical grounds, as the superstition of an unenlightened age. It is difficult, even for the rationalist or the mechanist, to account for the appearance of new ideas among men—especially new moral concepts—except by the occurrence of an act of revelation. The moral advance of a people from a condition of primitive selfishness and brutality to a condition of charity and humane principle is not easily explained as merely the consequence of increasing rationality and enlightened self-interest; while we have several examples of the purported direct revelation of ethical principle, most notably the life of Christ. That something cannot come out of nothing is a fixed principle of Western philosophy; and the claim of tradition to have originated in divine revelation remains perhaps as good an explanation as any that has been offered for the fact of a people's moral enlightenment. As for moral decay, that, from the view of the servant of tradition, is the consequence of a falling away from tradition; or perhaps of an unthinking obedience to the letter, rather than to the spirit, of tradition.

What purported revelations are true, and what are false; whether revelation still is possible in human experience, or whether it has ceased to work among men; whether a new revelation could undo a major tradition, and by what tests such a revelation ought to be judged—these grave questions, and certain others, are not easily answered. But much of life always remains veiled in mystery, and the simple existence of a tradition, accepted for many generations by a people, logically creates a presumption that such a tradition has purpose and significance, unless proof to the contrary is very strong.

Traditions also have been defended upon empirical grounds. That a society seems to have thrived when it obeyed the dictates of tradition, and seems to have suffered when it sought to substitute some new moral or social scheme for prescriptive wisdom—this test has been applied again and again by philosophers and moralists. The decay of tradition is the theme of the Roman satirists and historians: they judge the importance of tradition by the consequences of the disregard of tradition. And this argument is advanced by the Hebrew prophets and the early Christian fathers. Unfortunately for a society which neglects tradition, this proof can be afforded only when the decay of traditional belief has brought society near to catastrophe, if not actually to positive ruin. A society may for a great while appear to be thriving, despite its rejection of tradition, when in reality that society is decaying, and moving toward dissolution; an outward prosperity may mask a cultural and moral decay, the end of which is as sudden as its progress toward disaster has been gradual. The respecter of tradition argues that to abandon tradition—that is, to abandon respect for prescriptive wisdom, that Chesterton calls "the democracy of the dead," the voice of the wise men who have lived in ages past—is to commit a society inevitably to such dissolution.

The lamentations of Jeremiah very frequently are justified by the event, however much a complacent generation may have mocked at the adherents to traditions allegedly outworn. Yet sometimes such lamentations are merely splenetic or misguided, and some traditions actually do wear out each generation is compelled to judge for itself just how far to obey the letter of tradition, and just how far to modify tradition by the admission of salutary change. This faculty of distinguishing between needful and imprudent alteration seems to be granted only to a few persons in each generation. In general, the attitude of the respecter of tradition is that of the far-seeing Lord Falkland, in the English Civil Wars: "When it is not necessary to change, it is necessary *not* to change." The fact that humanity has gotten along tolerably well in obedience to a tradition creates a legitimate presumption, in short, in favor of retaining that tradition; the burden of proof rests upon the innovator. Most men and women are good only from habit, or out of deference to the opinions of their neighbors, the friend to tradition argues; and to deprive them of their habits, customs, and precepts, in order to benefit them in some novel way, may leave them morally and socially adrift, more harmed by their loss of ethical sanctions than helped by the fancied new benefit.

Tradition cannot suffice to guide a society, nevertheless, if it is not understood and expounded and, if need be, modified by the better intelligences and consciences in every generation. It is not possible for the living to see with the eyes of the dead. Whatever wisdom exists in any generation is, in a sense, born with that generation; and that generation's wisdom seeks sustenance in tradition, but cannot be kept alive merely by tradition.

Wisdom has to be born over and over again; tradition is the element of continuity which enables each generation's wisdom to profit from the wisdom of preceding generations. The past exists only in the living; yet whether the living are aware of it or not, most of their experience and their apprehension of their own experience is determined by their legacy from the past. This is a condition peculiar to man. The vegetable, unaware of its inheritance, is unable to use its inheritance for its own improvement. Man cannot be like the vegetable, for he has reason, conscience, and consciousness, and he inherits an awareness of his ancestors. He is either better or worse than a vegetable, and whether he is better or worse depends upon his relationship to the sources of his being. It is tradition which makes it possible for him, short of mystical experience, to know his part in the "contract of eternal society" which joins him to those who are dead and those who are not yet born, and also to a nature that is more than material and more than human.

If tradition sinks into mere unquestioning routine, it digs its own grave; for man then approximates vegetal nature, disavowing reason and conscience as correctors and restorers of tradition. It was one of the most eloquent apologists for tradition, Chateaubriand (in his *Memoires d'outre-tombe*) who lamented "the mania for adhering to the past, a mania which I never cease impugning.... Political stagnation is impossible; it is absolutely necessary to keep pace with human intelligence. Let us respect the majesty of time; let us reverentially contemplate past centuries, rendered sacred by the memory and the footsteps of our fathers; but let us not try to go back to them, for they no longer possess a vestige of our real nature, and if we endeavored to seize hold of them, they would fade away." This is the traditionalist of elevation, appealing to his generation to hold by living tradition, but not to be governed by a letter from which the spirit has departed.

The influence of tradition upon the modern world, though weakened by nineteenth-century rationalism and twentieth-century pragmatism, and yet more greatly reduced by the pace of technological change and the increased mobility of population, still is profound; and it might be possible to establish a direct ratio between the decline of order in the twentieth century, and the decline of belief in the truth of tradition. The expectation of change has come to exceed the expectation of continuity in almost the whole of America, even in the physical environment of the civil social existence. And the consequences are disquieting.

A consciousness of our spiritual inheritance, M. Gabriel Marcel writes in *The Decline of Wisdom*, is possible only in an atmosphere of diffuse gratitude: gratitude not merely to the generations that have preceded us in this life, but gratitude toward the eternal order, and the source of that order, which raises man above the brutes, and makes art man's nature. *Pietas*, in short, the veneration of man's sacred associations and of the wisdom of man's ancestors—this spirit survives only in holes and corners of modern society; and for lack of piety, modern men are bored, impatient, and ready enough to subvert the civil social state which is the source of their own material prosperity.

Now "the contract of eternal society," that phrase which describes the concept of social obligation presently decaying among us, is the idea which forms the kernel of Burke's *Reflections*. Society is indeed a contract, Burke says, but not a contract in any mere historical or commercial sense. It is a partnership between those who are living, those who are dead, and those who are yet to be born. It is a contract, too, between God and man, "linking the lower with the higher natures, connecting the visible and invisible worlds, according to a fixed compact sanctioned by the inviolable oath which holds all physical and all moral natures, each in their appointed place." We have no right to break this contract of eternal society; and if we do, we are cast out of this world of love and order into the antagonist world of hate and discord. Burke does not believe that wisdom began with the eighteenth century. He employs the words "contract" and "compact" in their most venerable meaning, the bond between God and man. "I do set my bow in the cloud, and it shall be for a token of a covenant between me and the earth." This is the thirteenth verse of the ninth chapter of the book of Genesis. This contract, this covenant, is the free promise of God, and its terms are obeyed by man in gratitude and in fear. Far from being a grandiloquent transcendence of real meaning, as some of Burke's critics have protested, Burke's employment of "contract" has the sanction of the Bible, the Schoolmen, and the whole body of ethical conviction which carries us back to Job and beyond Job.

Burke, then, spoke with the authority of a profound and practical intellect, not merely with the enthusiasm of an accomplished rhetorician, when he described the great primeval contract of eternal society; and I believe that our modern blindness to the reality of this contract, and to the sobriety of Burke's phrases, has mightily impeded any alleviation of our present discontents, our maladies of spirit and of the body politic. What Burke illuminates here is the necessity to any high and just civilization of a conscious belief in the value of continuity: continuity in religious and ethical conviction, continuity in literature and schooling, continuity in political and economic affairs, continuity in the physical fabric of life. I think we have neglected the principle of continuity to our present grave peril, so that with us, as Aristophanes said of his own generation, "Whirl is king, having overthrown Zeus." Men who do not look backward to their ancestors, Burke remarks elsewhere, will not look forward to their posterity.

If we retain any degree of concern for the future of our race, we need urgently to re-examine the idea of an eternal contract that joins the dead, the living, and those yet unborn. Even if we have lost most of that solicitude for posterity, still we may need to return to the principle of continuity out of simple anxiety for self-preservation. We live in a time when the fountains of the great deep are broken up; half the world has been drowned already, so far as the life of spirit and liberty and liberal learning is concerned; yet we are complacent, many of us, with Cyrus at the very gates. I think that these ideas of Burke's, rather than being vestiges of what Paine called "the

Quixot age of chivalry nonsense," are even more pertinent in our time than they were to his own society.

Burke wrote before the modern proletariat had become a distinct force in society, although even then its dim lineaments could be discerned in England and France. Yet in passage after passage, with his prophetic gift, Burke touches upon the terrible question of how men ignorant of tradition, impatient of any restraint upon appetite, and stripped of true community, may be kept from indulgence in a levelling envy that would fetch down in ruin the highest achievements of mind and spirit, and kept from releasing that congenital violence in fallen human nature which could reduce to ashes the venerable edifice of the civil social state. Once most men should forget the principle of continuity, once they should break the eternal contract, they would be thrown on the meagre resources of private judgment, having run recklessly through the bank and capital that is the wisdom of our ancestors. Under this new-fangled system, "laws are to be supported only by their own terrors, and by the concern which each individual may find in them from his own private speculations, or can spare to them from his own private interests. . . . Nothing is left which engages the affections on the part of the commonwealth. On the principles of this mechanic philosophy, our institutions can never be embodied, if I may use the expression, in persons; so as to create in us love, admiration, or attachment. But that sort of reason which banishes the affections is incapable of filling their place."

For, after all, abstract rationality cannot persuade us to observe the contract of eternal society. It is possible for Reason to persuade us to profit from the wisdom of our ancestors, true enough, even if pure Reason cannot teach us real veneration. But simple rationality, guided by self-interest, never can succeed in inducing us to look forward with solicitude to the interests of posterity. Men who are governed only by an abstract intellectuality will violate their obligations toward their ancestors by the destruction of tradition and the very monuments of the past, since we cannot learn veneration from mere logic; and such men will violate also their obligations toward posterity, for with them immediate appetite always must take precedence over the vague claims of future generations, and immediate appetites, if indulged without restraint, are insatiable in any society, however prosperous. Moreover, these men will snap that connection between the higher and the lower natures which is the sanction of the Eternal Contract, and thus will expose society to that conflagration of will and appetite which is checked, at length, only by force and a master. When men have repudiated the divine element in social institutions, then indeed power is everything.

Why, when all is said, do any of us look to the interest of the rising generation, and to the interest of the generations which shall exist in the remote future? Why do we not exhaust the heritage of the ages, spiritual and material, for our immediate pleasure, and let posterity go hang? So far as simple rationality is concerned, self-interest can advance no argument against the appetite of present possessors. Yet within some of us, a voice that is not the demand of self-interest or pure rationality says that we have no right to give ourselves enjoyment at the expense of our ancestors' memory and our descendants' prospects. We hold our present advantages only in trust. A profound sentiment informs us of this; yet this sentiment, however strong, is not ineradicable. In some ages and in some nations, the consciousness of a sacred continuity has been effaced almost totally. One may trace in the history of the Roman empire the decay of belief in the contract of eternal society, so that fewer and fewer men came to sustain greater and greater burdens; the unbought grace of life shrank until only scattered individuals partook of it—Seneca, Marcus Aurelius, here and there a governor or a scholar to knit together, by straining his every nerve, the torn fabric of community and spiritual continuity; until, at length, those men were too few, and the fresh dedication of Christian faith triumphed too late to redeem the structure of society and the larger part of culture from the ruin that accompanies the indulgence of present appetites in contempt of tradition and futurity.

Respect for the eternal contract is not a mere matter of instinct, then; it is implanted in our consciousness by the experience of the race and by a complex process of education. When the disciplines which impart this respect are imperilled by violence or by a passion for novelty, the spiritual bond which joins the generations and links our nature with the divine nature is correspondingly threatened.

Mr. Christopher Dawson, in his little book *Understanding Europe*, expresses this better than I can:

> Indeed the catastrophes of the last thirty years are not only a sign of the bankruptcy of secular humanism, they also go to show that a completely secularized civilization is inhuman in the absolute sense—hostile to human life and irreconcilable with human nature itself. For . . . the forces of violence and aggressiveness that threaten to destroy our world are the direct result of the starvation and frustration of man's spiritual nature. For a time Western civilization managed to live on the normal tradition of the past, maintained by a kind of sublimated humanitarian idealism. But this was essentially a transitional phenomenon, and as humanism and humanitarianism fade away, we see societies more and more animated by the blind will to power which drives them on to destroy one another and ultimately themselves. Civilization can only be creative and life-giving in the proportion that it is spiritualized. Otherwise the increase of power inevitably increases its power for evil and its destructiveness.

For the breaking of the contract of eternal society does not simply obliterate the wisdom of our ancestors: it commonly converts the future into a living death, also, since progress, beneficent change, is the work of men with a sense of continuity, who look forward to posterity out of love for the legacy of their ancestors and the dictates of an authority more than human. The man who truly understands the past does not detest all change; on the contrary, he welcomes change, as the means of renewing society; but he knows how to keep change in a continuous train, so that we will not lose that sense of gratitude which Marcel describes. As Burke puts it, "We must all obey the great law of change. It is the most powerful law of nature, and the means perhaps of its conservation. All we can do, and, that human wisdom can do, is to provide that the change shall proceed by insensible degrees. This has all the benefits which may be in change, without any of the inconveniences of mutation."

The outward fabric of our world must alter, as do our forms of society; but to demolish all that is old, out of a mere contempt for the past, is to impoverish that human faculty which yearns after continuity and things venerable. By such means of measurement as we possess—by such indices as suicide-rate, the incidence of madness and neurosis, the appetites and tastes of the masses, the obliteration of beauty, the increase of crime, the triumph of force over the law of nations—by these signs, it seems clear, all that complex of high aspiration and imaginative attainment which makes us civilized men is shrinking to a mere shadow of a shadow. If indeed society is governed by an eternal contract, then we may appeal to the Author of that covenant; but words without thoughts to Heaven never go, and the continuity which pertains directly to society must be repaired by those means which still are within the grasp of man.

The eternal contract, the sense of continuity among men, has been made known to succeeding generations, from the dawn of civilization, by the agency of tradition. Tradition is the process of handing on beliefs, not so much through formal schooling, or through books, as through the life of the family and the observances of the church. Until the end of the eighteenth century, no one thought it conceivable that most men could obtain most of their knowledge in any other way than this; and though cheap books and eleemosynary schooling have supplanted to some extent the old functions of traditionary instruction, still tradition remains the principal source of our moral beliefs and our worldly wisdom. Young persons do not acquire in school, to any considerable extent, the sense of continuity and the veneration for the eternal contract which makes possible willing obedience to social order; children acquire this sense from their parents and other elders, and from their gradual introduction to religion, if they obtain any; the process is illative, rather than deliberate. Now let us suppose that parents cease to impart such instruction, or come to regard tradition as superstition; suppose that young people never become acquainted with the church—what happens to tradition? Why, its empire is destroyed, and the young join the crowd of the other-directed whom Mr. David Riesman describes.

In a looser sense, by "tradition" we mean all that body of knowledge which is bound up with prescription and prejudice and authority, the accepted beliefs of a people, as distinguished from "scientific" knowledge; and this, too, is greatly weakened in its influence among the rising generation by a growing contempt for any belief that is not founded upon demonstrable "fact." Almost nothing of importance really can be irrefutably demonstrated by finally ascertained "facts"; but the limitations of science are not apprehended by the throng of the quarter-educated who think themselves emancipated from their spiritual heritage. When we confront these people, we are dealing not merely with persons ignorant of tradition, but actively hostile toward it.

Now cheap books and free schooling are not the principal reasons for this decay of the influence of tradition. The really decisive factors are the industrialization and urbanization of modern life. Tradition thrives where men follow naturally in the ways of their fathers, and live in the same houses, and experience in their own lives that continuity of existence which assures them that the great things in human nature do not much alter from one generation to another. This is the mood of Ecclesiastes. But the tremendous physical and social changes that have come with the later stages of our industrial growth, and the concentration of population in raw new cities, shake men's confidence that things will be with them as they were with their fathers. The sanction of permanence seems to have been dissolved. Men doubt the validity of their own opinions, founded upon tradition, and hesitate to impart them to their children—indeed, they may thrust all this vast obligation upon the unfortunate schoolteacher, and then grow annoyed when the teacher turns out to be incapable of bestowing moral certitude, scientific knowledge, and decent manners upon a class of fifty or sixty bewildered and distracted children. Most natural keepers of tradition, in short, abdicate their function when modern life makes them doubt their own virtue.

Our guardians of tradition have been recruited principally, although not wholly, from our farms and small towns; the incertitude of the cities disturbs the equanimity of the tradition-guided man. And our great cities have been swelling at the expense of our country and village population, so that the immense majority of young people today have no direct acquaintance with the old rural verities. Our reservoir of tradition will be drained dry within a very few decades, if we do not deliberately open up once more the springs of tradition. The size of the United States, and the comparative gradualness of industrial development in many regions, until now saved us from a complete exhaustion of tradition, such as Sweden seems to have experienced. At the beginning of this century, Sweden had seven people in the country for one in the city; now that ratio is precisely inverted; and one may obtain some hint of what the death of tradition means to a people from the fact that the Swedes, previously celebrated for their placidity and old-fashioned heartiness, now have the highest rates of abortion in the world, dismayed at the thought of bringing life into this world or even of enduring one's own life.[1]

I do not want our traditions to run out, because I do not believe that formal indoctrination, or pure rationality, or simple imitation of our contemporaries, can replace traditions. Traditions are the wisdom of the race; they are the only sure instruments of moral instruction; they have about them a solemnity and a mystery that Dr. Dryasdust the cultural anthropologist never can compensate for; and they teach us the solemn veneration of the eternal contract which cannot be imparted by pure reason. Even our political institutions are sustained principally by tradition, rather than by utilitarian expediency. A people who have exhausted their traditions are starved for imagination and devoid of any general assumptions to give coherence to their life.

Yet I do not say that tradition ought to be our only guide, nor that tradition is always beneficent. There have been ages and societies in which tradition, stifling the creative faculty among men, put an end to variety and change, and so oppressed mankind with the boredom of everlasting worship of the past. In a healthy nation, tradition must be balanced by some strong element of curiosity and individ-

---

1. A Scottish friend of mine invites young Swedish connections to his country house every summer; and what interests him most in their behavior is their pleasure at being emancipated from the boredom of the terrestrial paradise called the Third Way. The silent tyranny of democratic conformity, to which they had been always subjected at home, is lifted as soon as they arrive in Fife; at first they are surprised and suspicious, and look about for someone to reprove them for their indulgence of individuality; but once they have grown accustomed to the freedom of a society in which some elements of variety, tradition, and even irrational emotion are not eradicated, they loathe the notion of going home to the superior comforts, the abundant food, and the everlasting monotony of social-democratic Sweden.

ual dissent. Some people who today are conservatives because they protest against the tyranny of neoterism, in another age or nation would be radicals, because they could not endure the tyranny of tradition. It is a question of degree and balance. But I am writing of modern society, especially in the United States; and among us there is not the slightest danger that we shall be crushed beneath the dead weight of tradition; the danger is altogether on the other side. Our modern affliction is the flux of ceaseless change, the repudiation of all enduring values, the agonies of indecision and the social neuroses that come with a questioning of everything in heaven and earth. We are not in the plight of the old Egyptians or Peruvians; it is not prescription which enslaves us, but the lust for innovation. A young novelist, visiting George Santayana in his Roman convent in the last year of the philosopher's life, remarked that he could not endure to live in America, where everything was forever changing and shifting. Santayana replied, with urbane irony, that he supposed if it were not for kaleidoscopic change in America, life there would be unbearable. A people infatuated with novelty presently cannot bear to amble along; but the trouble with this is that the pace becomes vertiginous, and the laws of centrifugal force begin to operate.

I know that there are people who maintain that nothing is seriously wrong with life in the United States, and that we need not fret about tradition one way or the other; but I confess, at the risk of being accused of arrogance, that I take these people for fools, whether they call themselves liberals or conservatives. They have a fondness for pointing to the comfortable routine of our suburbs as a demonstration of our mastery over the ancient tragedy of life. Now I am not one of those critics of society who look upon residence in suburbia a stain worse than the mark of the beast; but neither am I disposed to think that a commuter's ticket and a lawn-sprinkler are the proofs of national greatness and personal exaltation. And I am convinced that, if the reservoir of our traditions is drained dry, there will not be ten thousand tidy little suburbs in America, very long thereafter; for the suburbs are dependent upon an older order of social organization, as well as upon an intricate modern apparatus of industrial technology, for their being.

When tradition is dissipated, men do not respond to the old

moral injunctions satisfactorily; and our circumstances and national character differing from Sweden's, I do not think we would experience the comparative good fortune to slip into an equalitarian boredom. The contract of eternal society forgotten, soon every lesser form of contract would lose its sanction. I say, then, that we need to shake out of their complacency the liberals who are smug in their conviction of the immortality of Liberal Democratic Folkways in the United States, and the conservatives who are smug in their conviction of the abiding superiority of the American Standard of Living. Political arrangements, and economic systems, rest upon the foundation of moral prejudices which find their expression in tradition.

Men who assail smugness cannot hope to be popular, in any climate of opinion; so the conservative ought not to expect to be thanked for reminding his age of the contract of eternal society. When he protests against the reduction of the mass of men to a condition below the dignity of true humanity, he will be attacked as an enemy of democracy, and ridiculed as a snob—when, in truth, he is endeavoring to save a democracy of elevation, and to put down the snobbery of a rootless new managerial elite. Mr. Wyndham Lewis, in Rude Assignment, refers to the abuse which many professors and publicists heap upon anyone who presumes to suggest that there is something wrong with modern minds and hearts: "To keep other people in mental leading-strings, to have beneath you a broad mass of humanity to which you (although no intellectual giant) can feel agreeably superior: this petty and disagreeable form of the will-to-power of the average 'smart' man counts for much in the degradation of the Many. And there is no action of this same 'smart' man that is more aggravating than the way in which he will turn upon the critic of the social scene (who has pointed out the degradation of the Many) and accuse him of 'despising the people.'" Nothing is more resented than the truth, and, as Mr. Lewis says, "people have deteriorated. They have neither the will nor common sense of the peasant or guildsman, and are more easily fooled. This can only be a source of concern and regret, to all except 'the leader of men.'"

Whenever human dignity is found, it is the product of a conviction that we are part of some great continuity and essence, which elevates us above the brutes; and wherever popular government is just and free, it is in consequence of a belief that there are standards superior to the interest of the hour and the will of a temporary majority. If these things are forgotten, then indeed the people will become despicable. The conservative, in endeavoring to restore a consciousness among men of the worth of tradition, is not acting in contempt of the masses; he is acting, instead, out of love for them, as human persons, and he is trying to preserve for them such a life as men should lead. The conservative does not believe that learning must be debased "because the people want it," or that a country's aspect must be made hideous "because the people want it," or that literature must vanish before the comic-book "because the people want it." He does not entertain so low an opinion of the people. The proletariat, shorn of tradition and roots, may crave such a degradation; but the conservative hopes to restore the lonely crowd who make up the faceless proletariat to character and individuality once more. And perhaps the first step in that restoration must be a renewed attention to the claims of tradition.

In the defense of tradition, as with the several other problems I have touched upon in this book, the conservative must not be daunted by the probability that he will be misunderstood by most people, and assaulted by everyone whose material interest seems to be bound up with the continued degradation of the masses. The doctrinaire liberal will call him names, and the unreflecting present possessor of property and power will give him no support. And the conservative must face the fact that he may very well be beaten; unlike the Marxist, the conservative does not profess a fanatic belief in an ultimate inevitable triumph of his cause. But the conservative, despite all this, will not surrender to the contagion of mass-opinion or the temptations of material aggrandizement and power. Convinced that he is a party to the contract of eternal society, he will abide by the sanctity of that contract, and do his appointed part under that compact. His back is to the wall, in our day, so that if he hopes to conserve anything at all, he must make his stand unflinchingly. He is not now defending mere ornaments and details of the civil social existence; he is not arguing simply about the Corn Laws, or the mode of electing senators, or the regulation of wages and hours. All these were important questions in their time, but the modern conservative has Medusa to contend with, and lesser matters shrink to insignificance beside the dilemma of humanity in this century.

The grand question before us is really this: Is life worth living? Are men and women to live as human persons, formed in God's image, with the minds and hearts and individuality of spiritual beings, or are they to become creatures less than human, herded by the masters of the total state, debauched by the indulgence of every appetite, deprived of the consolations of religion and tradition and learning and the sense of continuity, drenched in propaganda, aimless amusements, and the flood of sensual triviality which is supplanting the private reason? Are they to be themselves, endowed with personality and variety and hope, or are they to be the vague faces in the Lonely Crowd, devoid of all the traditional motives to integrity? The radical and the liberal, I think, have failed dismally to show us any road to the redemption of mankind from modern boredom and modern decadence. The conservative is become our guide, whether he likes it or not, and regardless of the will of the crowd. He may not succeed in covering the dry bones of this program with flesh and blood. If he is unequal to the task, the clock will strike, and Faustus will be damned.

Great civilizations do not fall at a single blow. Our civilization has sustained several terrible assaults already, and still it lives; but that does not mean that it can live forever, or even endure through another generation. Like a neglected old house, a society whose members have forgot the ends of society's being and of their own lives sinks by degrees almost imperceptible toward its ruin. The rain comes in at the broken pane; the dry-rot spreads like the corpse of a tree within the wall; the plaster drops upon the sodden floor; the joists groan with every wind; and the rat, creeping down the stair at midnight, gnaws his dirty way from the desolate kitchen to the mildewed satins of the parlor. We men of the twentieth century have this house only, and no other: the storm outside, in the winter of our discontent, will allow of no idle building of dream-castles; the summer indolence of the age of optimism is long gone by. The conservative, if he knows his own tradition, understands that his appointed part, in the present forlorn state of society, is to save man from fading into a ghost condemned to linger hopeless in a rotten tenement.

Books Mentioned

Adams, John. *Works.* Edited by C.F. Adams. 10 vols. Boston: Little, Brown, 1851–56.

America and the Intellectuals. Edited by the editors of *Partisan Review.* NY: Partisan Review Press, 1953.

Babbitt, Irving, *Democracy and Leadership.* Foreword by Russell Kirk. Indianapolis: Liberty Classics, 1979.

———. *Literature and the American College.* Introduction by Russell Kirk. Washington, DC: National Humanities Institute, 1986.

Bantock, C.H. *Freedom and Authority in Education.* Chicago: Regnery, 1952.

Bell, Bernard Iddings. *Crisis in Education.* NY: Whittlesey, 1948.

———. *Crowd Culture.* NY: Harper, 1953.

Bernanos, Georges. *The Diary of a Country Priest.* NY: Macmillan, 1937.

Bestor, Arthur. *Educational Wastelands.* University of Illinois Press, 1953.

Boorstin, Daniel J. *The Genius of American Politics.* University of Chicago Press, 1953.

Brogan, D.W. *The Price of Revolution.* London: Hamilton, 1951.

Brownson, Orestes. *Works.* 10 vols. Edited by H.F. Brownson. Detroit: Nourse, 1882–87.

Burke, Edmund. *Works.* 16 vols. London: Rivington, 1826–27.

Chalmers, Gordon Keith. *The Republic and the Person.* Chicago: Regnery, 1952.

Coleridge, Samuel Taylor. *The Constitution of Church and State.* London: Moxon, 1852.

———. *Table Talk.* London: Bell, 1884.

Cooper, James Fenimore. *The American Democrat.* Indianapolis: Liberty Classics, 1984.

Dawson, Christopher. *Understanding Europe.* London: Sheed and Ward, 1952.

Eliot, T.S. *The Idea of a Christian Society.* London: Faber and Faber, 1939.

———. *Notes Towards the Definition of Culture.* London: Faber and Faber, 1939.

———. *Selected Essays, 1917–1932.* NY: Harcourt, Brace, 1932.

Faguet, Emile. *Politicians and Moralists of the Nineteenth Century*. London: Benn, 1928.

Grazia, Sebastian de. *Of Time, Work and Leisure*. NY: Twentieth Century Fund, 1962.

Hayek, Friedrich A. *The Counter-Revolution of Science*. Glencoe, IL: Free Press, 1952.

Joad, C.E.M. *Decadence*. London: Gollancz, 1948.

———. *The Recovery of Belief*. London: Faber and Faber, 1952.

Juenger, Friedrich Georg. *The Failure of Technology*. Chicago: Regnery, 1949.

Kinsey, Alfred, et. al. *Sexual Behavior in the Human Male;—in the Human Female*. Philadelphia: Saunders, 1948 and 1953.

Kirk, Russell. *The Conservative Mind, from Burke to Eliot*. Seventh edition. Washington, DC: Regnery, 1986.

———. *Eliot and His Age*. Third edition. Peru, IL: Sugden, 1989.

Kirk, Russell, and McClellan, James. *The Political Principles of Robert A. Taft*. NY: Fleet, 1967.

Lancaster, Osbert. *Drayneflete Revealed*. London: John Murray, 1949.

Le Bon, Gustave. *The Crowd*. London: Unwin, 1917.

Lewis, Wyndham. *Rude Assignment*. London: Hutchinson, 1950.

Mallock, W.H. *A Critical Examination of Socialism*. Introduction by Russell Kirk. New Brunswick, NJ: Transaction Books, 1989.

———. *The Limits of Pure Democracy*. Fifth edition. London: Chapman and Hall, 1919.

———. *The New Republic*. Introduction by Sir John Squire. London: Michael Joseph, c. 1935.

Marcel, Gabriel. *The Decline of Wisdom*. NY: Philosophical Library, 1955.

———. *Man against Mass Society*. Chicago: Regnery, 1952.

McLuhan, Marshall. *The Mechanical Bride*. NY: Vanguard, 1951.

More, Paul Elmer. *Shelburne Essays*. Eleven vols. Boston: Houghton, Mifflin, 1904–21.

Muggeridge, Malcolm. *Things Past*. NY: Morrow, 1979.

Nisbet, Robert A. *The Quest for Community*. NY: Oxford University Press, 1953.

Ortega y Gasset, José. *The Revolt of the Masses*. Translated by Anthony Kerrigan. University of Notre Dame Press, 1985.

Orton, William A. *The Economic Role of the State*. University of Chicago Press, 1950.

Orwell, George. *Coming up for Air*. NY: Harcourt, Brace, 1950.

———. *Nineteen-Eighty-Four*. NY: Harcourt, Brace, 1949.

Parkinson, C. Northcote, and Le Compte, Herman. *The Law of Longer Life*. Troy, AL: Troy State University Press, 1980.

Picard, Max. *The Flight from God*. Chicago: Regnery, 1951.

Pieper, Josef. *Leisure, the Basis of Culture*. Introduction by T.S. Eliot. NY: Pantheon, 1952.

Riesman, David. *Individualism Reconsidered*. Glencoe, IL: Free Press, 1954.

———. *Thorstein Veblen: A Critical Interpretation*. NY: Scribners, 1953.

Riesman, David, et al. *Faces in the Crowd*. Yale University Press, 1953.

Roberts, Michael. *The Estate of Man*. London: Faber and Faber, 1951.

Röpke, Wilhelm. *Civitas Humana*. London: Hodge, 1948.

———. *The Social Crisis of Our Time*. University of Chicago Press, 1950.

Rougemont, Denis de. *The Devil's Share*. NY: Pantheon Books, 1944.

Rowntree, Seebohm, and Lavers, G.R. *English Life and Leisure*. London: Longmans, Green, 1951.

Santayana, George. *The Last Puritan*. NY: Scribners, 1935.

———. *Reason in Society*. NY: Scribners, 1905.

Seidenberg, Roderick. *Post-Historic Man*. University of North Carolina Press, 1950.

Sorokin, Pitirim. *The Crisis of Our Age*. NY: Dutton, 1941.

Stephen, J.F. *Liberty, Equality, Fraternity*. London: Smith, Elder, 1873.

Thibon, Gustave. *What Ails Mankind?* NY: Sheed and Ward, 1947.

Tocqueville, Alexis de. *Democracy in America*. Edited by J.P. Mayer. Garden City, NY: Doubleday, 1969.

Unamuno, Miguel de. *The Tragic Sense of Life*. Translated by Anthony Kerrigan. Princeton University Press, 1978.

Veblen, Thorstein. *The Theory of the Leisure Class*. Introduction by C. Wright Mills. NY: Mentor Books, 1953.

Weaver, Richard. *The Ethics of Rhetoric*. Chicago: Regnery, 1953.

Whitehead, A.N. *Science and the Modern World*. NY: Macmillan, 1925.

INDEX

Index

CPSIA information can be obtained at www.ICGtesting.com
Printed in the USA
LVOW12*2019211013

357970LV00001B/3/P